DISCOVER INTERNET EXPLORER 4

Getting Around in Internet Explorer 4

Launch Internet Explorer Browser

Launch Outlook Express

Show Desktop

View Channels

Internet Explorer Toolbar

Go back and forth between previously visited web pages

Refresh screen

Open Search pane

Open History pane

Print page

Link to a favorite page

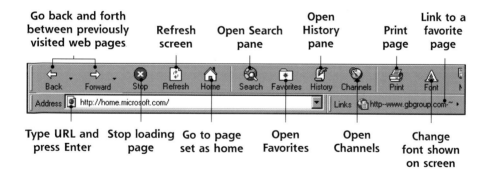

Type URL and press Enter

Stop loading page

Go to page set as home

Open Favorites

Open Channels

Change font shown on screen

Using AutoSearch and Links

Use AutoSearch

Drag the handle to expand or move the bar

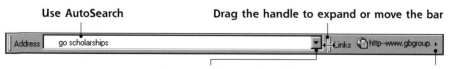

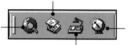

Show a list of previously visited websites

Scroll through links

Outlook Express Toolbar

Compose a new message

Reply to all recipients of current message

Send mail and get new mail

Open Address Book

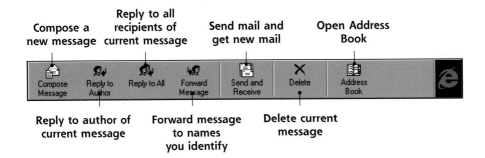

Reply to author of current message

Forward message to names you identify

Delete current message

Composing a New Message

Paste text **Check names** **Address Book** **Attach a file** **Insert signature** **Digitally sign message**

Send completed message

Undo

Cut text

Copy text

Type message

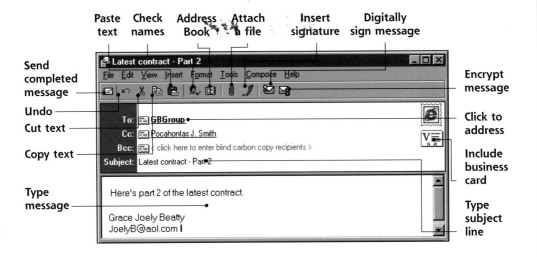

Encrypt message

Click to address

Include business card

Type subject line

Inbox icons

Icon	Indicates
!	The message has been marked high priority by the sender.
↓	The message has been marked low priority by the sender
₿	The message has an attachment.
✉	This message has not been read. The message listing appears in bold type.
✉	This message has been read. The message listing appears in light type.

WITHDRAWN

DISCOVER INTERNET EXPLORER 4

DISCOVER INTERNET EXPLORER 4

DAVID C. GARDNER, PH.D.
GRACE JOELY BEATTY, PH.D.
DAVID A. SAUER, M.S.

IDG BOOKS WORLDWIDE, INC.

AN INTERNATIONAL DATA
GROUP COMPANY

FOSTER CITY, CA • CHICAGO, IL •
INDIANAPOLIS, IN • SOUTHLAKE, TX

Discover Internet Explorer 4

Published by
IDG Books Worldwide, Inc.
An International Data Group Company
919 E. Hillsdale Blvd., Suite 400
Foster City, CA 94404
www.idgbooks.com (IDG Books Worldwide Web site)

Library of Congress Catalog Card No.: 97-70657

ISBN: 0-7645-3067-4

Printed in the United States of America

10 9 8 7 6 5 4 3 2 1

1E/SV/QZ/ZX/FC

Distributed in the United States by IDG Books Worldwide, Inc.

Distributed by Macmillan Canada for Canada; by Transworld Publishers Limited in the United Kingdom; by IDG Norge Books for Norway; by IDG Sweden Books for Sweden; by Woodslane Pty. Ltd. for Australia; by Woodslane Enterprises Ltd. for New Zealand; by Longman Singapore Publishers Ltd. for Singapore, Malaysia, Thailand, and Indonesia; by Simron Pty. Ltd. for South Africa; by Toppan Company Ltd. for Japan; by Distribuidora Cuspide for Argentina; by Livraria Cultura for Brazil; by Ediciencia S.A. for Ecuador; by Addison-Wesley Publishing Company for Korea; by Ediciones ZETA S.C.R. Ltda. for Peru; by WS Computer Publishing Corporation, Inc., for the Philippines; by Unalis Corporation for Taiwan; by Contemporanea de Ediciones for Venezuela; by Computer Book & Magazine Store for Puerto Rico; by Express Computer Distributors for the Caribbean and West Indies. Authorized Sales Agent: Anthony Rudkin Associates for the Middle East and North Africa.

For general information on IDG Books Worldwide's books in the U.S., please call our Consumer Customer Service department at 800-762-2974. For reseller information, including discounts and premium sales, please call our Reseller Customer Service department at 800-434-3422.

For information on where to purchase IDG Books Worldwide's books outside the U.S., please contact our International Sales department at 415-655-3200 or fax 415-655-3295.

For information on foreign language translations, please contact our Foreign & Subsidiary Rights department at 415-655-3021 or fax 415-655-3281.

For sales inquiries and special prices for bulk quantities, please contact our Sales department at 415-655-3200 or write to the address above.

For information on using IDG Books Worldwide's books in the classroom or for ordering examination copies, please contact our Educational Sales department at 800-434-2086 or fax 817-251-8174.

For press review copies, author interviews, or other publicity information, please contact our Public Relations department at 415-655-3000 or fax 415-655-3299.

For authorization to photocopy items for corporate, personal, or educational use, please contact Copyright Clearance Center, 222 Rosewood Drive, Danvers, MA 01923, or fax 508-750-4470.

 ™is a trademark under exclusive license to IDG Books Worldwide, Inc., from International Data Group, Inc.

IDG BOOKS WORLDWIDE

ABOUT IDG BOOKS WORLDWIDE

Welcome to the world of IDG Books Worldwide.

IDG Books Worldwide, Inc., is a subsidiary of International Data Group, the world's largest publisher of computer-related information and the leading global provider of information services on information technology. IDG was founded more than 25 years ago and now employs more than 8,500 people worldwide. IDG publishes more than 275 computer publications in over 75 countries (see listing below). More than 60 million people read one or more IDG publications each month.

Launched in 1990, IDG Books Worldwide is today the #1 publisher of best-selling computer books in the United States. We are proud to have received eight awards from the Computer Press Association in recognition of editorial excellence and three from *Computer Currents'* First Annual Readers' Choice Awards. Our best-selling *...For Dummies*® series has more than 30 million copies in print with translations in 30 languages. IDG Books Worldwide, through a joint venture with IDG's Hi-Tech Beijing, became the first U.S. publisher to publish a computer book in the People's Republic of China. In record time, IDG Books Worldwide has become the first choice for millions of readers around the world who want to learn how to better manage their businesses.

Our mission is simple: Every one of our books is designed to bring extra value and skill-building instructions to the reader. Our books are written by experts who understand and care about our readers. The knowledge base of our editorial staff comes from years of experience in publishing, education, and journalism — experience we use to produce books for the '90s. In short, we care about books, so we attract the best people. We devote special attention to details such as audience, interior design, use of icons, and illustrations. And because we use an efficient process of authoring, editing, and desktop publishing our books electronically, we can spend more time ensuring superior content and spend less time on the technicalities of making books.

You can count on our commitment to deliver high-quality books at competitive prices on topics you want to read about. At IDG Books Worldwide, we continue in the IDG tradition of delivering quality for more than 25 years. You'll find no better book on a subject than one from IDG Books Worldwide.

IDG
BOOKS
WORLDWIDE

John Kilcullen
CEO
IDG Books Worldwide, Inc.

Steven Berkowitz
President and Publisher
IDG Books Worldwide, Inc.

*Eighth Annual
Computer Press
Awards ≥1992*

*Ninth Annual
Computer Press
Awards ≥1993*

*Tenth Annual
Computer Press
Awards ≥1994*

*Eleventh Annual
Computer Press
Awards ≥1995*

IDG Books Worldwide, Inc., is a subsidiary of International Data Group, the world's largest publisher of computer-related information and the leading global provider of information services on information technology. International Data Group publishes over 275 computer publications in over 75 countries. Sixty million people read one or more International Data Group publications each month. International Data Group's publications include: ARGENTINA: Buyer's Guide, Computerworld Argentina, PC World Argentina; AUSTRALIA: Australian Macworld, Australian PC World, Australian Reseller News, Computerworld, IT Casebook, Network World, Publish, Webmaster; AUSTRIA: Computerwelt Osterreich, Networks Austria, PC Tip Austria; BANGLADESH: PC World Bangladesh; BELARUS: PC World Belarus; BELGIUM: Data News; BRAZIL: Annuário de Informática, Computerworld, Connections, Macworld, PC Player, PC World, Publish, Reseller News, Supergamepower; BULGARIA: Computerworld Bulgaria, Network World Bulgaria, PC & MacWorld Bulgaria; CANADA: CIO Canada, Client/Server World, ComputerWorld Canada, InfoWorld Canada, NetworkWorld Canada, WebWorld; CHILE: Computerworld Chile, PC World Chile; COLOMBIA: Computerworld Colombia, PC World Colombia; COSTA RICA: PC World Centro America; THE CZECH AND SLOVAK REPUBLICS: Computerworld Czechoslovakia, Macworld Czech Republic, PC World Czechoslovakia; DENMARK: Communications World Danmark, Computerworld Danmark, Macworld Danmark, PC World Danmark, Techworld Denmark; DOMINICAN REPUBLIC: PC World Republica Dominicana; ECUADOR: PC World Ecuador; EGYPT: Computerworld Middle East, PC World Middle East; EL SALVADOR: PC World Centro America; FINLAND: MikroPC, Tietoverkko, Tietoviikko; FRANCE: Distributique, Hebdo, Info PC, Le Monde Informatique, Macworld, Reseaux & Telecoms, WebMaster France; GERMANY: Computer Partner, Computerwoche, Computerwoche Extra, Computerwoche FOCUS, Global Online, Macwelt, PC Welt; GREECE: Amiga Computing, GamePro Greece, Multimedia World; GUATEMALA: PC World Centro America; HONDURAS: PC World Centro America; HONG KONG: Computerworld Hong Kong, PC World Hong Kong, Publish in Asia; HUNGARY: ABCD CD-ROM, Computerworld Szamitastechnika, Internetto online Magazine, PC World Hungary, PC-X Magazin Hungary; ICELAND: Tolvuheimur PC World Island; INDIA: Information Communications World, Information Systems Computerworld, PC World India, Publish in Asia; INDONESIA: InfoKomputer PC World, Komputek Computerworld, Publish in Asia; IRELAND: ComputerScope, PC Live!; ISRAEL: Macworld Israel, People & Computers/Computerworld; ITALY: Computerworld Italia, Macworld Italia, Networking Italia, PC World Italia; JAPAN: DTP World, Macworld Japan, Nikkei Personal Computing, OS/2 World Japan, SunWorld Japan, Windows NT World, Windows World Japan; KENYA: PC World East African; KOREA: Hi-Tech Information, Macworld Korea, PC World Korea; MACEDONIA: PC World Macedonia; MALAYSIA: Computerworld Malaysia, Mir PK, Publish, Seti; SINGAPORE: Computerworld Singapore, PC World Singapore, Publish in Asia; SLOVENIA: Monitor; SOUTH AFRICA: Computing SA, Network World SA, Software World SA; SPAIN: Communicaciones World España, Computerworld España, Dealer World España, Macworld España, PC World España; SRI LANKA: Infolink PC World; SWEDEN: CAP&Design, Computer Sweden, Corporate Computing Sweden, Internetworld Sweden, it.branschen, MaxiData Sweden, MikroDatorn, Nätverk & Kommunikation, PC World Sweden, PCaktiv, Windows World Sweden; SWITZERLAND: Computerworld Schweiz, Macworld Schweiz, PCtip; TAIWAN: Computerworld Taiwan, Macworld Taiwan, NEW ViSiON/Publish, PC World Taiwan, Windows World Taiwan; THAILAND: Publish in Asia, Thai Computerworld; TURKEY: Computerworld Turkiye, Network World Turkiye, PC World Turkiye; UKRAINE: Computerworld Kiev, Multimedia World Ukraine, PC World Ukraine; UNITED KINGDOM: Acorn User UK, Amiga Action UK, Amiga Computing UK, Apple Talk UK, Computing, Macworld, Parents and Computers UK, PC Advisor, PC Home, PSX Pro, The WEB; UNITED STATES: Cable in the Classroom, CIO Magazine, Computerworld, DOS World, Federal Computer Week, GamePro Magazine, InfoWorld, I-Way, Macworld, Network World, PC Games, PC World, Publish, Video Event, THE WEB Magazine, and WebMaster; online webzines: JavaWorld, NetscapeWorld, and SunWorld Online; URUGUAY: InfoWorld Uruguay; VENEZUELA: Computerworld Venezuela, PC World Venezuela; and VIETNAM: PC World Vietnam.
3/24/97

Welcome to the Discover Series

Do you want to discover the best and most efficient ways to use your computer and learn about technology? Books in the Discover series teach you the essentials of technology with a friendly, confident approach. You'll find a Discover book on almost any subject — from the Internet to intranets, from Web design and programming to the business programs that make your life easier.

We've provided valuable, real-world examples that help you relate to topics faster. Discover books begin by introducing you to the main features of programs, so you start by doing something *immediately*. The focus is to teach you how to perform tasks that are useful and meaningful in your day-to-day work. You might create a document or graphic, explore your computer, surf the Web, or write a program. Whatever the task, you learn the most commonly used features, and focus on the best tips and techniques for doing your work. You'll get results quickly, and discover the best ways to use software and technology in your everyday life.

You may find the following elements and features in this book:

Discovery Central: This tearout card is a handy quick reference to important tasks or ideas covered in the book.

Quick Tour: The Quick Tour gets you started working with the book right away.

Real-Life Vignettes: Throughout the book you'll see one-page scenarios illustrating a real-life application of a topic covered.

Goals: Each chapter opens with a list of goals you can achieve by reading the chapter.

Side Trips: These asides include additional information about alternative or advanced ways to approach the topic covered.

Bonuses: Timesaving tips and more advanced techniques are covered in each chapter.

Discovery Center: This guide illustrates key procedures covered throughout the book.

Visual Index: You'll find real-world documents in the Visual Index, with page numbers pointing you to where you should turn to achieve the effects shown.

Throughout the book, you'll also notice some special icons and formatting:

FEATURE FOCUS A Feature Focus icon highlights new features in the software's latest release, and points out significant differences between it and the previous version.

WEB PATH Web Paths refer you to Web sites that provide additional information about the topic.

TIP Tips offer timesaving shortcuts, expert advice, quick techniques, or brief reminders.

X-REF The X-Ref icon refers you to other chapters or sections for more information.

Pull Quotes emphasize important ideas that are covered in the chapter.

NOTE Notes provide additional information or highlight special points of interest about a topic.

CAUTION The Caution icon alerts you to potential problems you should watch out for.

The Discover series delivers interesting, insightful, and inspiring information about technology to help you learn faster and retain more. So the next time you want to find answers to your technology questions, reach for a Discover book. We hope the entertaining, easy-to-read style puts you at ease and makes learning fun.

Credits

ACQUISITIONS EDITOR
Andy Cummings

DEVELOPMENT EDITOR
Susannah D. Pfalzer

TECHNICAL EDITOR
Keith Underdah

COPY EDITORS
Luann Rouff
Larisa North
Nicole Fountain
Carolyn Welch

PRODUCTION COORDINATOR
Susan Parini

GRAPHICS AND PRODUCTION SPECIALISTS
Mario F. Amador
Stephanie Hollier
Ed Penslien
Mark Schumann
Trevor Wilson

PROOFREADER
Annie Sheldon

INDEXER
James Minkin

BOOK DESIGN
Seventeenth Street Studios
Phyllis Beaty
Kurt Krames

About the Authors

David C. Gardner, Ph.D., and **Grace Joely Beatty, Ph.D.**, are licensed psychologists who specialize in the human interface to computers. They are a husband-and-wife team and the coauthors of over 35 computer books, with more than a million copies in print. Many of their titles have been bestsellers. The Golden Gate Computer Society suggested that their books serve as a model for how to put together a book about a computer program. In their corporate consulting, they work with organizations undergoing major computer conversions.

David A. Sauer, M.S., is currently Vice President of Information Services at CyberHelp, Inc. He has over 20 years' experience in electronic information management, database design and administration, and online services. He designed and managed the online information management system at the Stone Science Library, Boston University, and is the coauthor of more than a dozen computer books.

The book is dedicated to the memory of Joseph B. Beatty (1924-1997) — father, friend, and cheerleader! He is sorely missed.

PREFACE

Internet Explorer 4.0 is actually a number of programs all rolled into one suite. When Internet Explorer first appeared a few years ago, it was instantly called a Johnny-come-lately and was definitely not in the same league with Netscape, the granddaddy of browsers. Since then, it has evolved into a state-of-the-art Internet suite containing an HTML editor, conferencing and collaborating programs, and programs for reading and responding to electronic mail and Usenet newsgroups. In addition, Internet Explorer 4 uses the Web's latest "push" technology to bring you updated information on news, finance, and dozens of other subjects.

Discover Internet Explorer 4 is designed to give you a basic understanding of how to use the Explorer suite of programs to explore the Internet and tap into its potential. While we could easily have written an entire book on every one of Internet Explorer's parts, we have made an effort to introduce all the important elements of each component in the suite of programs. It is our hope that the book will show you both what Explorer can do for you, and what you can do with it.

Who Should Read This Book

If you're just starting to investigate the Internet but have a little experience with your computer, this book is for you. We don't cover every detail of every aspect of Internet Explorer's operation, but we will point you in the right direction for learning how to use the program's most important and interesting features and for finding out more on your own. Our goal in previous books was to make technical matters easy to understand for nontechnically minded people. That is our goal here, too, and we hope the book will give you confidence to feel good about and get the most out of Internet Explorer.

How This Book Is Organized

We start by introducing you to some basics, and then divide the rest of the book into sections that correspond to Internet Explorer's parts. Throughout the book, you'll find real-life stories, pointers, and bonuses that will help you get the most from what the Internet has to offer. At the end of the book are three appendixes that give you guidelines on selecting an Internet service provider, installing Internet Explorer, and finding help for some common problems.

Quick Tour

First, we show you Internet Explorer's Web browser. We'll show you around Microsoft's Web site (the ultimate source for anything having to do with Explorer) and explain the basics for using Internet Explorer to move around on the World Wide Web.

Part One: Getting Started

Part One continues your introduction to the Web browser. In addition, this part shows you how to tailor Internet Explorer's interface and background operations to suit your computer, and how to set up your desktop options—the way you use the program and the way you want the program to "look and feel."

Part Two: Exploring the Internet

Once you have the basics under your belt and have set up Internet Explorer the way you want it, we'll show you some of the more advanced features the browser has to offer. We'll also show you ways to bring the Internet under control, how to find your way to World Wide Web resources, and how to save them on your computer.

Part Three: Communicating with Explorer

Here's where we introduce e-mail, which accounts for most of the use the Internet gets by far. E-mail can keep you in touch with friends and family with electronic letters that contain all that a written letter can, but with a fraction of the time and effort involved. And if you work at home, or hope to one day, we'll show you how Outlook Express's e-mail offers all the features you need to maintain your professional business correspondence.

In addition, you will learn how to take advantage of newsgroups. Newsgroups started out as a way for researchers to keep each other up to date and to collaborate on solving problems. Now, with several tens of thousands of newsgroups available, you can use them to keep up with any topic you can imagine. In this part, you'll see how to use Outlook Express and its common interface with Internet Explorer to help you become an active member of the global newsgroup community.

Part Four: Holding a NetMeeting

In this part, you'll get a chance to work with Internet Explorer's NetMeeting program. You'll learn how to set up NetMeeting for your computer, chat with people anywhere in the world, share the "Whiteboard" with them, exchange files, and actually "browse together"—all live and online.

Part Five: Creating HTML Documents with FrontPage Express

It used to be that you had to be a programmer to put together an HTML document, the code file that makes up Web pages. With FrontPage Express, you'll be creating Web pages like a pro right from the get-go. This part will show you how to plan a Web page, how to avoid Web page pitfalls, how to create a Web page of your own, and how to mount it on the Web for all the world to see.

Appendixes

We've included three brief appendixes in the back of the book to help you out in case this is your first foray onto the 'Net. Appendix A helps you with installation and your first use of Internet Explorer; Appendix B gives you pointers on choosing the Internet service provider that's right for you; and Appendix C gives you tips on common problems and where to find the latest and best information on solving them. In addition, you'll find the Discovery Center, Visual Index and Glossary in the back of the book.

Getting Updates on Internet Explorer 4

iscover Internet Explorer 4 **is based on the beta release of Internet Explorer 4.0.** Because Microsoft reserves the right to change Internet Explorer, there may be some differences between the descriptions in this book and the final release of Internet Explorer 4.0. Please check the IDG Books Worldwide Web site at http://www.idgbooks.com for updates.

To help you easily retrieve and print Internet Explorer 4.0 updates from the Web, you can download an evaluation version of WebPrinter for Windows 3.x/95 v2.0 from the IDG Books Worldwide Web site. WebPrinter enables you to print Web pages as mini-booklets. This application automatically intercepts standard-sized pages as they are sent to your laser/ink jet printer and then reduces, rotates, and paginates the pages to print as double-sided booklets.

NOTE **You can print up to four documents before you have to purchase the full version of WebPrinter. For more information, visit the ForeFront Group's Web site at** http://www.ffg.com, **or call (800) 475-5831.**

Now, fire up your computer, turn to the Quick Tour, and get ready to see what all the fuss over the Internet is about.

ACKNOWLEDGMENTS

Chris Alan, President of ElectriCiti, Inc., our Internet service provider, gave us accounts to make things go more smoothly, and he and his staff, especially Karen Stiner, were there for us when we had technical problems or questions!

Frank Straw and Dan Terhark of Computer Service and Maintenance provided the technical support for this project and furnished us with ongoing computer troubleshooting and maintenance. Thanks, guys!

We are delighted to be working with the professionals at IDG Books Worldwide: Andy Cummings, acquisitions editor, Carolyn Welch and Luann Rouff, copy editors, and Keith Underdahl, technical editor. They were all incredibly supportive and helped us produce this book in record time. Susannah Pfalzer, our development editor, contributed greatly to the book and made the process a pleasure as we worked our way up to "Purgatory."

We can't sign off without thanking Bill Gladstone and Matt Wagner of Waterside Productions. They've been good friends and terrific agents.

Finally, we must acknowledge the continuing support of Carolyn and Ray Holder. They have always been there for us during every book crunch. We forgive them for sneaking off to Paris in the middle of this one!

CONTENTS AT A GLANCE

CONTENTS

DISCOVER INTERNET EXPLORER QUICK TOUR

PRACTICE USING THESE SKILLS

Internet Explorer 4.0 (IE 4) goes far beyond Web browsers that you may have used in the past, integrating your computer and many of the programs in it with the Internet. It lets you go back and forth between resources on your own computer and those at any Web site in the world with just one click of your mouse. You can set it up to automatically keep track of updates to your favorite Web pages and to use "Active Desktop" components to keep you up-to-date about things that change continuously throughout the day, such as news and financial data.

IE 4's many new features also alter the way in which you interact with your computer. It changes several familiar Windows 95 procedures, but also lets you turn those features off if you don't want to use them. You'll find that your desktop works more like a Web page with IE 4, whether you use the Active Desktop and its components or not.

So follow along for a quick tour of a few of the most noticeable changes that IE 4 has in store for you. In the chapters that follow, we'll give you more details about the changes; and tell you how to use them, how to turn features off and on, and how to customize them to suit your tastes and work habits.

Turning the Active Desktop Off and On

I f you selected the Web Integrated Desktop when you installed IE 4, it automatically enabled the Active Desktop (see Figure QT-1). For some, the dramatic and sudden change to your desktop may be "too much, too soon." Also, if your computer has only the minimum random access memory (RAM) required for running IE 4 (8MB for Windows 95, 16MB for NT4), you may find that nearly everything you do takes longer than it used to. This is because the Active Desktop needs a lot of RAM.

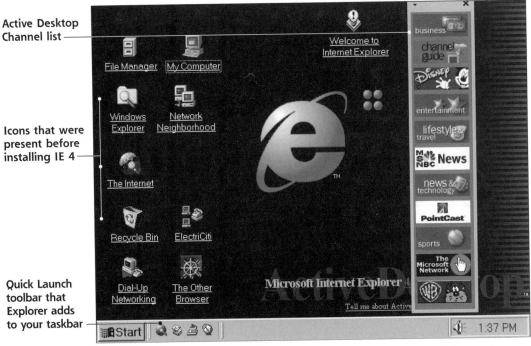

Active Desktop Channel list

Icons that were present before installing IE 4

Quick Launch toolbar that Explorer adds to your taskbar

Figure QT-1 IE 4's Active Desktop, showing the channel list and Quick Launch toolbar.

If either of these apply to you, it's easy to turn the Active Desktop off for the time being. After you read about all that you can do using the Active Desktop in Chapter 4, you will probably want to re-enable it, customizing its features and/or upgrading your computer's RAM so that it runs at its former speed.

 X-REF **If you didn't install the Web Integrated Desktop and would like to try it out, see "Updating Explorer," the Bonus at the end of Chapter 3.**

After a day or two, the black background and welcome message on the Active Desktop that you see in Figure QT-1 go away, and the background you had for your regular desktop before installing IE 4 replaces it. In Chapters 2 and 4 we show you how to customize desktop backgrounds.

The Active Desktop automatically includes any icons or folders that you installed on your Windows 95 or Windows NT4 desktop. In addition, it adds a black background with an animated welcome message and the Channel bar. Channels are part of the Internet's new *push* technology, which lets various services send information that you select to your desktop. The Channel bar itself is an example of an Active Desktop item. These "items" are one of IE 4's hot, new features, including such things as weather maps, news services, and stock market data.

Follow these steps to turn the Active Desktop off and on:

1. Right-click the mouse on an empty part of the desktop. A shortcut menu appears (see Figure QT-2).

Figure QT-2 Right-click a blank space on IE 4's Active Desktop to open the shortcut menu.

2. Move the mouse pointer over Active Desktop to open the Active Desktop menu.

3. Click View as Web Page to remove the ✓ next to it. The menus close and your desktop returns to the way it looked before you installed IE 4.

4. Repeat Steps 1-3 to replace the ✓ next to View as Web Page if you want to turn the Active Desktop back on.

NOTE Some older video cards can't "refresh" the view to show the difference between the Active Desktop and your regular desktop until you reboot your computer.

Browsing Your Computer

I E 4 lets you browse your own computer in the same way that you browse the Web. Icons on your desktop show up like links on a Web page and, just like Web page links, are activated with one click instead of two. (We'll show you how to change things back to their former state, should you want to, in Chapter 2, "Getting Familiar with Explorer.") The new IE 4 replaces three separate programs that come with the standard Windows 95 operating system: Internet Explorer 3.0, My Computer, and Windows Explorer. In fact, any time you open a folder, IE 4 will be lurking in the background.

To see how IE 4 and the new desktop work, follow these steps:

1. Move the mouse pointer over the My Computer icon but don't click it yet. Notice that the pointer turns into a hand and the icon's underlined title becomes highlighted, just as if it were a link on a Web page. After the pointer has been over the icon for a moment, the icon's background turns dark. This indicates that the icon has been selected. (See Chapter 1 for more information about selecting icons and the files that they represent.)

2. Click the My Computer icon once. The My Computer window opens (see Figure QT-3).

3. Click the maximize button so that the window fills the screen.

Notice that IE 4 displays the My Computer resources in a split screen. When you move the mouse pointer over an icon, information about the resource that the icon represents appears on the left. Try resting the mouse pointer over the icon for your computer's C: drive to see what happens. IE 4 also uses a split screen to show resources in the Control Panel folder and for Windows Explorer. This feature can also be disabled (we show you how in Chapter 1), if you don't care for it.

Now, click the icon for your computer's C: drive. When you do, the C: drive's resources will appear in the Explorer window. Notice that the Back (left-pointing) arrow to the right of the Address text box in the toolbar turns white (see Figure QT-4). Just like the Back arrow on a Web browser's toolbar, you can click it to return to the My Computer information.

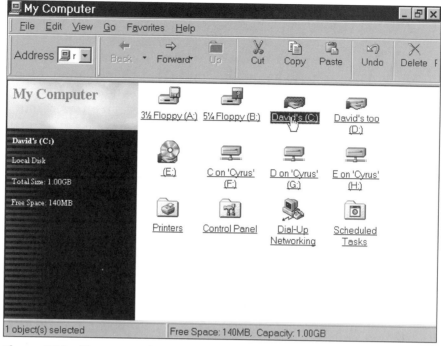

Figure QT-3 The open Explorer window, showing My Computer. When the mouse pointer is over an icon, it turns into a hand as if it were over a link on a Web page.

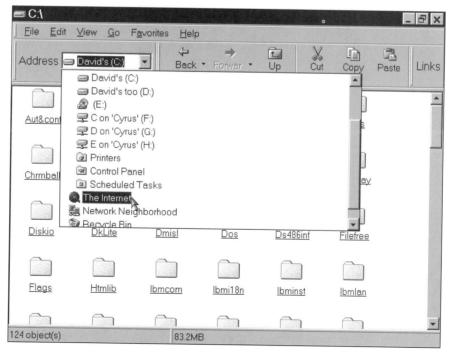

Figure QT-4 The Explorer window, showing resources on the C: drive and with the Address box list open.

Browsing the Web

With the Explorer window open, you can get to Internet resources in a flash. Notice that in Figure QT-4 the toolbar has an Address text box, something the old My Computer didn't have. You can use the Address box just like the Address box or Location box in a browser. That is, you can type in an Internet address, or URL (Uniform Resource Locator), press the Enter key on your keyboard, and go to the Web page it represents. Another way you can use IE 4's Address box is to select a resource from its drop-down list. For example, you can instantly display the resources on another drive or in the Control Panel folder by clicking the resource's name in the drop-down list.

Follow these steps to use the Address box to connect to the Internet:

1. Click the arrow at the right side of the Address box. A drop-down list appears. Notice that all of your computer's drives, the Control Panel, and other resources are in this list.

2. Click The Internet. If you use a dial-up ISP (Internet Service Provider), the Connection Manager dialog box appears (see Figure QT-5).

Figure QT-5   The Connection Manager dialog box appears when you need to connect to the Internet.

3. By default (the standard setting), the Connection Manager is set to dial into your ISP automatically and make the Internet connection. If for some reason your Connection Manager is not set to automatically dial

for you (see the Troubleshooting appendix at the end of the book), click Connect. Once the Internet connection is made, IE 4 goes to an Explorer page at Microsoft's Web site unless you have changed IE 4's default home page. The one that appeared at the time this was written is shown in Figure QT-6.

Figure QT-6 IE 4, showing the Internet Explorer 4.0 home page.
Screen shot reprinted by permission from Microsoft Corporation.

NOTE If you're on a company network with a direct Internet connection, IE 4 goes directly to a Web page when The Internet is clicked. See Appendix A to find out how you can set Internet Explorer to go to the home page (the page that's displayed when the program is opened) of your choice, or to open with a blank page and not connect to the Internet when you start Internet Explorer.

Once you're on the Web with Internet Explorer 4, browsing is a snap. The toolbar changes to include buttons that you'd see in any Web browser, including those for Forward, Back, Stop, Home, and Print. In addition, if you click the Back arrow at this point, you'll go back to the resources on your C: drive that you saw using My Computer.

Follow these steps to use the IE 4 browser:

1. Move the mouse pointer around the screen. When you see it change into a hand, it's over a link to another Web page.

2. Click any link on the page to go to another Web page.

3. Experiment with IE 4's various toolbar buttons and Web page links.

4. When you're through exploring, click [**File**] → [**Close**] to close IE 4. Don't forget to disconnect from your ISP after you close IE 4.

Next, in Chapter 1, we tell you more about the Explorer program and how you can set it to suit the way you browse the Web and manage your own desktop.

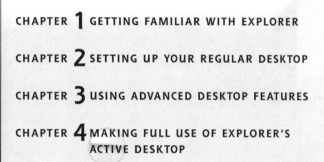

Microsoft Internet Explorer version 4 is a complete departure from the way Web browsers worked in the past. It is integrated into the operating system of your computer to give you a seamless link with the Internet, making the resources of every computer on the Net as accessible as those in your home or office PC. In addition, it gives you the ability to tap into the new "push" technology that information vendors on the Web use to provide continuously updated information to your computer without any effort on your part.

Any software that does this much is bound to be complicated and seem a bit intimidating at first. But Explorer's developers had lots of tricks up their collective sleeves and included them in the program. Explorer lets you customize it in dozens of ways to make it as personalized and easy for you to use as possible. You can take advantage of the Active Desktop's "live" content or ignore it completely. And you can create a customized interface that's yours alone or turn off all the new features and go back to the way Windows 95 looked and worked. The choices are all yours.

THE NAME GAME

Internet...Gopher...Web... Ever wonder how these things got their names? We're not sure who coined the term *Internet*, but it came into being to describe the global connection of computer networks that started developing only during the last twenty years. In 1973, Robert Kahn and Vinton Cerf published a paper on networking titled "A Protocol for Packet Network Internetworking." It's very possible that this title was the source for the term Internet.

In its early days, the Internet's potential was unrealized because there were no directories to what was on it and no easy way to search it. You had to ask your colleagues what computer held which data, and then you had to contact the computer's operator to get permission to use it. Then you had to use a program called Telnet to connect to the computer and read through its directories. Since the directories only listed the names of the files and not what was in them, you couldn't really be sure whether the files would be useful. Finally, you had to use another program called FTP to copy any files to your computer, where you could read through them to see what they contained. One method people came up with to make the Internet more usuable is called Gopher.

In 1991, the University of Minnesota Microcomputer, Workstation, Networks Center developed a program for searching the Internet using menus. The program was named Gopher, after the University's mascot. Gopher organizes files on a computer into menus that list and describe the files. Each choice on the first menu leads to another, more detailed, menu. The choices on the second menu may lead to another menu, or to a document that you can read or print out. Gophers work faster than Web pages because they don't contain graphics. In recent years, many gophers have been replaced by Web pages and shut down. However, hundreds are still in operation.

At about the same time Gopher was being developed, people were working on the idea of sending graphics and hypertext over the Internet. The authors of the original proposal for what eventually became the World Wide Web, Tim Berners-Lee and Robert Cailliau, referred to this idea for linking information all over the world using hypertext and graphic links as the World-Wide Web. People who insist on proper English would say that "World Wide" isn't correct and should be "Worldwide," but the Berners-Lee/Cailliau name for it stuck. The word "web" came from the spider web model used for thinking about the World Wide Web.

GETTING FAMILIAR WITH EXPLORER

T he biggest difference you'll notice between older browsers and Internet Explorer 4.0 (IE 4) is that IE 4 changes the way your desktop looks and the ways in which you interact with your computer. With IE 4, your desktop behaves like a Web page, and icons on your desktop work like Web page links. In fact, you can even use a Web page for your desktop wallpaper (see Chapter 4).

In this chapter, we show you some basic uses of IE 4 for browsing your computer and managing files. For the examples in this chapter, we turned the Active Desktop off, but you don't have to in order to follow along. To turn your Active Desktop off, right-click a blank space on the desktop and select Active Desktop→ View as Web Page from the shortcut menu that appears.

Checking Out the Changes

Y ou'll probably notice two things after installing IE 4: you have a black desktop with IE 4's welcome message on it, and your Windows 95 taskbar has a "Quick Launch toolbar" with some little buttons that weren't there before.

(After a day or two the black background and welcome message of the Active Desktop mysteriously disappear, and whatever background you had for your regular desktop before you installed IE 4 replaces it.) Any icons and folders that were on your old desktop will still be there, but their names will be underlined, just like links on a Web page. This is IE 4's Active Desktop, and we'll cover its many features and uses in Chapter 4. You may find it easier to follow along in this chapter with the Active Desktop turned off.

FEATURE FOCUS Internet Explorer 4's biggest news is the Active Desktop, in which you can create custom backgrounds, install "live" components, and subscribe to continuously updated "channels" of information. Another new feature, hover select, makes opening programs and files easier.

Next, you'll notice IE 4's *hover select* feature. When you move the mouse pointer over an icon on your desktop, the icon's name becomes highlighted, like the text links on Web pages. If you let the pointer "hover" over the icon for a moment, the icon and its name become dark, indicating that the icon has been selected. The programs, files, and folders represented by icons are opened with one click instead of two. Just as before you installed IE 4, icons can be renamed, deleted, and so forth, by using the shortcut menu that appears when you right-click the icon. Also, you can still drag icons to different places on your desktop. All of the changes that IE 4 makes to your desktop can be reversed.

NOTE We simplified the screen examples for this chapter by hiding the taskbar and turning off the Active Desktop. Also, some of the examples were made using Windows NT4, which has a desktop almost identical to Windows 95. Because of this, your screen may not look exactly like the examples shown, and some of the icons may have names that are slightly different (for example, "NT Explorer" instead of "Windows Explorer").

To see how hover select works, follow these steps:

1. Move the mouse pointer over an icon on your desktop but don't click it. The pointer turns into a hand and the icon's name is highlighted (see Figure 1-1).

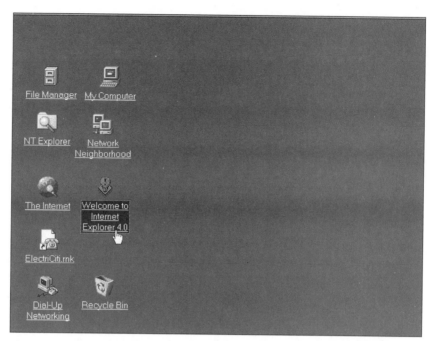

Figure 1-1   Resting the mouse pointer over an icon turns it into a hand and highlights the icon's name, just like on a Web page.

Figure 1-2   Right-click an icon to open its shortcut menu.

2. Leave the pointer over the icon for a moment. The icon and its name become dark, indicating that it is selected.

3. Right-click the icon. A shortcut menu appears (see Figure 1-2).

4. Click in a blank area of the desktop to close the shortcut menu.

Exploring IE 4

When you open My Computer or Windows Explorer, or any folder for that matter, the window that appears looks similar to the window you saw before IE 4 was installed. Also, changes that you make (to toolbars, sort order, etc.) in each of these windows can be saved separately so that each one is customized. However, what you're seeing is actually IE 4 in disguise. The browser is there in the background no matter what folder you open, and it fully integrates your computer with the Web. You can still manage files using My Computer and Windows Explorer, but because of hover select and something that Microsoft calls *Web View,* IE 4 looks and works just a little differently. The first time you open My Computer or Windows Explorer, their windows will not be maximized. We'll start showing you the changes by using Windows Explorer.

FEATURE FOCUS IE 4 updates three programs that came with Windows 95 or Windows NT 4: Internet Explorer, Windows Explorer (or NT Explorer), and My Computer. Shortcuts and menu choices for them are still there, and each still looks and functions differently, but in reality it's IE 4 working in the background. Any folder you open also includes IE 4 toolbars and menus.

Follow these steps to open Windows Explorer:

1. Click Start on your taskbar to open the Start menu (see Figure 1-2). Notice that IE 4 added new menu choices for Favorites and Log Off to the Start menu.

2. Click Programs → Windows Explorer to open Windows Explorer.

3. Maximize the Windows Explorer window by clicking the ☐ in the upper-right corner of the title bar.

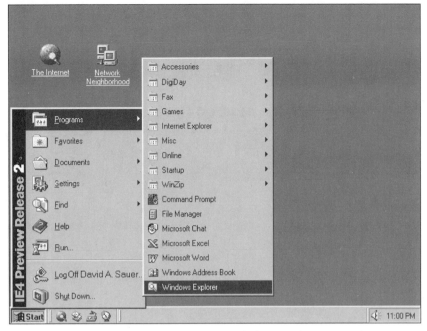

Figure 1-3 Using the Start menu to open Windows Explorer.

The new Windows Explorer displays a "tree view" of your computer's resources in the left side of the window, and details about the selected resource in the right side of the window. The two sides of the window are called *panes*. If you want to, you can create a background pattern for the right pane. Customizing folder backgrounds are discussed in Chapter 2.

Scroll down the left pane of the window until you see the Windows folder and click it. (Hover select works in the right pane, but not in the left one.) When you do, the folders and files inside the Windows folder will appear in the right pane of the window (see Figure 1-4).

FEATURE FOCUS IE 4 adds to your folders toolbars and menus that resemble those in a Web browser. These give you instant access to any resource on your computer, your network, or the Internet, from any open folder.

Notice that the toolbar in Figure 1-4 contains an Address box and, next to the box, arrows pointing left and right. These arrows work like the forward and back buttons in a Web browser. Your Windows Explorer window may not look exactly like the one shown in Figure 1-4. For one thing, we have selected the Large Icons option on the View menu (see Figure 1-9 to see the View menu open), and you may have Details or List selected. Also, we set our view options to display all file types and file extensions. These settings are discussed later in this chapter.

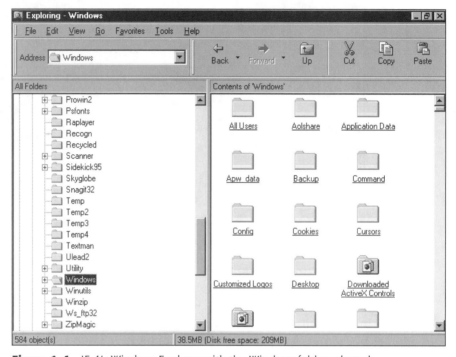

Figure 1-4   IE 4's Windows Explorer with the Windows folder selected.

Opening Programs with Windows Explorer

As with the original Windows Explorer, you can open programs from within the new version.

Follow these steps to open a program using Windows Explorer:

1. Scroll down or across the right pane of the window until you see "Calc," "Calc.exe," or a calculator icon named "Calc" or "Calc.exe" (see Figure 1-5).

2. Move the mouse pointer over Calc and click it once. The Calculator program opens.

3. Click the close button in the upper-right corner of the Calculator title bar to close the program.

Figure 1-5   The Windows folder selected in the left pane, with "Calc.exe" selected in the right pane.

Managing Files with Windows Explorer

Routine file management tasks, such as copying, cutting and pasting, deleting, and renaming, also work the same way that they did with the old Windows Explorer. However, if you want to select a *group* of files for any of these actions, you have to be a little careful because of the hover select feature. Hover select is tricky and takes a while to get used to.

Follow these steps for managing a file with Windows Explorer:

1. Right-click a file in Windows Explorer's right pane to open the shortcut menu (see Figure 1-6). The shortcut menu gives you the options to copy, cut and paste, delete, or rename the file. You also use the shortcut menu to send (copy) the file to one of the places listed in the Send To menu, or to create a shortcut icon for the file.

Figure 1-6 Right-click a file to open the shortcut menu for most file management tasks.

2. To cut and paste a file, select **Cut** from the shortcut menu.

3. Next, scroll through the left pane to select the drive and directory you want to paste the file into, then click **Edit** → **Paste** .

As mentioned before, the new hover select feature can make selecting a group of files tricky if you're used to the old procedures. All you really have to remember is not to click any of the files you're selecting for file management tasks.

Follow these steps to select a group of files that are all next to one another in the right pane:

1. Select the first file in the group by resting the mouse pointer over the file's name or icon. When the file's name or icon turns dark, it is selected (see Figure 1-5). Remember not to click the file.

2. Hold down the Shift key on your keyboard.

3. Rest the pointer over the last file in the group that you want to select. Again, remember not to click the file. The group of files all turn dark to indicate that they are selected as a group (see Figure 1-7).

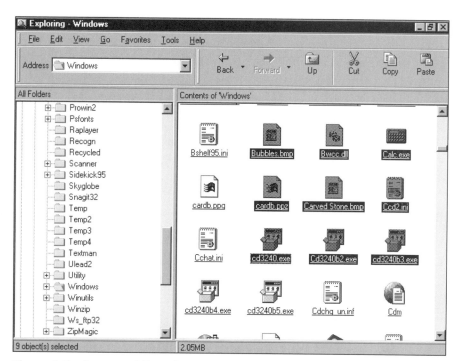

Figure 1-7   A group of files selected using the hover select feature.

In our example, shown in Figure 1-7, we selected a block of nine icons, starting in the upper right with the Calc.exe icon and ending in the lower left with the cd3240.exe icon. The group of files that you can select using the hover select technique depends on how you have the view (selected on the View menu) set—to Large Icons, Details, etc. In the Large Icons view, you can select blocks, columns, or rows of adjacent icons. Try this with different views to see how selecting groups of files changes with each view. For more on changing the view, see the next section.

NOTE   To select several files that are not next to one another, rest the mouse pointer over the first file to select it; hold down the Control key; and rest the mouse pointer over the next file that you want to select, and so forth. Remember not to click the files; just let the pointer hover over them.

Now You See It, Now You Don't

Internet Explorer lets you customize many of the ways it looks and works. You can hide or show toolbars, choose what buttons show on the toolbars, move the toolbars around, view your files as icons or in a list, sort files by name or type, and so on. But don't let the "gee whiz" factor fool you. These options aren't there just to impress; they're there to enable you to set up Explorer and other programs so that they work the way that's best for you.

By including so many ways for you to customize its look and feel, Internet Explorer 4 lets you turn it into your own personalized version.

The files you see and how they're sorted in Windows Explorer, My Computer, and other folders can be set using the View menu.

Follow these steps to change the way files are sorted:

1. Click **View** → **Arrange Icons** to show the menu options for arranging (sorting) your icons or files (see Figure 1-8).

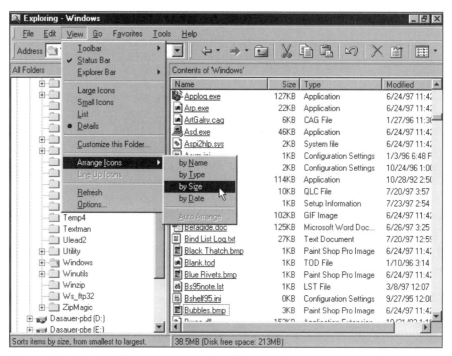

Figure 1-8 Use the View menu to set how files are displayed and sorted.

2. Click your choice for the way you want the icons (or files) sorted. The menu closes and the icons are sorted the way you want.

When the View menu is open, notice the options named Large Icons, Small Icons, List, and Details. These options determine how the files are displayed in the right pane. Open the menu again and click any of these to see how it changes the view. Try all four to see which one is best for you. Then try the different options for arranging icons to see which of those you want to use. You can have one setup for the view and arrangement in Windows Explorer and another in My Computer. Each can be customized independently of the other.

Tooling Around

The toolbars in Windows Explorer, the IE 4 browser, My Computer, and the Control Panel can be individually customized, or you can set the toolbars to look the same in all of them. The procedure for customizing toolbars is the same no matter what folder or IE 4 program you have open.

Table 1-1 provides a brief description of several elements common to the IE 4 toolbars. For our example, in Figure 1-9, we'll show you the My Computer toolbar. If you have Windows Explorer open, close it and click the My Computer icon on your desktop to open My Computer.

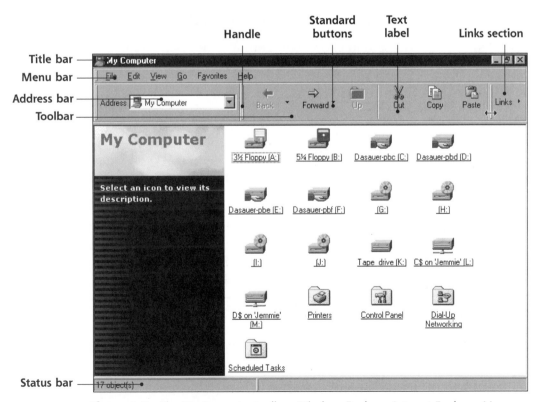

Figure 1-9   The My Computer toolbar. Windows Explorer, Internet Explorer, My Computer, and folders also share these same elements.

TABLE 1-1 Elements of IE 4 windows and toolbars

Toolbar Item	Description
Title bar	The horizontal segment at the top of the window that includes the open program or folder's name, and buttons to minimize, maximize, or close the window.
Menu bar	The horizontal segment at the top of the window that holds menu options.
Toolbar	The horizontal segment at the top of the window that holds command buttons and other sections, such as the Address bar.
Status bar	The horizontal segment at the bottom of the window that shows information such as how much hard disk space you have available.
Explorer bar	A section of the toolbar for buttons that open a special pane in the left part of the window. By default, it's only part of the toolbar when you open Internet Explorer, but the special panes can be opened in other programs as well.
Standard buttons	The toolbar buttons for Forward, Back, Copy, etc.
Address bar	The section of the toolbar that contains the Address box.
Links	The section of the toolbar that contains customizable buttons for links.
Handle	A small, vertical line at the left end of a toolbar section that is used to expand or reduce the section's width or drag the section to a different part of the toolbar.
Text labels	Labels under toolbar buttons that can be turned off or on.

You can set the IE 4 toolbars to include (or not include) standard buttons, the Address bar, and links. The Explorer bar can be part of the toolbar only in Internet Explorer, or when Internet Explorer is selected from within another window or folder. Each of these sections can be moved around on the toolbar, expanded or reduced in height, and expanded or reduced in width. The menu bar can also be moved around, and you can have more than one row of buttons and sections in the toolbar.

Each of the sections of the toolbar has a short vertical line at its left end. This line is called the *handle*. (We've also seen it called the *tab* and the *grabber bar*.) Notice in Figure 1-9 that the mouse pointer, positioned over the handle for the Links bar, has turned into a two-headed arrow pointing left and right. When the pointer changes in this way over a handle, you can drag the handle left or right to expand or close the section, or drag the entire section from one part of the toolbar to another. If you move the pointer over the bottom border of the toolbar, it turns into a two-headed arrow pointing up and down. When the pointer changes like this, you can drag the bottom border up or down to make the toolbar expand or reduce in size.

Follow these steps to open, close, or drag a section of the toolbar:

1. Move the mouse pointer over the handle of a toolbar section.

2. Press and hold the mouse button and drag the handle to the left or right. As you do so, the toolbar section will expand or contract.

3. Press and hold the mouse button and drag the handle to another part of the toolbar. In our example, we dragged it to the right end of the menu bar and dragged it open, to the left, to reveal a few of the link buttons (see Figure 1-10).

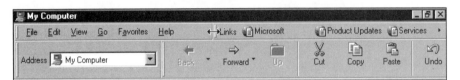

Figure 1-10   The My Computer toolbar. The links have been moved to the right of the menu options.

4. Release the mouse button when the toolbar section is where you want it to be.

Follow these steps to remove or restore the text labels on the toolbar buttons:

1. Click **View** → **Toolbar** to open the menu of toolbar options (see Figure 1-11).

2. Click **Text Labels** to remove the ✓ next to it. The menus close and the toolbar buttons are without text and reduced in size. Repeat Steps 1 and 2 if you want to restore the text labels.

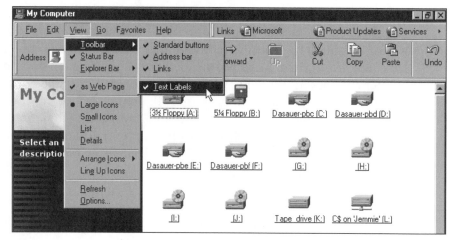

Figure 1-11   The View menu, with Text Labels selected.

Follow these steps to expand or reduce the toolbar in height; or to add or remove rows:

1. Move the mouse pointer over the bottom border of the toolbar so that it turns into a two-headed arrow pointing up and down (see Figure 1-12).

Figure 1-12   Drag the bottom border of the toolbar to expand it or add another row.

2. Press and hold the mouse button as you slowly drag the border down. At first, the height of the row of toolbars will increase and the text labels, if removed, will return (see Figure 1-13). As you continue to drag, another row will be added to the toolbar and one of the sections, such as standard buttons, that used to be in the single toolbar row will "jump" into the new row.

Figure 1-13   The My Computer toolbar with a row added for the standard buttons.

3. Continue dragging the border down if you want to add another row, so that each section of the toolbar has its own row.

4. Reverse this process—that is, drag the border up—to remove rows from the toolbar.

As noted above, the Explorer bar is automatically included in the toolbar when you open Internet Explorer or select Internet Explorer from within another window or folder. The Explorer bar lets you open special panes that are particularly useful while you're browsing the Web. You can also open these panes in My Computer or other folders.

Follow these steps to open one of the Explorer bar's special panes:

1. Click [View] → [Explorer Bar] → [Favorites]. Your Favorites will appear in a list in the left pane (see Figure 1-14). The My Computer panes will be squeezed into the right pane.

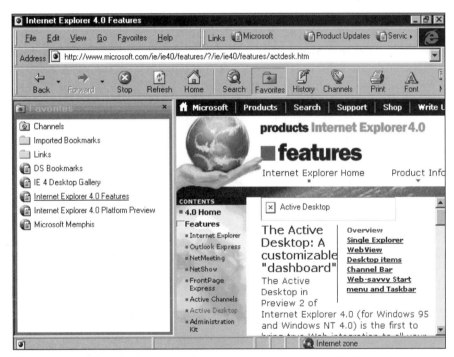

Figure 1-14 The My Computer window turns into an Internet Explorer window when a Favorite is selected.

Screen shot reprinted by permission from Microsoft Corporation.

2. To connect to the Internet and go to a Favorite, click the Favorite in the left pane. In our example, we clicked on Internet Explorer 4.0 Features (your Favorites list will be different). If you do this, the My Computer window changes into an Internet Explorer window, and the following option won't work.

or

To close the Favorites pane without connecting to the Internet, either click the Back button in the toolbar or select [View] → [Explorer Bar] → [None].

With the Favorites pane open, you can right-click a Favorite and use the shortcut menu that appears to cut, copy and paste, or delete it. You can also select Properties from the shortcut menu and edit the Favorite's name or URL.

X-REF **For more information about managing Favorites, see Chapter 6; to learn more about using the special panes that open from the Explorer bar, see Chapters 5 and 7.**

Notice the toolbar in Figure 1-14. When you open the Favorites pane, the Explorer bar does not appear in the toolbar. That only happens when you click the Favorite and connect to the Internet. At that point, the My Computer window is transformed into an Internet Explorer window; and the Explorer bar—with the Search, Favorites, History, and Channels buttons—appears in the toolbar. Once the window has turned into Internet Explorer, you can't go back to the My Computer window format. To continue following along in this chapter, you'll have to close the Explorer window and open My Computer again. (Don't forget to disconnect from your ISP if you have connected to the Internet.)

Traveling Back in Time

For those who want their desktop to work the way it used to, without hover select and other IE 4 features, it's easy to turn these things off. In "Microsoft-speak," such features are collectively called *Web View*. However, Web View may also refer to the enhanced displays available in the My Computer and Control Panel windows, where information about resources in the right pane is displayed in the left pane.

Going Retro, Part 1

IE 4's new look and ways of working aren't for everyone. You may want to turn off the split-pane view that IE 4 adds to My Computer and the Control Panel folder.

Follow these steps to return My Computer and Control Panel to their old look:

1. Click the My Computer icon on your desktop to open My Computer, or click [Start] → [Settings] → [Control Panel] to open the Control Panel folder. You only have to make this change to one of them for it to apply to both.

2. Click **View** → **as Web Page** to remove the ✓ next to **as Web Page**. The menu closes and the enhanced information in the left panel disappears (see Figure 1-15).

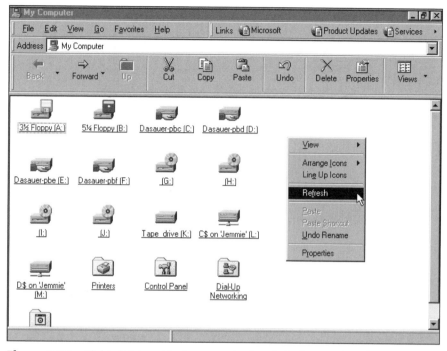

Figure 1-15 Right-click in a blank area and select Refresh to update the view in a folder.

3. Repeat Steps 1 and 2 to replace the ✓ next to **as Web Page** if you want to restore the enhanced information.

4. Right-click in a blank part of the window and select **Refresh** from the shortcut menu that appears to update the view in the folder (see Figure 1-15). You can also update the view by pressing the F5 key on your keyboard.

NOTE With as Web Page turned off, you cannot add a customized background to a folder (see Chapter 2).

Going Retro, Part 2

Next, we'll show you how to turn most of the other Web View features off and on. These are handled in a dialog box that you open from the View menu in My Computer, Windows Explorer, the IE 4 browser, or other folders.

Follow these steps to modify or turn off Web View features:

1. Select ⬚ **View** ⬚ → ⬚ **Options** ⬚ to open the Options dialog box. The General tab will be at the front (see Figure 1-16).

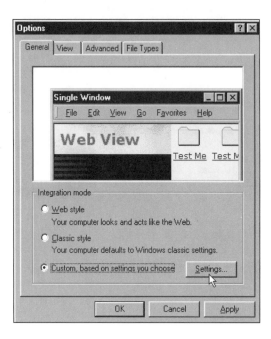

Figure 1-16 The Options dialog box with the General tab selected.

2. On the General tab, click Classic style (the old Windows 95 look and feel) to go back to the old way of doing things, then click OK to save your choice and close the dialog box.

   or

   Click Custom if you want to select IE 4 features, then click Settings to open the Web Integration Settings dialog box (see Figure 1-17).

The Web Integration Settings dialog box contains places to choose a variety of options. If your computer was set up to browse folders in separate windows, here's where you can tell it to browse them all in one, and vice versa. In the middle of the dialog box, you can tell IE 4 that you want to be able to select which folders look like Web pages.

The lower section of the dialog box has several settings. This is where you can go back to single- and double-clicking to select and open icons ("Select when single-clicked..."). If you stick with hover select ("Select when pointed at..."), you can choose whether icons will look like Web links all the time or only when you point at them.

Click a choice (to place a dot next to it) to select it. When you're done, click OK to save your choices and close the Web Integration Settings dialog box, but don't exit the Options dialog box just yet. There are two more things to take a look at.

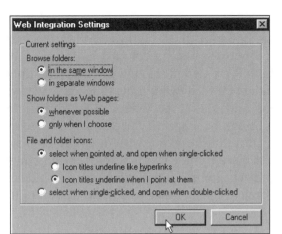

Figure 1-17 The Web Integration Settings dialog box, for selecting some but not all of IE 4's new features.

Picky, Picky, Picky

A few things in the Options dialog box don't have anything to do with turning IE 4 features off and on, but we thought you could use some information about them anyway. These settings control how you interact with your computer whether you enable all of IE 4's features or not. If necessary, go back through the previous "Going Retro" sections to open the Options dialog box.

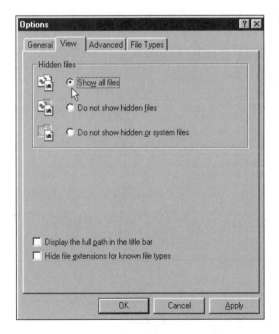

Figure 1-18 The Options dialog box with the View tab selected.

Click the View tab in the Options dialog box to bring the tab to the front.

The View tab (see Figure 1-18) lets you select which files you can see in Windows Explorer, My Computer, and so forth. We've always been in favor of full disclosure and don't like our operating systems keeping things secret from us, so we opted for the "Show all files" setting at the top of the tab. But the choice is yours. Click an option to place a dot next to it to select it.

At the bottom of the tab are two more view options. The upper one lets you see the full path to a folder you're viewing in its title bar. The lower one displays file extensions (the dot and last three letters of its name) in lists of files. Displaying file extensions can be extremely useful if you have several files in a folder with names that start the same, but with different extensions at the end. For example, you might have a folder with several graphic files in it such as "cats.jpg," "cats.gif," and "cats.bmp." If the extensions are hidden, all three files would seem to be the same. Click a choice to place a ✓ next to it if you want to select it.

The Advanced tab is our last stop in the view customization tour (see Figure 1-19).

Click the Advanced tab in the Options dialog box to bring the tab to the front. Click a choice to place a ✓ next to it to select it.

The Advanced tab includes the following:

* *Show Map Network Drive button in toolbar.* This button may be useful for restoring a connection to another computer if you're on a network.

* *Show file attributes in Detail View.* File attributes tell you things such as whether a file is "read only" (can't be edited or deleted) or a system file (usually necessary in order for the operating system to function correctly).

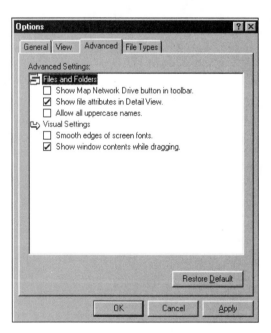

Figure 1-19 The Options dialog box with the Advanced tab selected.

* *Allow all uppercase names.* It isn't necessary to check this in order to name files with a combination of uppercase and lowercase letters, as you can already do so in "Save As" dialog boxes. Checking this option may change several files and folders already on your computer to have all uppercase names.

* *Smooth edges of screen fonts.* We didn't notice any difference with this checked or unchecked, but maybe we aren't using the right screen fonts. Try it both ways to see if it makes a difference for you.

* *Show window contents while dragging.* If your video card supports this, it's kind of neat. Instead of seeing just the outline of a window while you are adjusting its size, you see the contents as well.

The File Types tab shows you what programs automatically open when you click a file. For example, if you click a file that ends with the ".txt" extension, the Notepad accessory program opens by default to display it. Generally, you won't need to deal with these settings. Click OK to save your choices and close the Options dialog box.

Saving the Look

Once you have a custom "look" in Explorer, My Computer, etc., IE 4 will remember it. The next time you open the program, it should look the way it was when you closed it. If this is not the case, you can "remind" IE 4 that you want it to save the look you've set up.

Follow these steps to be sure IE 4 remembers the look you've set up:

1. Press and hold down the Control (or Ctrl) key on your keyboard.

2. Select File → Close to close the program.

BONUS

Opening Explorer Where You Want It

It's easy to make a shortcut for Windows Explorer for your desktop so that opening it is more convenient. But when it opens, it automatically selects your C: drive and expands the folders on it (as shown in Figure 1-4). By adding a few things to the shortcut's properties, you can have Explorer open to

My Computer so that you can select which drive on your computer or network you want to explore without a lot of scrolling around.

Follow these steps to set Windows Explorer to open to My Computer:

1. Make a shortcut for Windows Explorer on your desktop. (Right-click the desktop, select `New` → `Shortcut`, and browse to C:\Windows\Explorer.exe.)

2. Right-click the shortcut and select `Properties` from the shortcut menu that appears. The Windows Explorer Properties dialog box appears.

3. Click the Shortcut tab in the dialog box to bring it to the front. The text in the Target box will be selected (highlighted).

4. Press the right arrow key on your keyboard. A cursor will appear at the right end of the text, right after "EXPLORER.EXE" in the Target box.

5. Press the spacebar on your keyboard to enter a blank space, then type **/n, /e, /select, c:**. The text in the Target box should read:

   C:\WINDOWS\EXPLORER.EXE /n, /e, /select, c:\
   when you're done.

6. While you have the Shortcut tab showing, click the Change Icon button if you want to select a different icon for the desktop shortcut.

7. Click OK. The dialog box closes.

Now, whenever you use this shortcut to open Windows Explorer, it'll automatically open to My Computer, not to the C: drive.

To have Windows Explorer open to a specific folder, substitute the path to the folder (such as d:\files) for the "c:\" at the end of the string of text in the Target box.

Summary

In this chapter, we've seen how IE 4 changes the look and feel of Windows 95 to make your desktop work much like a Web page on the Internet. IE 4 also works in the background in My Computer and Windows Explorer. It handles all of the file management routines that these formerly separate programs used to do, and adds instant access to World Wide Web resources. You can also customize IE 4 to suit the way you use your computer, or turn off its new features if they're not to your liking.

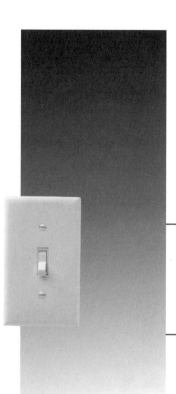

SETTING UP YOUR REGULAR DESKTOP

2

IN THIS CHAPTER YOU LEARN THESE KEY SKILLS

HOW TO CUSTOMIZE THE DESKTOP   PAGE   33

HOW TO CUSTOMIZE FOLDERS   PAGE   35

HOW TO CUSTOMIZE THE START MENU   PAGE   46

If you opt to include the Web Integrated Desktop when you install IE 4 (see Appendix A), your copy of Internet Explorer includes many convenience features that affect your desktop, folders, and the way you interact with your computer. In this chapter, we'll show you how you can personalize your desktop, your folder backgrounds, and the choices that appear on your start menu. (Customizing and using the Active Desktop is covered in Chapter 4.) And for a bonus, we'll tell you about a program you can install that may take care of some minor annoyances.

Shaking Up Your Desktop

The biggest changes that IE 4 can make to the way your regular desktop looks and works are covered in the section of Chapter 1 titled, "Traveling Back in Time." If you haven't already, read through that section to learn how you can change your desktop back to the way it worked before you installed IE 4, or combine some of the new features with some of the old ones.

IE 4 makes a couple of changes to the way you add color or colorful patterns to your desktop. If you customize your Active Desktop with an HTML background, (see Chapter 4), any "wallpaper" (a design or picture), colors, or patterns that you have added to the regular desktop may get covered up while the Active Desktop feature is turned on. But when you turn the Active Desktop off, they will return.

Follow these steps to see the changes IE 4 makes for customizing your regular desktop:

1. Turn off the Active Desktop if it's on (see the Quick Tour if you need to know how).

2. Right-click a blank space on the desktop to open the shortcut menu.

3. Click **Properties** . The Display Properties dialog box appears (see Figure 2-1).

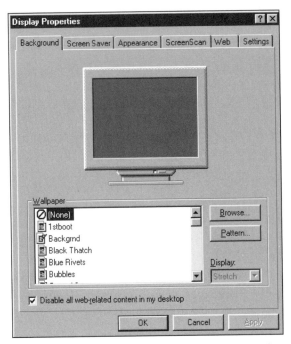

Figure 2-1 The Display Properties dialog box with the Background tab at the front.

4. Click the Background tab, if needed, to bring it to the front.

The Display Properties dialog box includes two tabs where you can change the colors and patterns on your desktop: the Background tab and the Appearance tab. The Appearance tab lets you select colors for the various elements of your Windows 95 interface, and we won't go into detail about that. Basically, you click the element you want to change, click a color, and save the scheme with a unique name. (See Windows 95 Help for details.)

IE 4 changes the Background tab, where you select wallpaper or a pattern for your desktop background. (The patterns only apply to solid colors that you select on the Appearance tab; they won't work for wallpaper.) Instead of giving you two columns of background choices, one for a pattern and one for wallpaper, IE 4's background tab has only one, for wallpaper. To select a pattern, you have to click the Pattern button. Otherwise, the procedures for selecting wallpaper or a pattern remain the same (see Windows 95 Help for details). If you do decide to create an HTML background for your Active Desktop (see Chapter 4), the Background tab is where you select it.

Before we leave the Display Properties dialog box, we'd like to point out some other changes that IE 4 makes here when it's installed. You'll notice two new tabs in the dialog box. One, named ScreenScan, lets you tell the ScanDisk program that it can run while the screen saver is in operation, and lets you set operating parameters for ScanDisk. The other new tab, Web, is where you tell IE 4 which Active Desktop items you want to display, and which you want to hide (see Chapter 4 for more about Active Desktop items).

Customizing Folders

Ever get bored with the same old, plain backgrounds you see inside your folders? Well, with IE 4's "Web View" feature, you can customize each and every folder's background to be different. Just as you can have pictures or wallpaper for the background on your desktop, you can use favorite pictures or an HTML (Hypertext Markup Language) editor to create custom backgrounds like the ones shown in Figures 2-5 and 2-11. For our examples, we're using the Programs folder and the Games folder, but you can use almost any folder you'd like. The only exceptions are the My Computer and Control Panel folders; these two have predefined HTML backgrounds. The changes you make to one folder won't show up in any others; you can make every one of them unique.

With IE 4's "Web View" feature, you can make every folder's background different.

FEATURE FOCUS   IE 4 lets you liven up folder backgrounds with pictures or even interactive HTML features.

Picture This

First we'll show you how to use a picture for a folder's background. You can use pictures that come with Windows, or any that have been saved on your computer in bitmap, JPEG, or GIF format (these are different file formats for image files). By default, the Customize This Folder Wizard looks for bitmap images (files that end with ".bmp").

Follow these steps to select a picture for a folder's background:

1. Right-click **Start** on your taskbar and click **Open** to open the Start Menu folder (see Figure 2-2).

Figure 2-2 Right-click the Start button and select Open to open its folder.

2. Click the Programs icon to open the Programs folder.

3. Right-click a blank part of the folder's background to open the shortcut menu, or click **View** in the menu bar to open the View menu.

4. Click **Customize this Folder**. The Customize This Folder Wizard will open (see Figure 2-3). In the Wizard's first dialog box you select whether you want to create an HTML document for the folder's background, select a picture for the background, or remove customization that you may have made previously.

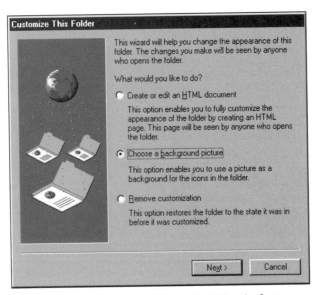

Figure 2-3 The Customize This Folder Wizard's first dialog box.

5. Click "Choose a background picture" to select it.

6. Click Next. The dialog box changes to show the bitmap (".bmp") images that are available in your C:\Windows folder (see Figure 2-4).

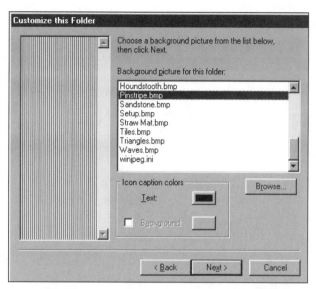

Figure 2-4 The Customize This Folder Wizard's dialog box for choosing a picture.

7. If you want to use an image file that came with Windows 95, scroll through the list and click an image's name to select it. A sample of the image appears in the box on the left. In our example (Figure 2-4) we clicked on Pinstripe.

8. If you want to use a picture that's on your computer, click the Browse button. Use the Open dialog box that appears to browse to the folder where the picture you want to use is located and select it. If you're not using a ".bmp" image, you can click the arrow at the right end of the Files of Type list box and select ".JPG" or ".gif." A sample of the image appears in the Wizard's dialog box. For our example (see Figure 2-5), we selected a picture named "clouds.bmp" that we copied to the computer from our Windows 95 CD. (You can find it in the Pictures folder inside the Funstuff folder on your copy of the CD.)

9. To select a unique color for the icon captions in your folder, click the color box to the right of "Text:" in the part of the dialog box labeled "Icon caption colors" to open the color palette, and click the color you want.

10. To select a background color for the icon captions, click the box to the left of "Background" to place a ✓ in it, click the color box to the right of "Background," and then click the color you want in the palette that appears.

11. Click Next. The Wizard congratulates you in its last dialog box.

12. Click Finish to save your choice, or Cancel to cancel the operation without making any changes. If you click Finish, the background picture appears in the folder (see Figure 2-5).

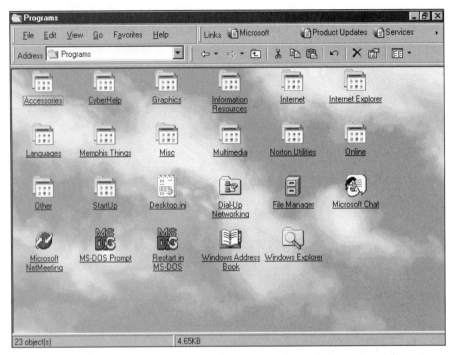

Figure 2-5 The Programs folder customized with a picture ("clouds.bmp" from the Windows 95 CD) for its background.

Making an HTML Folder Background

If you choose to customize your folder background, another option is to create a background using an HTML document. Using an HTML document for your background lets you include images, text (such as explanations of what's in the folder or what an icon leads to), or, for advanced HTML authors, interactive controls, tables, animation, or anything else that you may see on HTML documents such as Web pages.

For our example, we'll just show you some basics by making a background that uses the folder template provided by IE 4. We'll change the template a little and put our own pictures and text into it. This section assumes that you chose an install option that includes FrontPage Express during the IE 4 installation. If you did not, and you don't already have an HTML editor installed on your computer, this procedure will not work. See the Bonus section at the end of Chapter 3 if you want to add FrontPage Express to your suite of IE 4 programs.

Follow these steps to make an HTML folder background:

1. Follow Steps 1–4 under "Picture This" (above) to start the Customize This Folder Wizard (see Figure 2-3).

2. Click "Create or edit an HTML document" to select it.

3. Click Next. The Wizard gives you directions for this process (see Figure 2-6). In short, you create the document using your HTML editor, save the document, then close the HTML editor and automatically return to the Wizard.

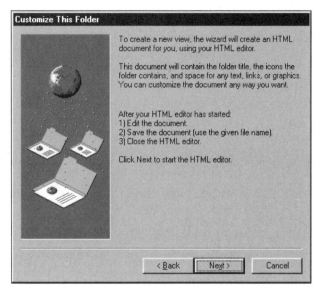

Figure 2-6   The Customize This Folder Wizard gives you brief instructions for using an HTML editor to make a background.

4. Click Next. Your HTML editor opens.

Unless you have installed another HTML editor, FrontPage Express will open as your default HTML editor. The examples we use from this point to the end of this section use FrontPage Express and the folder template that comes with IE 4. If another program is your default HTML editor, the template will open in it, but it may not look like our examples.

EDITING THE FOLDER TEMPLATE WITH FRONTPAGE EXPRESS

As noted above, we'll only be showing you a couple of tricks you can do with IE 4's folder template. You don't have to worry about losing the template in this process. Any time you repeat the "Customize This Folder" steps, another copy of the template will be provided by IE 4. The template creates backgrounds like the ones that come with IE 4 for the Control Panel and My Computer folders (see Figure 1-6 in Chapter 1 for an example). That is, the background will display the icons in the folder on the right, with information about the folder and icons in a pane on the left. Other arrangements are possible, of course, but at the time of this writing, the only folder template available created a background with this arrangement.

FrontPage Express opens with four things already showing in it (see Figure 2-7): a little square in the upper-left corner, a white rectangle with "Web View Folder Title" in it, a black block with little squares with question marks in them, and a large block labeled "Folder Data" (partially obscured in Figure 2-7—scroll down to see the whole thing).

The white rectangle and the black block below it represent the folder's title and the pane along the folder background's left side. You saw these elements back in Chapter 1, in Figure 1-6. The little squares in the block and the one above the black block represent the HTML code that automatically puts the folder's name in the pane and causes information about the icons to appear in the pane when the icons are selected. The large "Folder Data" block represents a script that automatically adds information about whatever may be in the folder to the HTML document.

First, we'll delete some of these elements; then we'll put in some text and pictures. You can, of course, keep all of these elements and also add text and/or pictures, but because of the limited space in the pane that the black block represents, all of it may not show.

Follow these steps to create a sample HTML folder background:

1. Click to the right of the last little square with a question mark in it in the black block to place the cursor (see Figure 2-7).

2. Press the Enter key on your keyboard a couple of times to introduce a few blank lines into the black block.

3. Click to the right of the last little square with a question mark in it in the black block to place the cursor next to it again.

4. Press and hold the mouse button as you drag the cursor back and up, to select all of the little squares in the black block, everything in the white rectangle, and the little square in the upper-left corner of the screen.

5. Press the Delete key on your keyboard. You will be left with two things in the FrontPage Express screen: a much smaller black block and the large "Folder Data" block (see Figure 2-8).

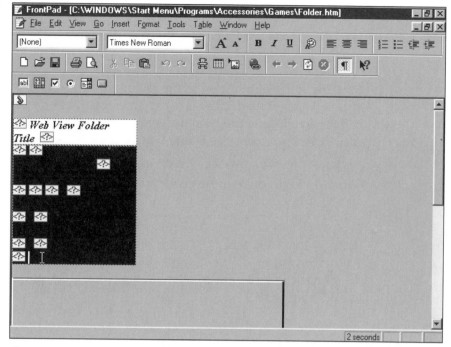

Figure 2-7 The Wizard opens FrontPage Express with a fresh copy of the folder template.

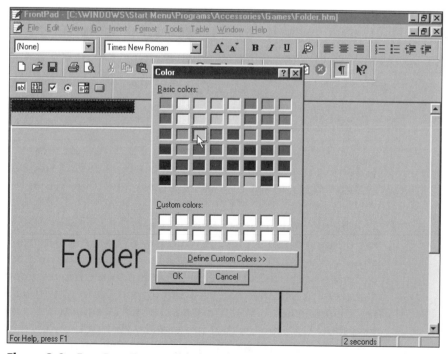

Figure 2-8 FrontPage Express with the color palette open.

ADDING TEXT

Follow these steps to add text to the sample HTML document:

1. Click in the black block to place the cursor.

2. Click the Text Color button in the toolbar. It's the one that looks like a little artist's palette. (To be sure you have the right one, rest the mouse pointer over it for a moment until you see the "Text Color" label.) The color palette appears (see Figure 2-8).

3. Click a bright color for text so it'll show up against the black background (in our example we chose bright green), then click OK. The color palette closes.

4. Type some text and press the Enter key. As you type, the text will appear in the black block. Since this is for the Games folder, we typed **Jemmie's Favorite Games** in our example, but you can type anything you'd like. Pressing the Enter key adds a line to the black block and moves the cursor down to it.

ADDING AND SIZING A PICTURE

Follow these steps to add a picture to the sample HTML document:

1. Click the Insert Image button in the toolbar. It's in the middle of the second row of toolbar buttons, and looks like a little picture with an arrow next to it. The Image dialog box appears (see Figure 2-9).

2. Click the Browse button. Another dialog box appears, also named "Image," which is used to browse for image files on your computer. You can use images in several different formats. Click the arrow at the end of the "Files of Type" box in the Image (browse) dialog box to see all of the formats that you can use. For our example, we used a JPEG picture.

3. Browse to a folder on your computer that contains a picture to include in the document, select it, and click Open. The Image dialog box shown in Figure 2-9 reappears, with the file's name in the "From File" box.

NOTE The Image dialog box shown in Figure 2-9 contains other options, including getting an image from the Web ("From Location") or using clipart, if you have any on your computer. For the purposes of this example, we're using the easiest option, inserting an image file that IE 4 users who installed the Web Integrated Desktop will be able to find on their computers. If you browse to the C:\Windows\Web folder, you'll find some GIF images that are used by IE 4's Channels feature. You can use one of these images for this sample document.

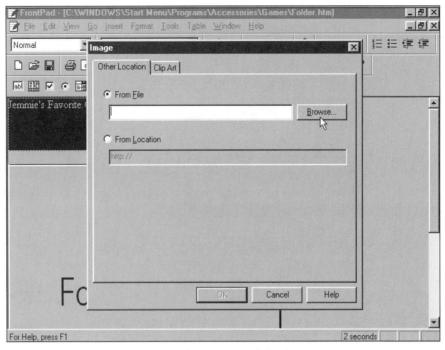

Figure 2-9 FrontPage Express with the Image dialog box open.

4. After selecting an image, click OK in the Image dialog box. The dialog box closes and the image will be added to the black block.

5. If the image you added is wider than the black block was originally, move the mouse pointer to the lower-right corner of the image so that the pointer turns into a two-headed, diagonal arrow. Then press and hold the mouse button and drag the corner up and to the left until the image's width is slightly smaller than the black block. As you drag the pointer, you can see lines that represent the image's outline (see Figure 2-10). This reduces the size of the entire image proportionally; it doesn't just cut part of it off.

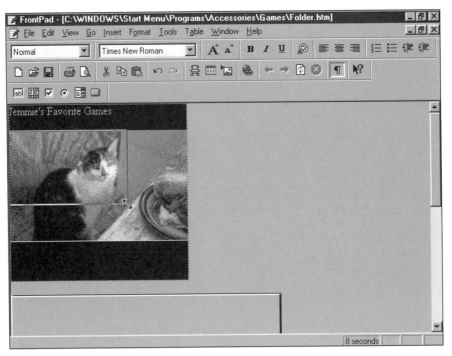

Figure 2-10   Sizing the image in FrontPage Express.

FINISHING THE SAMPLE

Now it's time to save the sample HTML document and finish up with the Customize This Folder Wizard.

Follow these steps to complete the customization process:

1. Click **File** → **Save** to save the sample document.

2. Click **File** → **Exit** to close FrontPage Express and return to the Wizard. The Wizard's congratulatory dialog box appears.

3. Click Finish. The Wizard closes and after a moment the customized folder background appears (see Figure 2-11).

In our example, we added some more text and a second image before saving and closing FrontPage Express. We also dragged the icons around so that some of them lined up next to the upper image and text, while others lined up with the lower image and text.

Figure 2-11 The customized folder background.

SIDE TRIP

MAKING A FOLDER INTO A FAVORITE

If you always launch programs from your Start menu, you may not ever see your folders again after you've customized them. One way to get to folders fairly easily is to add them to your Favorites.

Follow these steps to add a folder to your Favorites:

1. Use My Computer or Windows Explorer, or right-click ⎡ Start ⎤ and browse to open the folder you want to add to your Favorites.

2. Click ⎡ Favorites ⎤ → ⎡ Add to Favorites ⎤. The Add to Favorites dialog box appears.

(*continued*)

MAKING A FOLDER INTO A FAVORITE *(CONTINUED)*

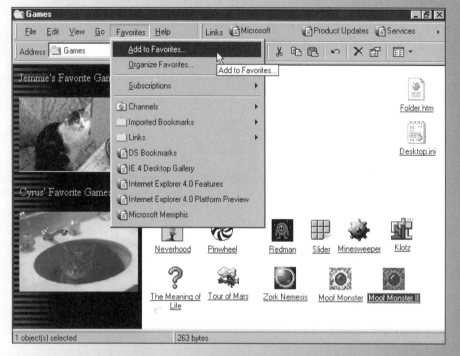

3. **Click OK. The dialog box closes and the folder is added to your Favorites. Whenever the My Computer or Explorer window is open, you can go to the folder instantly by selecting it from your Favorites.**

Customizing the Start Menu

I E 4 adds "drag-and-drop" editing to the Start menu. Previously, you had to open the Start menu folder and the folders within it and cut or copy and paste icons to make the Start menu look the way you wanted it. Before we show you how this works, let's take a look at a couple of new things that appear on your Start menu after IE 4 is installed.

IE 4 adds your Favorites and new capabilities to the Find function on
your Start menu.

Follow these steps to check out the changes in your Start menu:

1. Click **Start** on your taskbar. The Start menu opens.

2. Move the mouse pointer over **Favorites** . The same favorite items appear
   here that appear when you click **Favorites** on the My Computer or
   Explorer menu bar. In our example (see Figure 2-12), we selected the
   Links option to show the links that are installed with IE 4.

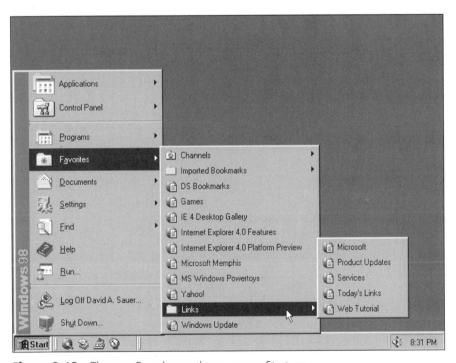

Figure 2-12 The new Favorites options on your Start menu.

3. Move the mouse pointer down the Start menu to **Find** . The Find menu
   appears (see Figure 2-13).

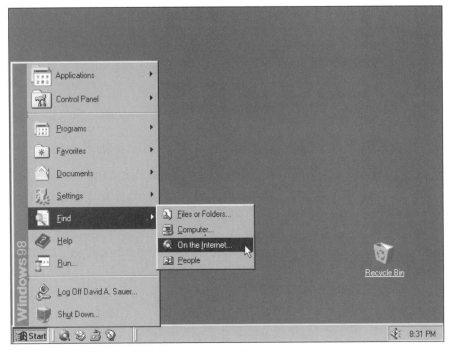

Figure 2-13 The new Find options on your Start menu.

The Find menu has some new choices:

✳ If you click the Internet, Explorer opens and goes to Microsoft's Find It Fast page.

✳ If you click People, a dialog box opens that lets you specify where you want to search for people (in your Address Book, in Internet directories, etc.), and the person you're looking for.

✳ If you're on a network, the Computer option lets you search other computers on the network.

✳ If you have an account on MSN (The Microsoft Network), that's an option on the Find menu too.

FEATURE FOCUS **IE 4 adds the convenience of drag-and-drop editing to your Start menu.**

Drag and drop is a feature that some people have been hoping for. It makes moving icons and folders (menus) from one part of the Start menu to another a snap. For our example, we'll move the Games folder from within the Programs\

Accessories menu to the Programs menu to make it easier to open. If you have already moved your Games folder, use any other folder in the Accessories folder to see how this works. (Our example in Figure 2-14 shows some folders and icons that may not appear on your computer.)

Follow these steps to move items from one place on your Start menu to another:

1. Click Start on your taskbar to open the Start menu.

2. Select Programs → Accessories → Games and continue to press and hold the mouse button. The Games menu will open, but it will close as soon as you start dragging.

3. Drag the Games folder away from the Accessories menu so that the Accessories menu closes but the Programs menu remains open. The mouse pointer will have a little rectangle attached to it (see Figure 2-14), indicating that you're dragging something.

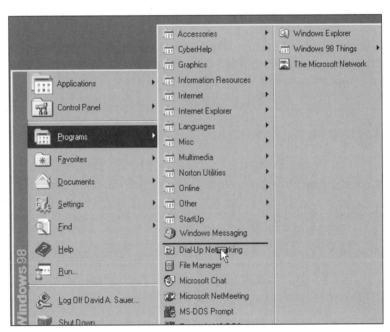

Figure 2-14 Dragging a folder to a new Start menu location.

4. Continue dragging the Games folder over the Programs menu until you see a horizontal line appear between the choices on the Programs menu (see Figure 2-14). The line indicates where the Games folder would be placed if you released the mouse button.

5. Release the mouse button when the horizontal line is where you want the Games folder.

BONUS

Tweaking the Interface

Try as they may, companies that produce operating systems just don't seem to be able to please everyone with their constant upgrades. As soon as a new version appears, people find problems with it or ways they could improve it. Windows 95 is no exception. Soon after it was released, some programmers at Microsoft came up with a little program called *Tweak UI* that takes care of a few things that some people consider pesky problems. These range from having to sign on to the network each time you boot up the computer to safely removing icons that you never use from your desktop.

Tweak UI is not guaranteed or supported by Microsoft, nor by us. Read the information and cautionary statements at Microsoft's Web site regarding the use of Tweak UI and the other "Power Toys" that they offer there. While we have never had any problems with Tweak UI, you should understand that you install and use it at your own risk.

Follow these steps to download, install, and use Tweak UI:

1. Open Explorer and go to

   http://microsoft.com/windows/windows95/info/powertoys.htm

2. Scroll down the page until you see the link for Tweak UI.

3. Right-click the link, select **Save Target As** from the shortcut menu, and browse to the folder where you want to save the file. (We suggest that you make a folder for Tweak UI and keep the file there so that you can reinstall it in the future if necessary. In our example in Figure 2-15, we copied it to a folder that we made and named tweak, inside another folder we made and named winutils.)

4. Click Save and, after the file is transferred to your computer, close Explorer and disconnect from your ISP.

5. Click **Start** → **Run** to open the Run dialog box.

6. Browse to where you saved the Tweak UI file, select it, and then click OK in the Run dialog box. A DOS window will open. When "Finished" appears in the DOS window's title bar, several files will have been extracted and you can close the DOS window.

7. Click **Start** → **Settings** → **Control Panel** to open your Control Panel window, and then click Add/Remove Programs. The Add/Remove Programs dialog box appears (shown in Figure 2-15, behind the open dialog boxes).

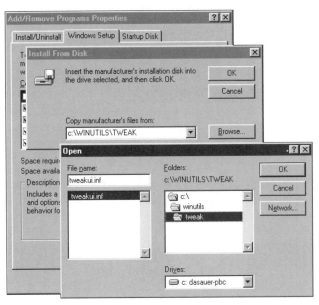

Figure 2-15 Locate the Tweak UI files to install them in Windows Setup.

8. In the Add/Remove Programs dialog box, click the Windows Setup tab to bring it to the front.

9. Click Have Disk on the Windows Setup tab, and then click Browse in the Install From Disk dialog box that appears (shown in Figure 2-15, behind the Open dialog box). The Open dialog box appears.

10. Browse to the folder where the Tweak UI files are located. The file named tweakui.inf should appear in the File name box in the Open dialog box (see Figure 2-15).

11. Click OK. The Have Disk dialog box will appear, with Tweak UI listed in the Components box (see Figure 2-16).

12. Click Tweak UI to place a ✓ next to it, and then click Install. In a few moments, installation will be complete. We suggest that you reboot your computer after installing Tweak UI.

13. Open the Control Panel again. You'll see a new icon for Tweak UI.

14. Click Tweak UI to open the Tweak UI dialog box.

Each tab in the Tweak UI dialog box contains some information about the options that it presents. For more information, click the ? in the upper-right corner of the title bar, and then click whatever item on the tab you want more information about.

Figure 2-16 Select Tweak UI and click Install
to complete installation.

Our favorite Tweak UI options are on the Desktop and Network tabs, where we set which desktop icons show and automatic network logon, respectively. (Don't set automatic logon if you're in a networked situation where this could compromise important data.) Other Tweak options let you do such things as turn "Auto-Run" for CDs off and on, clear the Start→Documents list each time you reboot, and customize the appearance of shortcut icons. Have fun with it!

Summary

I E 4's Web Integrated Desktop can change your whole outlook on computing. By taking advantage of its many customization features, you can personalize your computer's interface for maximum fun and efficiency. In the next chapter, we'll show you some of the more advanced features IE 4 adds to your computer, including customizable toolbars for your desktop.

CHAPTER THREE

USING ADVANCED DESKTOP FEATURES

IN THIS CHAPTER YOU LEARN THESE KEY SKILLS

HOW TO CUSTOMIZE THE TASKBAR   PAGE 53

HOW TO CREATE TOOLBARS   PAGE 57

HOW TO SCHEDULE ROUTINE TASKS   PAGE 62

W e keep saying this, but it bears repeating: when you install IE 4 you get much more than just a new browser. If you choose to install the Web Integrated Desktop during IE 4 setup (see Appendix A), you get a number of enhancements to the Windows 95 interface.

One of the new IE 4 features covered in this chapter that we're particularly impressed with is the ability to customize the taskbar and set up multiple toolbars for launching programs or opening documents and Web site shortcuts. If you're like us and have lots of programs and documents that you use or refer to frequently, you may never again have to hunt through layer after layer of menus under your Start menu to get to them.

The other feature we'll tell you about in this chapter is the Task Scheduler. This little program lets you set up routine operations such as hard disk scanning or defragmenting so that they take place automatically on a regular basis.

Customizing the Taskbar

A fter you installed IE 4, one of the first changes you probably noticed were some little icons on your Windows 95 taskbar that weren't there before. What you were actually seeing is a toolbar on your taskbar that includes icons (we may also call these "buttons" or "shortcuts") for programs in the IE 4 suite. The number of buttons on the toolbar depends on how many of the IE 4 component programs you installed.

**FEATURE
FOCUS**   IE 4 automatically installs a new toolbar on your Windows 95 taskbar
for quickly launching programs in the IE 4 suite.

Adding a Button to a Toolbar

IE 4 calls the new toolbar on your taskbar the *Quick Launch toolbar,* and initially it contains buttons for IE 4 and its related programs. However, you can place buttons on this toolbar for opening any program, document, or Web page shortcut that you want. You can also delete the IE 4 buttons if you choose. Later, we'll also show you how to add toolbars to the taskbar or create new toolbars elsewhere on your desktop. The procedure for adding a button (shortcut) is the same for any of these toolbars.

NOTE   One of the buttons IE 4 installed on this toolbar is not related to IE 4
programs. It looks like a little desktop and lamp, and if you rest your
mouse pointer over it for a moment a label that says "Show Desktop"
appears. If you have a number of programs open and want to get to
your desktop quickly, click this button. Any windows that are open will
instantly be minimized on the taskbar and your desktop will appear.
Click it again and all the windows open up again.

Notice the Quick Launch toolbar and the rest of the taskbar shown in Figure 3-1. At the left end of the Quick Launch toolbar, next to the Start button, are two vertical lines. This is called a *handle* (we've also seen it called a *grabber bar* and a *tab*). In most cases, you can drag the handle left and right (or up and down on a vertical toolbar) to expand or reduce the size of the toolbar. You can also double-click the handle to quickly expand or reduce the toolbar.

There is another handle at the right side of the Quick Launch toolbar. This one adjusts the size of that part of the taskbar where icons for open windows are displayed. Try dragging this handle left and right and you'll see what we mean. As you drag it to the right, closer to the taskbar "tray" (the space where the clock and speaker icon are showing), any icons for open windows will get smaller, and the Quick Launch toolbar will get larger. You may want to expand the Quick Launch toolbar in this way before you drag new shortcuts to it.

Follow these steps to add a button to a toolbar:

1. Create a shortcut to the program, document, or Web page that you want a button for on your desktop. For our example, we're using the "Welcome to Internet Explorer 4.0" shortcut that IE 4 installs on the desktop during setup.

2. Drag the shortcut from your desktop to the Quick Launch toolbar on your taskbar (see Figure 3-1). If you have set the taskbar to "Auto Hide," it will open as you drag the shortcut to where the taskbar is hidden. A dark line will appear as you move the shortcut over the Quick Launch toolbar, indicating where the shortcut will be placed when you release the mouse button.

Figure 3-1   Drag a shortcut to a toolbar to add a copy of it to the toolbar.

3. Release the mouse button to drop the shortcut on the toolbar. The original shortcut will remain where it was (a copy is placed on the toolbar).

4. Right-click the original shortcut and select Delete from the menu that appears if you wish to remove it from the desktop. The shortcut that you placed on the toolbar will not be deleted if you do this.

Deleting a Button from a Toolbar

It's even quicker and easier to remove a button from a toolbar.

Follow these steps to delete a button (shortcut) from a toolbar:

1. Right-click the toolbar button to open its shortcut menu.

2. Select Delete . The menu will close and a message asking you if you really want to delete the button appears.

3. Click Yes if you're sure you want to delete it. The message disappears and the button is deleted.

Changing a Shortcut's Icon

If you add a shortcut for a Web page to a toolbar, it will have the same icon as any other Web page shortcuts on the toolbar, or the shortcut for IE 4. Although each icon will have a unique "tooltip" (the little label that appears when you rest the mouse pointer over the icon for a moment), you may want to change the shortcut's icon to make it easier to remember. The procedure we show here applies to any shortcut icon, not just the ones on your toolbars.

Follow these steps to change a shortcut's icon:

1. Right-click the icon that you want to change. A shortcut menu appears.

2. Click [**Properties**]. The shortcut's Properties dialog box appears (see Figure 3-2).

Figure 3-2   Right-click a shortcut and select
Properties to open the shortcut's
Properties dialog box.

3. Click the Shortcut tab if necessary to bring it to the front and click the Change Icon button. The Change Icon dialog box opens. If you don't want to select one of the icons in the Change Icon dialog box, click the Browse button, browse to your C:\Windows folder, and double-click the file named moricons.dll to open it. It contains several more icons that you can choose from.

4. Double-click the icon you want to use. The Change Icon dialog box closes.

5. Click OK in the Properties dialog box to save your choice and close the dialog box, or click Cancel to close the dialog box without making any changes.

6. If the icon doesn't change right away, right-click a blank space on the desktop and select [**Refresh**] from the shortcut menu that appears.

GETTING RID OF MEMORY-HOGGING TOOLBARS

If you use Microsoft Office or any other suite of programs that comes with a toolbar that you can install on your desktop, you can save RAM (Random Access Memory)—and make your computer run faster—by deleting or turning it off and using one of the new IE 4 toolbars instead. Simply make shortcuts for the programs in the suite that you use and place them on the Quick Launch toolbar or a toolbar that you make (see the next section, "Creating Toolbars").

Next, turn off the suite's toolbar or delete it. Use Windows Explorer or My Computer to check the C:\Windows\Start Menu\Programs\StartUp folder—any shortcuts in this folder are for programs that start up automatically when you boot up your computer. There may be a shortcut for the suite's toolbar in this folder that you will have to move to another folder or delete in order to keep the toolbar from loading.

Creating Toolbars

E 4 lets you create a variety of toolbars on your desktop. They can be free-floating over the desktop, or, like the Windows 95 taskbar, they can be placed along either side or at the top or bottom of the desktop.

FEATURE FOCUS

Custom toolbars are a new feature of Internet Explorer 4.

You can create so many different types of toolbars with IE 4 that it may be impossible to describe all of the possibilities. So instead of devoting the rest of this book to toolbars, we'll just show you a few toolbar tricks and let you take it from there.

Showing or Hiding IE 4 Toolbars

IE 4 lets you show or hide four "predefined" toolbars on the taskbar. Once one of these is showing on the taskbar, it can be dragged to the desktop or to another toolbar (we'll show this later). The four IE 4 toolbars are the Address and Links toolbars (discussed in the next section, "Adding an IE 4 Toolbar to the Desktop"); a Desktop toolbar (that includes copies of all of the shortcuts on your desktop);

and the Quick Launch toolbar. Choices for the four predefined toolbars or a "New" toolbar, are listed on the toolbar's submenu.

Follow these steps to show or hide IE 4's toolbars:

1. Right-click a blank space on the taskbar (not on the Quick Launch toolbar). A shortcut menu appears.

2. Select Toolbars . Another menu opens.

3. Select a toolbar that doesn't have a ✓ next to it. The menus close and the toolbar appears on the taskbar.

4. Repeat Steps 1–3 to remove the ✓ next to the toolbar's name and hide it.

Adding an IE 4 Toolbar to the Desktop

Two of the toolbars that IE 4 lets you add to your desktop are copies of toolbars from the Internet Explorer browser program. These are the Address toolbar and the Links toolbar. The Address toolbar consists entirely of an Address box, just like the one in Internet Explorer. To open the browser and go to a Web site, you just type an Internet address, or URL (Uniform Resource Locator), into it and press the Enter key on your keyboard.

The Links toolbar includes whatever links you have on the Links toolbar in the browser. Just as with the Address toolbar, you can use it to open the browser and go to whatever Web page or site a link on the toolbar represents. (See "Adding a Page to Your Links Bar" in Chapter 5 for more information about using the Links toolbar or adding links to it from within the browser program.)

In this section we'll show you how to add the Address toolbar to your desktop. You can use the same procedures to add the Links toolbar (and others) if you choose to.

Follow these steps to add the Address toolbar to your desktop:

1. Right-click a blank space on the taskbar (not on the Quick Launch toolbar). A shortcut menu appears.

2. Select Toolbars → Address . The menu closes and an Address toolbar appears on the taskbar.

3. Move the mouse pointer over the Address toolbar's handle (the two vertical lines to the left of "Address"). The pointer turns into a two-headed arrow.

4. Press and hold the mouse button and drag the handle off of the taskbar and over the desktop.

5. Release the mouse button. The Address toolbar moves to the desktop (see Figure 3-3). When you first move it to the desktop, the Address toolbar is

much larger than it needs to be. You will probably want to drag the lower edge of the toolbar up to reduce its size.

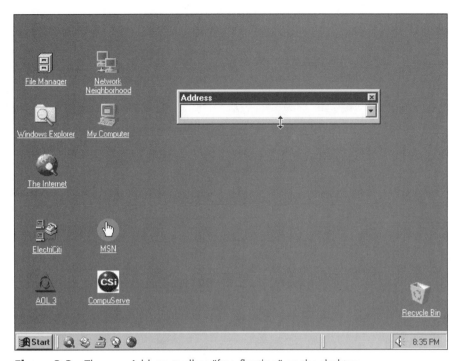

Figure 3-3   The new Address toolbar "free-floating" on the desktop.

6. Move the mouse pointer to the lower edge of the toolbar so that the pointer turns into a two-headed arrow and then press and hold the mouse button and drag the lower edge of the toolbar up to make the toolbar smaller.

You can drag the Address toolbar to any position on the desktop where you may want it. You can also drag it back to the taskbar, or onto another toolbar that you make. Just click and hold the mouse button when the mouse pointer is over the toolbar's Title bar (where the word "Address" appears) and drag it.

Making and Modifying New Toolbars

Now comes the real fun part, creating your own toolbar. You can make a toolbar for any folder on your hard disk. If you want to make a "blank" toolbar, create a new folder and give it whatever name you want. Later, you can create whatever shortcuts you want for the toolbar and drag them onto it. For our example, we'll use a folder that's already set up, the Games folder. On most Windows 95 computers it is located in the C:\Windows\Start Menu\Programs\Accessories folder. This exercise will not affect the original Games folder in any way, so it won't hurt anything to follow along.

Follow these steps to create a new toolbar:

1. Right-click a blank space on the taskbar (not on the Quick Launch toolbar). A shortcut menu appears.

2. Select `Toolbars` → `New Toolbar`. The New Toolbar dialog box appears (see Figure 3-4).

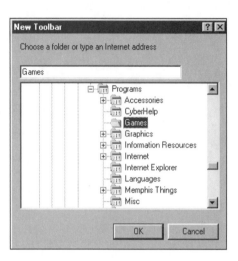

Figure 3-4 Browse to the folder you want to copy to create a new toolbar.

3. Browse to the C:\Windows\Start Menu\Programs\Accessories folder and click the Games folder to select it.

4. Click OK. A new toolbar named "Games" will appear on the taskbar.

5. Move the mouse pointer over the new toolbar's handle so that the pointer turns into a two-headed arrow.

6. Press and hold the mouse button and drag the handle as far as you can to the opposite side of the screen (that is, to the top edge of the screen if your taskbar is at the bottom of the screen, etc.).

7. Release the mouse button. The new toolbar will open.

Your new toolbar may be bigger than you want it to be, or have other characteristics that you don't care for. However, it's easily modified. It can also be dragged to a different edge of your screen. You could, hypothetically, have toolbars at the top, bottom, and along both sides of your screen. To alter the toolbar's appearance or behavior, you first have to open its shortcut menu. To do this, right-click the toolbar's name. Now you have a number of options:

✱ To remove the text from the toolbar's buttons, select Show Text to remove the ✓ next to it. Select Show Text again to replace the ✓ to restore the text.

✱ To select large icons instead of small ones, select View→Large. Select View→Small to go back to small icons.

✱ To hide the toolbar title, select Show Title to remove the ✓ next to it. Select Show Title to replace the ✓ to restore the title.

✱ To add another toolbar to share the space your new toolbar is in, select Toolbar, then select the type of toolbar you want to add.

✱ To reduce or increase a horizontal toolbar's height or a vertical toolbar's width, move the mouse pointer to the outer edge of the toolbar so that the pointer turns into a two-headed arrow, press and hold the mouse button, and drag the edge of the toolbar toward or away from the edge of the screen.

✱ To force the toolbar to keep showing on top of any programs or windows you have open, select Always on Top to place a ✓ next to it. Select Always on Top again to remove the ✓ to turn this off.

✱ To "Auto Hide" the toolbar, select Always on Top, and then select Auto Hide so that there is a ✓ next to each of these options. (When Auto Hide is turned on, the toolbar only appears when you move your mouse pointer close to the edge of the screen where it's located.)

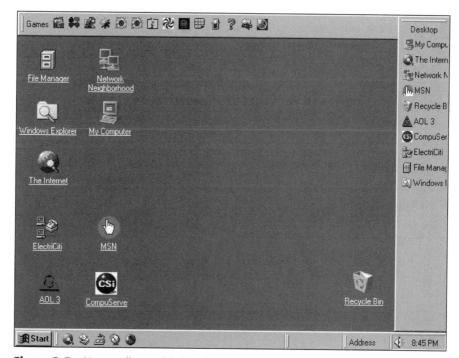

Figure 3-5 New toolbars added to the desktop.

For our example in Figure 3-5, we removed text, reduced the size of the Games toolbar, and created a Desktop toolbar that we dragged to the right side of the screen.

Try all of these options to see how they change the toolbar's looks and the way it works. Toolbars, like the taskbar, can be dragged to different edges of the screen (top, bottom, or left or right side). However, after dragging a toolbar to a different edge of the screen you will probably want to modify such things as icon size and text. You will have to reset Auto Hide if you move a toolbar to a different edge of the screen.

Deleting a New Toolbar

You can easily delete a toolbar that you have made. This is not the same as showing or hiding IE 4 toolbars, shown earlier in this chapter. Once a toolbar that you have created is deleted, it's gone. If you decide you want it back later, you'll have to create it all over again.

Follow these steps if you want to remove a toolbar that you created:

1. Right-click the toolbar's title to open the shortcut menu and select
   Toolbars . The name of the toolbar you made will be listed among the
   other toolbars on the menu, and it will have a ✓ next to it.

2. Select the toolbar's name from the shortcut menu. The menu will close
   and the toolbar will disappear.

Scheduling Routine Tasks

I E 4 adds a utility program called Task Scheduler to your computer that will automatically run other programs for you. For example, you can set it to run routine tasks for you during the night or while you're at lunch. You select the program that you want to run, set up a schedule for it, and Task Scheduler does the rest. Task Scheduler is similar to the System Agent program included in the Windows 95 Plus! CD. We've had reports that Task Scheduler does not show up on some computers on which System Agent is installed.

The only snag to using Task Scheduler is that some programs require that you change settings in two different places in order for them to run in a completely automatic mode. (We're hoping that future versions of Task Scheduler will eliminate this problem.) For example, programs such as ScanDisk and Disk Defragmenter (two utility programs for routine hard disk maintenance that come with Windows 95) will start up automatically. But in the course of doing their work, they stop for input from you, such as specifying which hard disk you want them to work on. We'll show you where to find the two places in which you change settings for ScanDisk and how you change them in our examples.

Getting a Program Ready to Run

For our example, we're using the ScanDisk program. It comes with Windows 95 and checks your hard disk for errors. In most cases it can automatically fix any errors that it finds. ScanDisk has several settings that must be checked in order for Task Scheduler to run it in totally automatic mode. Consult the help files or manuals that come with any other programs that you want Task Scheduler to run automatically to find out if they require special settings or parameters in order to run unattended.

Follow these steps to prepare ScanDisk for automatic operation:

1. Click Start on your taskbar to open the Start menu.

2. Select **Programs** → **Accessories** → **System Tools** → **ScanDisk** . The ScanDisk dialog box appears (see Figure 3-6).

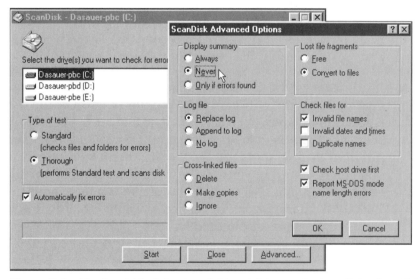

Figure 3-6   The ScanDisk dialog box (left) and Advance Options dialog box (right).

The ScanDisk dialog box (shown on the left in Figure 3-6) includes three options that affect automatic operation:

* Click "Standard" to select it if you want ScanDisk to check only your files and folders (directories) for errors (this setting is optional for automatic operation).

* Click "Thorough" to select it if you want ScanDisk to check files, folders, and the surface of the hard disk for errors; this takes longer, and ordinarily does not have to be done as often as checking files and folders (this setting is optional for automatic operation).

* Click "Automatically fix errors" so that ScanDisk won't pause for input from you if it detects errors (this setting is <u>not</u> optional for automatic operation).

Next, there is an "Advanced" setting to check. Click the Advanced button in the ScanDisk dialog box to open the Advanced Options dialog box (shown on the right in Figure 3-6). There is only one setting among the Advanced Options that affects automatic operation:

* Click "Never" in the "Display summary" section. This will keep ScanDisk from pausing to display a summary of what it did after it finishes checking your hard disk.

Now you're ready to use Task Scheduler to select and schedule ScanDisk for automatic operation. If you want to see what the other advanced options do, click the question mark in the Advanced Options dialog box's Title bar, then click the option you want to know about.

Changes you make to the program's settings in this way will apply any time the program runs; that is, whether you use Task Scheduler to run it automatically or start it manually using your Start menu.

NOTE If you want to check on what ScanDisk did during an automatic operation, set the option in the "Log file" section of the Advanced Options dialog box to either "Replace log" or "Append to log." This tells ScanDisk to make a log (record) of its operations. Then use the Notepad program to open and read the log file; it will be named scandisk.log and can be found in your C:\ (root) folder. We recommend the "Append to log" setting, so that the log of a previous operation is not deleted. This could be important if you occasionally forget to check the log after ScanDisk has run automatically.

Opening the Scheduled Tasks Folder

The Scheduled Tasks folder keeps track of any tasks that you may set up. It's listed in the "All Folders" pane (the left pane) in Windows Explorer, and is also accessible through the Start menu.

Follow these steps to open the Scheduled Tasks folder:

1. Click Start on your taskbar to open the Start menu.

2. Select Programs → Accessories → System Tools → Scheduled Tasks . The Scheduled Tasks folder appears.

Like many other folders and windows when first opened, the Scheduled Tasks folder is not maximized. Click the ▢ in the upper-right corner of its title bar to maximize the folder's window.

Setting Up a Schedule

The folder includes one item: an entry that you use to start the Add Scheduled Task Wizard. As you set up scheduled tasks, they will be added to the folder.

Follow these steps to set up a scheduled task:

1. Click Add Scheduled Task. The Add Scheduled Task Wizard dialog box opens.

2. Read the information on the opening screen and click Next. The Wizard will begin to create a list of all of the programs on your computer's hard disks. Depending on how many programs and hard disks you have, it could take several minutes for the Wizard to do its thing. When it finishes, a new screen displaying the list appears in the dialog box (see Figure 3-7).

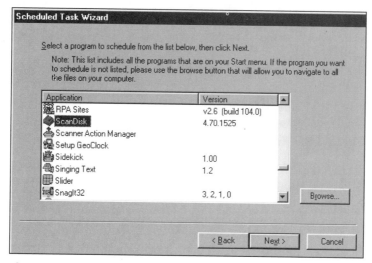

Figure 3-7 The Wizard makes a list of all of your programs for you to choose from.

3. Scroll through the list of programs ("Applications") until you find the one you want to run. If the Wizard missed the one you want to run, click the Browse button, browse to the folder that contains the program and select it.

4. Click the program to select it from the Wizard's list and click Next. The first of two scheduling screens appears in the dialog box.

5. Select the frequency (daily, weekly, etc.) for running the program. Click your choice to place a dot next to it to select it, and click Next. If you select Daily, Weekly, Monthly, or One time only, a second scheduling screen will appear in the dialog box (see Figure 3-8).

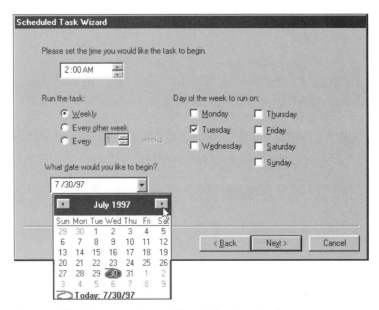

Figure 3-8 The second scheduling dialog box is where you set frequency details.

6. Set the details in the dialog box as shown in Figure 3-8:

* Click your choice to place a dot or ✓ next to it in the "Run the task" and "Days of the week ..." categories.

* To set the time, click the hour or minute, then click the up or down arrow next to the time box to change the numbers.

* To set the date you want the routine task to start, click the arrow at the right end of the "What date ..." box to open a calendar for the current month. Then click the date you want, or click the forward arrow at the top of the calendar to move to a later month and make your choice.

* Click Next when all of these details are set.

7. The Wizard's last dialog box gives you the option of opening the program's Properties dialog box to set special parameters, something you need to do for ScanDisk (see the next section, "Setting Special Parameters"). Click "Open advanced properties of the task" to place a ✓ next to it, and click Finish. The program's Properties dialog box will appear (see Figure 3-9).

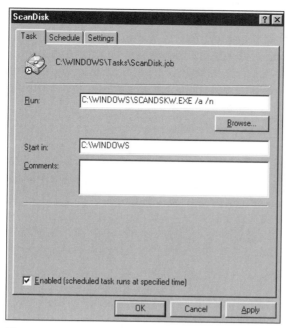

Figure 3-9 The Properties dialog box for ScanDisk, with parameters added to the "Run" box.

Setting Special Parameters

After selecting the program you want to run automatically and setting up a schedule, you may have to set special parameters for it. Otherwise, the program may stop before it is finished doing its work. In our example, we use the ScanDisk program that comes with Windows 95. This program checks your hard disk for errors, and it can fix most errors that it finds for you. We'll set up ScanDisk to run without stopping to ask you which disk you want it to scan.

Follow these steps to add special parameters for running ScanDisk with Task Scheduler:

1. Follow through the previous sections "Getting a Program Ready to Run" and "Setting Up a Schedule" if you have not already done so, to get to the stage of having ScanDisk's Properties dialog box open to the Task tab (shown in Figure 3-9).

2. Click to the right of the text in the "Run" box to place the cursor.

3. Press the spacebar once to enter a blank space, then type **/a /n**. The "/a" tells ScanDisk to check all of your computer's hard disks. The "/n" tells it to run without stopping. When you finish, your "Run" text box should look like the one in Figure 3-9.

4. Click the Setup tab to bring it to the front (see Figure 3-10). The Setup tab lets you set other parameters. For example, if the program you want to run interferes with other programs that may be running, you may want to select "Stop the scheduled task if computer is in use." Also, notice the Power Management options for laptop computers.

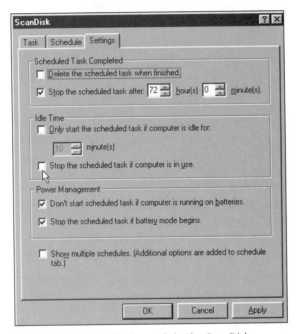

Figure 3-10 The Settings tab in the ScanDisk Properties dialog box.

5. When you're done setting special parameters, click OK to save your settings and close the dialog box.

Managing Scheduled Tasks

Once you have a scheduled task or two set up in your Scheduled Tasks folder, you may want to make some changes to them or delete them.

Follow these steps to manage your scheduled tasks:

1. Open the Scheduled Tasks folder.

2. Right-click a task to open its shortcut menu (see Figure 3-11).

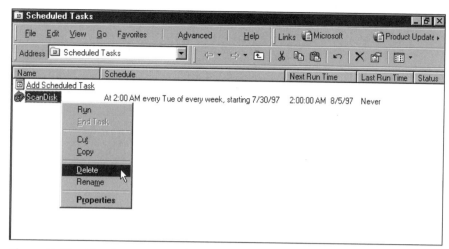

Figure 3-11 The shortcut menu for tasks in the Scheduled Tasks folder.

The shortcut menu gives you access to the following commands for each scheduled task as shown in Table 3-1.

TABLE 3-1 Shortcut menu commands

Command	Function
RUN	Runs the task now
CUT	Cuts the task (to paste it into another folder)
COPY	Copies the task (if, for example, you want two different parameter setups for the same task)
DELETE	Deletes the task (a message box appears asking you to confirm the deletion)
END TASK	Stops the task (this is grayed out if the task isn't running)
RENAME	Gives the task a new name
PROPERTIES	Opens the Properties dialog box to change parameters or the task's schedule

Pausing, Shutting Down, or Checking Task Scheduler

There may be times when you want Task Scheduler to pause or shut down completely. For example, you may not want a scheduled program to slow down the computer or interrupt you in the middle of an important project. Also, once you set up scheduled tasks, Task Scheduler will always be running in the background, even if you delete all of the tasks you've set up. A small icon appears in the taskbar tray to remind you that Task Scheduler is running (see Figure 3-12).

The Task Scheduler Icon

Figure 3-12 The Task Scheduler icon and its shortcut menu.

Follow these steps to pause, shut down, or check on Task Scheduler:

1. Right-click the Task Scheduler icon in your taskbar tray. The icon's shortcut menu appears. Notice that you can select **Pause Task Scheduler** from this menu.

2. Select **Open** from the Task Scheduler icon's shortcut menu. The Scheduled Tasks folder appears.

3. Click **Advanced** to open the Advanced menu.

4. Select **Pause Task Scheduler** if you want the scheduler to pause.

5. Select **Stop Using Task Scheduler** to shut the program down completely (no scheduled tasks will be run automatically if you select this option).

6. Select **View Log** if you want to see what Task Scheduler's been doing.

BONUS

Updating Explorer

Microsoft has introduced a new way for you to enhance or update IE 4 by downloading self-installing upgrade files from their Web site. Our example shows adding features to IE 4 after the basic program has been installed. Updating IE 4 itself works in a very similar manner.

Follow these steps to upgrade IE 4:

1. Open Explorer and go to the IE 4 Web site at http://www.microsoft. com/ie/ie40/. The page may take a while to load because it uses ActiveX scripts for menus that are part of the page. If you are prompted to approve loading the scripts, click Yes. Once the page finishes loading,

you may want to select Favorites → Add to Favorites to add IE 4's home page to your Favorites.

2. Click the word "Download" to open the Download menu.

3. Click Internet Explorer 4.0 Components on the Download menu. The Internet Explorer Download page appears.

4. Read the information on the Download page, then scroll down the page and click the "Internet Explorer 4.0 Components (Windows 95, Windows NT)" link. The Microsoft Internet Explorer 4 Components page begins to load. The page takes a while to load because it uses ActiveX scripts for its interactive interface. If you're prompted to approve loading the scripts, click Yes. A message box appears, asking you if it's OK for "Active Setup" to search your computer to determine what IE 4 components are already installed.

5. Click Yes in the Active Setup message box. After a few moments, Active Setup presents you with a list of IE 4 components (see Figure 3-13). To the left of each component is a little square that you click to indicate that you want to install the component. To the right of each component are two columns of information. The first tells you how large the upgrade file is and about how long it will take to download. The second column tells you whether or not the component is installed. You may see "Not Installed" for a component that you *have* already installed. This indicates that the component has been upgraded since you installed it and that a newer version is available.

6. Scroll through the list and click the square to the left of any component you want to install to place a ✓ in the square. Alternately, you can click the "upgrade all" button near the top of the page to install all components that aren't installed or that have been upgraded. After you have made your selection, the total size for the files you will download and the approximate time the download will take appear at the bottom of the page, next to the "NEXT" button.

7. Click NEXT. After a moment, a page where you can select the download site appears.

8. Click the arrow at the right end of the "Please Select a Download Site" list box to open the list, scroll through the list, and click a download site location that's near you. The list closes. If you want to review your selection, scroll down the page.

9. Click Install Now. The page changes to show an animated globe traveling across the page and an Active Setup message box appears to show you the progress of the download and installation. Once the file(s) are downloaded, they will install themselves automatically. When installation is complete, an Active Setup Engine message box appears and reports on the installation.

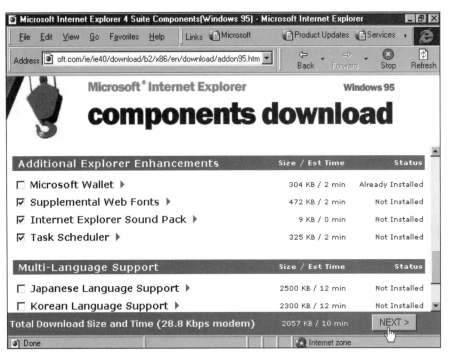

Figure 3-13   The Microsoft Internet Explorer 4 Suite Components page.
Screen shot reprinted by permission from Microsoft Corporation.

10. Click OK in the Active Setup Engine message box. The message disappears.

At this point you will either be finished with the upgrade or you will see an Active Setup Engine message box that says you must restart your computer to complete installation. If the message doesn't appear, you're done; you may close IE 4 and disconnect from your ISP. If the message does appear, click Yes in the message box. Your computer restarts, IE 4 opens again, your ISP connection is made, and the Microsoft Internet Explorer 4 Suite Components page appears again. At this point you can close IE 4 and disconnect from your ISP.

Summary

IE 4 lets you customize your Windows 95 taskbar and create toolbars to simplify the way you work and play with your computer. You can move toolbars to different places on your screen, and set them to hide away when they're not needed. Another great new IE 4 feature, Task Scheduler, lets you schedule routine computer maintenance programs to run at times when you're not using the computer for other things.

CHAPTER FOUR

MAKING FULL USE OF EXPLORER'S ACTIVE DESKTOP

IN THIS CHAPTER YOU LEARN THESE KEY SKILLS

HOW TO CREATE A CUSTOM ACTIVE DESKTOP
PAGE 73

HOW TO ADD ACTIVE DESKTOP ITEMS   PAGE 82

HOW TO GET SPECIAL SERVICES FROM CHANNELS
PAGE 89

A s interesting as the many new features discussed in Chapters 1–3 are, IE 4's greatest development is the Active Desktop. In this chapter we discuss the three major features of the Active Desktop: a customizable background, Active Desktop items, and Channels.

For your desktop's background, you can create an HTML document containing text, graphics, and even interactive elements that use ActiveX and Java programming. In addition, your desktop can contain "Active Desktop Items." These can include such things as a regularly updated weather map or a three-dimensional digital clock. The star of IE 4's show is its Channels feature. Channels deliver information to your desktop from a wide variety of Web sources, everything from up-to-the-minute stock quotes to new recipes for your dinner.

Getting Creative

F or your first venture into using the Active Desktop, you'll learn how to create a simple HTML document to use for the desktop's background. Once you understand the basics, you can go on to experiment with more complex HTML elements on your own.

The Active Desktop can be thought of as having two layers: one for your icons and one for the background. The icon layer consists of the shortcuts that were on your desktop before you installed IE 4 (and any that you added since). The background shows through, behind the shortcuts. Because your desktop icons will always be visible, you'll want to plan the HTML background accordingly.

Before starting up the FrontPage Express program to create your HTML background, make sure that you have the Active Desktop turned on. If IE 4's Channel bar is showing (shown on the right in Figure 4-1), the Active Desktop is on. You may also want to turn off the "Welcome" HTML background that comes with IE 4 (see "Customizing the Desktop" in Chapter 2 and select "None" for your desktop background).

If your Active Desktop isn't on, right-click a blank space on the desktop and select Active Desktop→View as Web Page to turn it on. The IE 4 Channel bar appears on the right side of your screen (see Figure 4-1).

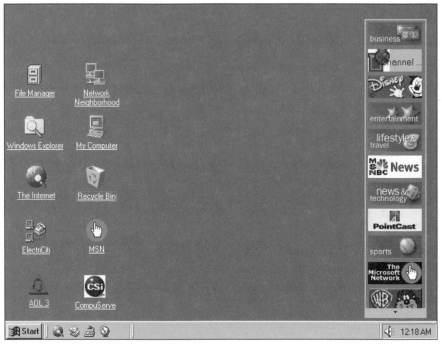

Figure 4-1   The Active Desktop with the "Welcome" background turned off.

Starting Out and Saving Your Work

Now you're ready to open FrontPage Express and create an HTML document to serve as the background for your desktop. First we'll show you how to create a basic document with some text and color and designate it as your desktop background.

Follow these steps to open FrontPage Express and begin to make an HTML background:

1. Click **Start** on your taskbar to open the Start menu.

2. Select **Programs** → **Internet Explorer** → **FrontPage Express** . FrontPage Express opens with a blank document. The cursor will be blinking in the upper-left corner of the document.

3. Type some text. This can be anything you want; you can always delete this document or edit it later. For our example, we typed **Welcome to the custom desktop (Enter) created especially for you. (Enter) Here are your most-used programs:**.

4. Click at the end of the text and hold the mouse button as you drag the cursor back and up to select (highlight) the text.

5. Release the mouse button, and then click the bold button in the toolbar. The text will become bold.

6. Click anywhere away from the text to deselect it.

That's it! You're on your way. Now you should save the document and go on to give it a little color.

Follow these steps to save your HTML document:

1. Click **File** → **Save As** . FrontPage Express' Save As dialog box appears (see Figure 4-2). The text in the Page Title box will be selected.

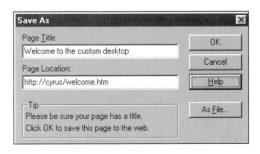

Figure 4-2 The Save As dialog box lets you name your document and save it as a file on your hard disk.

2. Type a new title in the Page Title box if you want a title other than what's there. FrontPage Express automatically uses the first several words of text that you enter in the document as a title.

3. Drag the cursor over the text in the Page Location box to select it, and then press the Delete (or Del) key on your keyboard to remove the text.

4. Click the As File button. A regular Windows 95 Save As dialog box appears.

5. Browse to the folder where you want to save the file, name the file, and click Save. For our example, we saved the file in the Windows folder. The dialog boxes disappear.

Adding Some Color to Your Life

FrontPage Express lets you choose a standard color or create one of your own. In the steps that follow, we show how to create a custom color. You can skip Steps 4–6 if you want to use one of the standard colors or the default color in your background, but we suggest that you at least read through the steps for creating a custom color to see how it works.

Follow these steps to give your background a custom color:

1. Click   Format → Background . The Page Properties dialog box appears with the Background tab at the front. The default colors for Background, Text, etc., appear in the lower part of the Background tab. Note that you can select a picture for your background instead of a color by clicking "Background image" and then clicking the Browse button and locating the picture that you want to use.

2. Click the arrow at the right end of the Background box. A menu of colors appears.

3. Click the color you want to use or click Custom (at the bottom of the list of colors) to proceed with creating a custom color. If you click Custom, a Color dialog box appears (see Figure 4-3).

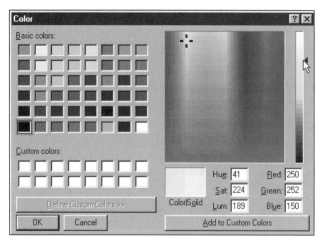

Figure 4-3 The Color dialog box, for selecting custom colors.

4. Click any point within the color square in the upper-right portion of the Color dialog box. In our example, we clicked in a yellow area (see

Figure 4-3). A range of the colors available for the area you click appears in the narrow column to the right of the color square.

5. Click any point along the narrow column to select a color. The color appears in the small rectangle below the color square. The color's numerical values appear below and to the right of the color square. You can duplicate the color for other purposes by using these numbers. (Write down the numbers and what each number applies to now; this will come in handy later.) Try as many different colors as you want to see what's available.

6. When you've found a color you want to use for the background, click the Add to Custom Color button, then click OK. The Color dialog box disappears, and the color you selected appears in the Background box on the Background tab of the Page Properties dialog box.

7. Repeat Steps 2–6 to choose alternative colors for Text, Hyperlinks, etc., if you wish to do so.

8. Click OK in the Page Properties dialog box to save your choices and close the dialog box. The color(s) you select will appear in your HTML document.

9. Save your document and close FrontPage Express.

Trying It Out

Now you're ready to see what your work so far looks like as a desktop background. Some of what you'll see may surprise you!

Follow these steps to make your HTML document the Active Desktop's background:

1. Right-click a blank space on the desktop to open the shortcut menu.

2. Select `Properties`, or select `Active Desktop` → `Customize My Desktop` to open the Display Properties dialog box (see Figure 4-4). The Background tab will be at the front (click it to bring it there if it is not).

3. Click the Browse button and use the Browse dialog box that appears to locate and select the HTML file you created. The file's name appears in the Wallpaper box on the Background tab. In a moment, a sample of the background file will appear in the monitor on the Background tab.

4. Click OK. The Display Properties dialog box closes and after a moment your new background appears.

NOTE   You may have to right-click a blank space on the desktop and select Refresh from the shortcut menu to cause the HTML background to appear.

The new Active Desktop background includes the color and text that you created with FrontPage Express. In our example in Figure 4-5, we moved the icons around so that they appear under the text that says "Here are your most-used programs." But there is a minor problem with the color surrounding the text that appears under the icons.

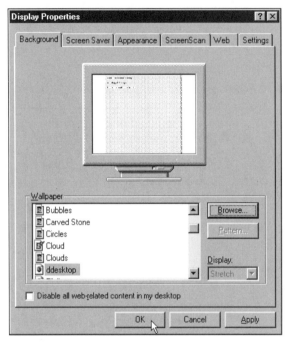

Figure 4-4   The Display Properties dialog box.

Fixing a Little Problem

In our example in Figure 4-5, the color that outlines the icon text is the old, regular desktop's background color, held over from before the HTML document was created. This is where writing down the numerical values for the custom background color (described in "Adding Some Color to Your Life") comes in handy.

Follow these steps if you want the color outlining the icon text to match the custom HTML background color:

1. Turn off the Active Desktop, open the Display Properties dialog box as you learned in the "Trying It Out" section, and click the Appearance tab to bring it to the front. "Desktop" should appear in the Item box on the Appearance tab.

2. Click the arrow by the Color box to open the color palette and click Other. A Color dialog box like the one shown in Figure 4-3 appears.

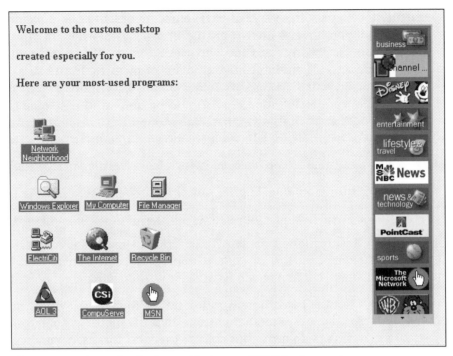

Welcome to the custom desktop

created especially for you.

Here are your most-used programs:

Network Neighborhood

Windows Explorer   My Computer   File Manager

ElectriCiti   The Internet   Recycle Bin

AOL 3   CompuServe   MSN

business

channel ...

DISNEY

entertainment

lifestyle & travel

MSNBC News

news & technology

PointCast

sports

The Microsoft Network

Figure 4-5 The Active Desktop with the new HTML background.

3. Double-click in each box for the color's numerical value and enter the values for the HTML document's background color that you wrote down. (If you didn't write them down, you can retrace your steps by reopening the document in FrontPage Express to get them.) The color you selected before will be duplicated.

4. Click Add to Custom Colors, and then click OK to close the Color dialog box.

5. Click Save As in the Appearance tab. A Save Scheme dialog box appears.

6. Give the new color scheme a name and click OK in the Save Scheme dialog box.

7. Click OK in the Display Properties dialog box to save your choice and close the dialog box. The new color for the regular desktop appears.

When you turn the Active Desktop back on, the color you selected for the HTML background and the color outlining the icon text should be identical.

Getting the Picture

To make your HTML background a little more interesting, you can add graphics or pictures. FrontPage Express' WYSIWYG ("What you see is what you get") interface makes this very easy. Of course, in order to add a picture to your background, you have to have a picture in a file somewhere in your computer that you can use. Nearly everyone who uses Windows 95 has some, though they may not know it. If you don't have a folder of pictures, in the steps that follow try looking in your C:\Windows folder or the C:\Windows\Web folder that IE 4 added during installation. You should be able to locate some files that end in ".gif" or ".bmp" in these folders. If you don't have any other picture files, these will do as examples of what you can do with images in your HTML background.

Follow these steps to add a picture to your Active Desktop's background:

1. Open FrontPage Express and select ⬚File → ⬚Open .

2. Browse to where you saved your background file and open it.

3. If you followed the previous FrontPage Express example, click to the right of the first row of text to place the cursor there. This indicates where the image will be added to the document.

4. Click the Insert Image button on the toolbar. (It's in the middle of the middle row of toolbar buttons. Rest the mouse pointer for a moment on each one in turn until you see the label for Insert Image.) The Image dialog box appears.

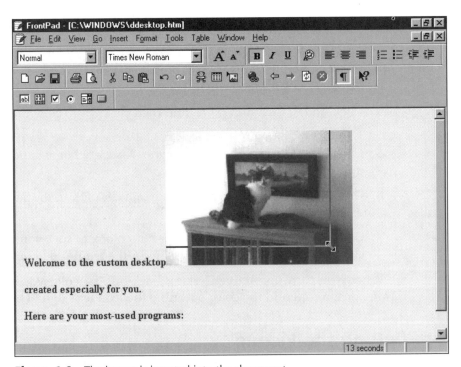

Figure 4-6 The image is inserted into the document.

5. Click the Browse button, use the Open dialog box to browse to the folder that contains the picture file that you want to use, and select the picture file. FrontPage Express looks for ".gif" and ".jpg" files by default. If you're not using a GIF or JPEG image, you can click the arrow at the right end of the Files of Type list box in the Open dialog box and select the type of image file you want to use.

6. Click OK in the Image dialog box. The image will appear where the cursor was located in the HTML document (see Figure 4-6).

Fine-Tuning the Image

Next, unless the image happens to be exactly the right size and managed to end up exactly where you wanted it, you'll probably want to adjust its size, position, and some other details relating to it.

Follow these steps to fine-tune the image's size and placement:

1. Click the image. Little squares appear at each corner and at the midpoint along each edge of the image. These are called *handles,* and you can drag them to adjust the image's height and width.

2. Drag the lower-right handle up and to the left to make the image smaller, or down and to the right to make the image larger, so that the image is about one-third as wide as the HTML page (the height will adjust in proportion automatically when you drag one of the corner handles).

3. Right-click the image. A shortcut menu appears.

4. Select **Image Properties** on the shortcut menu. The Image Properties dialog box appears.

5. Click the Appearance tab to bring it to the front.

6. Click the arrow at the right end of the Alignment box to open its menu and select "right" from the menu. This positions the image along the right edge of the document.

7. Click the little up arrow at the right end of the Border Thickness box until the number 2 appears. This creates a small, 2-pixel–wide border around the image. The border will be the same color as the text.

8. Click the little up arrow at the right end of the Horizontal Spacing box until the number 5 appears. This keeps any text at least 5 pixels away from the sides of the image. You won't need to adjust the Vertical Spacing or Size values for this example.

9. Click OK to save the adjustments and close the dialog box.

10. Save the document and close FrontPage Express.

11. Right-click the desktop and select ⟦ **Refresh** ⟧ from the shortcut menu. The HTML background with the image in it appears (see Figure 4-7).

Unless you have already moved it, the Channel bar will cover part of the image on your desktop. But don't worry about that. You'll take care of this minor conflict between desktop elements in the next section.

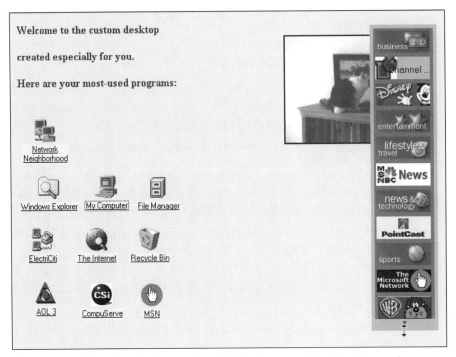

Figure 4-7   The Active Desktop with an HTML document for its background.

Keeping Active

The second Active Desktop feature we'll show you is something Microsoft calls "Active Desktop items." These are little windows on your desktop that can contain a variety of things: a weather map that's updated throughout the day, a favorite Web page, or other items available for download. For our download example, we use items available from Microsoft at their Web site. However, as IE 4 becomes more widely used, you're likely to see buttons with labels such as "Add to My Desktop," indicating Active Desktop items available for download, at lots of Web sites.

Your desktop comes with one Active Desktop item already installed: the Channel bar. When the Active Desktop is turned on, it appears near the right edge of your screen. We discuss the Channel bar's use later in this chapter. In this section, we use it to demonstrate how Active Desktop items can be moved around or resized to suit the way you want your desktop arranged. For the examples in this chapter, your Active Desktop must be turned on.

Moving Things Around

The Channel bar is an Active Desktop item and, like others, it can be resized or moved so that your desktop is arranged the way you want it. For our example, you'll resize and move the Channel bar. If you followed along in the chapter so far, you have an HTML background for your Active Desktop that includes an image, and the image will be partially obscured by the Channel bar (see Figure 4-7).

Follow these steps to resize or move an Active Desktop item:

1. Move the mouse pointer to the middle of the lower edge of the Channel bar. The frame around the Channel bar becomes wider and the pointer turns into a two-headed arrow pointing up and down, as you saw in Figure 4-7. The pointer will also turn into a two-headed arrow when it's at a corner, on the top, or at either side edge. Whenever the pointer becomes a two-headed arrow, you can drag the edge or corner it's at to enlarge the item or make it smaller.

2. Drag the lower edge of the Channel bar up until only five or six buttons in the Channel bar are showing.

3. Move the mouse pointer to the upper edge of the Channel bar. The frame along the upper edge becomes wider than it is along the other edges, and it contains a small arrow in the left corner and an X in the right corner (see Figure 4-8).

4. With the mouse pointer in the middle of the upper part of the frame, drag the Channel bar down so that it no longer covers the image on the HTML background.

Now all of the elements on the Active Desktop are showing. You can still look at the Channel bar buttons that don't show by clicking on the little arrow on the lower edge of the Channel bar to scroll down through the buttons. When you've scrolled down a little bit, another little arrow appears at the upper edge of the Channel bar for scrolling back up.

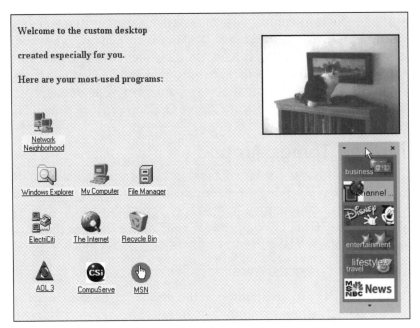

Figure 4-8   Active Desktop items can be resized and moved to suit your tastes.

Adding Active Desktop Items

You can find several examples of Active Desktop items available for download at Microsoft's IE 4 Web site. The items are available at the "Active Desktop Gallery" at `http://www.microsoft.com/ie/ie40/gallery/`. (You should also be able to locate links to the gallery at IE 4's home page: `http://www.microsoft.com/ie/ie40/`.) For our example, we'll download a weather map that can be updated regularly.

Follow these steps to download an Active Desktop item from Microsoft:

1. Open IE 4, type the URL for the gallery shown above into the Address box, and press Enter to go to the Active Desktop Gallery Web page (see Figure 4-9).

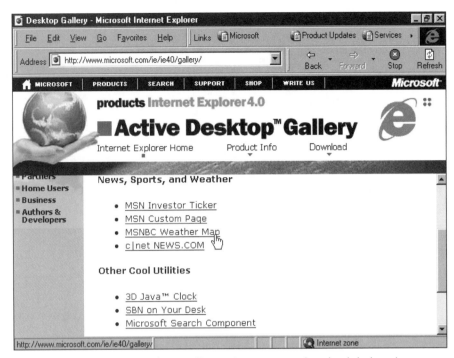

Figure 4-9 The Active Desktop Gallery, where you can download desktop items.
Screen shot reprinted by permission from Microsoft Corporation.

2. Scroll through the list of Active Desktop items until you see MSNBC weather map or another desktop item that interests you.

3. Click the link for the desktop item that you want to download. A page of information about the item appears. In our example, we selected the MSNBC weather map.

4. Scroll down the information page and click the "Add to my Desktop" button. A Subscribe dialog box appears.

5. Click Customize in the Schedule dialog box. The New Active Desktop item dialog box appears (see Figure 4-10).

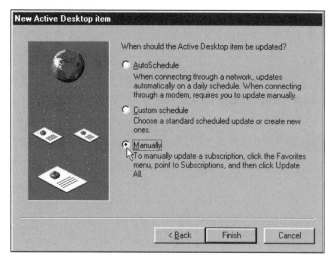

Figure 4-10 You control the update frequency for Active Desktop items.

The New Active Desktop item dialog box gives you three options for updating the information in your desktop item:

✳ AutoSchedule—Select this for automatic updates if you're always connected to a network (LAN, or Local Area Network) and have your Internet access through it. If you're not connected to a network and select this, you'll have to update the item manually (the same as selecting "Manually," below).

✳ Custom schedule—Select this if you want to designate a specific schedule for automatic updates whether you dial into the Internet or are on a LAN. If you select Custom schedule, there will be two more dialog boxes to go through in which you 1) choose between daily, weekly, or monthly updates; and 2) select particular times, days of the week, etc. These dialog boxes work like the ones in Task Scheduler, discussed in Chapter 3.

✳ Manually—Select this if you want to control the time of the update completely by using "manual" updates. We'll discuss manual updates later in this chapter.

Follow these steps to finish installing the item:

1. Select the update option you want to use and click Finish. (If you select Custom schedule, the button will be labeled "Next"; click it to bring up the two dialog boxes for specifying a custom schedule, and then click OK in the second scheduling dialog box.) After clicking Finish (or OK for Custom schedule), the Subscribe dialog box is again at the front.

2. Click OK in the Subscribe dialog box to complete the subscription process for the Active Desktop item. A Download Progress box appears while the files for the desktop item are transferred to your computer's hard disk.

3. When the desktop item has been downloaded to your computer, close Explorer and disconnect from your ISP. The Active Desktop item will be on your desktop (see Figure 4-11), and it can be resized and moved about as previously shown for the Channel bar.

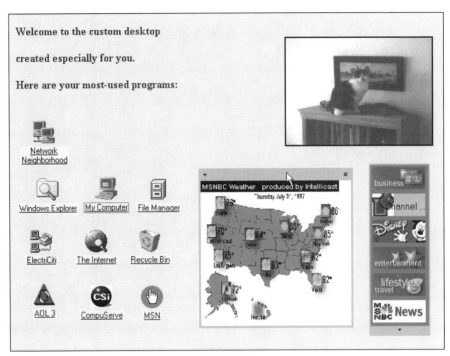

Figure 4-11 The new item (the weather map) on the Active Desktop.

Making a Web Page an Active Desktop Item

We can think of a couple of reasons for making a Web page into an Active Desktop item. For one thing, you could include a favorite Web page and set it to be updated regularly so that you can keep track of it. For another, you could use your own Web page, or an HTML document that you store on your computer's hard disk, and include your favorite links on it for instant access to them.

Follow these steps to include a Web page as an Active Desktop item:

1. Right-click the desktop and select Properties from the shortcut menu. The Display Properties dialog box appears.

2. Click the Web tab to bring it to the front (see Figure 4-12). The Web tab includes a representation of your computer's monitor that shows the placement of Active Desktop items and a list of the items you have installed. The top item in the list will be highlighted, as will its counterpart in the monitor.

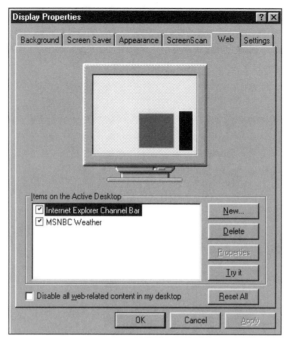

Figure 4-12 The Web tab in the Display Properties dialog box.

3. Click New. A New Active Desktop Item dialog box appears. This dialog box gives you instant access to the Active Desktop Gallery if you want to use it for adding desktop items.

4. Click No. Another New Active Desktop Item dialog box that includes a "Location" box appears. The Location box is where you indicate whether you want to use a page on the Web or an HTML file on your computer for the desktop item.

Type either the URL for a page on the Web, or the path and filename for an HTML document on your computer into the Location box in the New Active Desktop Item dialog box and click OK. (You can also use the Browse button to browse to a file on your computer.) What happens next is different for Web pages and files on your computer. If you typed the path and filename for an HTML file on your computer, the New Active Desktop Item dialog box closes, and the file appears in the list of items in the Web tab of the Display Properties dialog box.

If you typed a Web page URL into the Location box, you have some choices to make. When you use a Web page as a desktop item, IE 4 treats it like a "Channel." (Channels will be discussed later in this chapter.) The first dialog box that appears in this instance is a Subscribe dialog box. You can click OK to accept the default settings or click Customize to set custom options for updating the Web page. For now, click OK. We'll discuss default and custom Channel settings later in this chapter in the "Tuning In" section, and you can set custom options for the desktop item later if you want to. When you click OK, the Subscribe dialog box closes and the Web page URL appears in the list of items in the Web tab of the Display Properties dialog box.

Once you have the new desktop item listed on the Web tab, click OK to close the Display Properties dialog box. The new item appears on your desktop, and you can resize or move it as you wish. (You may have to right-click the desktop and select Refresh from the shortcut menu to see the new item.)

TIP **There's another way to add a Web page to your Active Desktop. If you have IE 4 open (but not maximized) and you're at a Web page that you want to use as a desktop item, use the right mouse button (instead of the left one) to drag the little icon in the upper-left corner of the IE 4 Title bar to your desktop. The page appears as a desktop item, and the Subscribe dialog box opens, as described above.**

Managing Active Desktop Items

The Web tab in the Display Properties dialog box (see Figure 4-12) is where you manage your desktop items. From there, you can turn the items off or on, delete them, or change their update schedules. Notice the checkboxes to the left of each item. Click to remove the ✓ if you want to turn the item off (stop it from displaying and being updated). Click again to replace the ✓ to turn it back on. To delete an item, click it to select (highlight) it, then click the Delete button. To change the update schedule, click the Properties button. A Properties dialog box, with tabs for changing how and when updates are received, appears.

Tuning In

We saved the biggest Active Desktop feature for last: Channels. Channels are a little like special cable television channels, periodically sending out information on a variety of topics. IE 4's Channels let you take advantage of the new "push" technology on the Web. Using push, information suppliers send out Channel updates on a regular schedule. When you subscribe to a Channel, you set up how and when the information in the Channel is delivered to your computer.

Channels take advantage of the new "push" technology on the Web by periodically sending you information on a variety of topics.

Channel Surfing

You can quickly start "channel surfing" in two ways:

* Click the Channel guide button on the Channel bar

   or

* Click the View Channels button that IE 4 installed on the Quick Launch toolbar (on your taskbar).

Either way, the IE 4 Channel viewer opens. This is IE 4 in a special "full screen" mode. Next, IE 4 connects you to the Internet, and loads up samples and options for subscribing to Channels (see Figure 4-13).

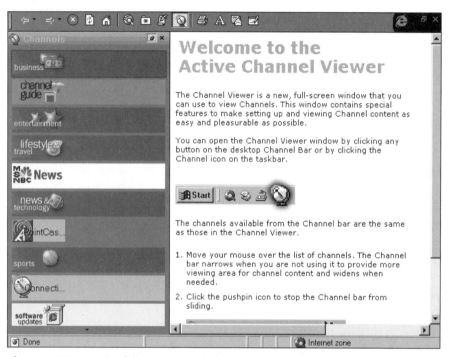

Figure 4-13   IE 4 in "full screen" mode for subscribing to and viewing Channels.

At first you'll see a larger version of the Channel bar along the left side of the screen that includes buttons for some sample Channels and, in dark blue, buttons for categories of Channels. These are actually category folders, containing links to Channels. If you click one of the category buttons, a list of links for Channels in the category appears. The Channel bar in the Channel viewer is the same as the Channel bar on your desktop, but you can only open the category folders from the Channel bar in the Channel viewer.

The Channel viewer's Channel bar gradually closes by moving to the left and disappearing. If you move your mouse pointer to the left side of the screen, it opens again. When the Channel bar is all the way open, you can click the little pushpin icon in its upper-right corner to make it stay open (don't do this now if you're going to follow along with the example that follows).

At the top of the Channel viewer is a toolbar with buttons for the browser. A tab at the right end of the toolbar includes a Minimize button and a Close button. This tab opens and shows a revolving globe when the browser is in the process of connecting to a Web page or Channel, and then partially closes.

If you clicked the View Channels button on the Quick Launch toolbar, you'll see a welcome screen on the right. If you clicked the Channel guide button in the Channel bar, the Channel guide page appears with information about a Channel that it picked at random.

Finding Channels

IE 4 comes with links to sample pages for a multitude of Channels in its Channel bar. The Channel bar also includes a button for the Channel guide, where you can find an extensive list of available Channels. Not every Channel shows up in it, but we'll use the Channel guide for our examples. (Many Web sites offer Channel subscriptions, but they don't show up in the Channel guide. In such cases, you'll see a button or link at the Web site that you can click to subscribe.) Whichever way you open the IE 4 Channel viewer, you're on your way to finding what's available.

Follow these steps to check out the Channels:

1. Open the IE 4 Channel viewer by clicking the Channel guide button on the Channel bar, or by clicking the View Channels button in the Quick Launch toolbar. If you use the View Channels button, click the Channel guide button in the viewer after it opens. The Channel guide appears with information about a random Channel. At the top of the Channel guide page are links to pages with information about Channels (What's New, Coming Soon, and Learn About Channels). Below these are links to Channel categories: Business, Entertainment, Lifestyles & Travel, News & Technology, etc.

2. Click the News & Technology link. A frame on the left appears with button links for various Channels; directions appear in the frame on the right (see Figure 4-14).

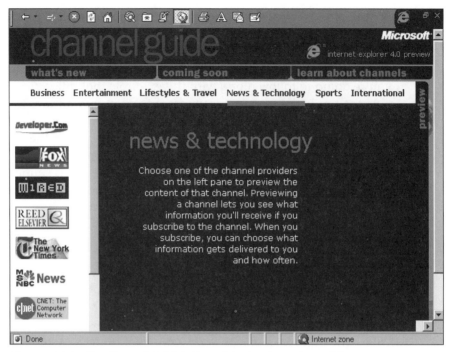

Figure 4-14 The Channel Guide's News & Technology Channel list.
Screen shot reprinted by permission from Microsoft Corporation.

3. Scroll down the left frame until you see the button for the Microsoft Channel.

4. Click the Microsoft Channel button. A page with information about the Channel appears in the right frame. At some place on the page in the right frame will be a button or link for subscribing to the Channel.

Subscribing to a Channel

Once you've found a Channel in the Channel guide that looks interesting, subscribing to it is a snap. Many of the dialog boxes that appear as part of subscribing to Channels will be familiar if you've been following along in this chapter.

Follow these steps to subscribe to a Channel:

1. Locate a Channel using the Channel guide (see the previous section in this chapter if you haven't been following along). The page that tells about the Channel will have a button on it for subscribing to the Channel marked "Subscribe," "Add to Channels," or something similar.

2. Click the Subscribe button. A Subscribe dialog box appears.

3. Click the Customize button in the Subscribe dialog box. The first Channel Subscription Wizard dialog box appears and gives you two

choices. When a Channel's content changes, you can either be notified about the change or have the new Channel content downloaded automatically for offline viewing. If hard disk space is at a premium on your computer, you may wish to select notification. If, however, you want to view the changed Channel content offline, select that.

4. Click your choice to select it, and click Next. Another Channel Subscription Wizard dialog box appears. This one asks if you want to include the Channel in the Channel Screen Saver.

5. To follow along in the Bonus for this chapter where we discuss the Channel Screen Saver, click Yes, and then click Next. Another Channel Subscription Wizard dialog box appears. This dialog box tells you that IE 4 will notify you about changes to the Channel's content by adding a "gleam" (a little red star) to the channel's icon, and asks if you also want to be notified by e-mail. The e-mail would be sent to whatever address you set up for yourself in Outlook Express (if you've done so). If you select Yes, you get the option of having the e-mail sent to a different address, if you have more than one.

6. Click your choice to select it, and click Next. Another Channel Subscription Wizard dialog box appears. This one is identical to the dialog box for setting up schedules shown in Figure 4-10. Your options are the same as those for scheduling updates for desktop items, covered in the section "Setting Update Options." Refer to that section for details.

7. After setting your update schedule options, click Finish, and the Channel Subscription Wizard dialog box closes.

8. Click OK in the Subscribe dialog box and it closes. If you chose to include the Channel in the Channel Screen Saver, a dialog box appears and asks if you want to replace the current screen saver with the Channel Screen Saver. Click Yes and the dialog box closes.

Procedures for all Channel subscriptions are not identical. Some Channels—PointCast, for example—include desktop components that can be downloaded for displaying information that is updated throughout the day. This adds extra steps to the subscription process.

Viewing Channels

After setting up a subscription, the IE 4 channel viewer will open a new window and display the Channel you have subscribed to. A button for the channel is added to your Channel bar. To view the Channel in the future, click its button on the Channel bar and the Channel viewer will open to display it. If you have moved the button inside one of the category folders (see "Customizing the Channel Bar," later in this chapter), click the Category button to open the viewer and select the Channel. You can also open the Channel viewer using the View Channels button, and then click the Channel's icon to view it. Depending on how you set up the subscription, the viewer may or may not connect to the Internet to download new content when you open the viewer.

If your Channels are set up for scheduled, automatic updates, remember to have your computer turned on at the scheduled time. IE 4 will automatically dial into your ISP and download the updated Channel content, or notify you that the content changed by adding a gleam to the Channel icons and/or sending you an e-mail notification.

Managing Channels

You can check the Channel icons, change Channel update schedules, and do other Channel management through the Subscriptions folder (see Figure 4-15). To make this process easier, we recommend placing a shortcut to the folder on your desktop.

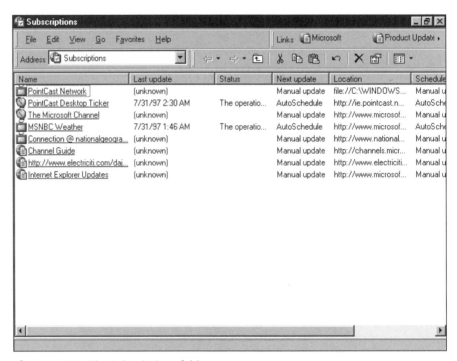

Figure 4-15   The Subscriptions folder.

Follow these steps to open the Subscriptions folder and make a desktop shortcut for it:

1. Click the My Computer icon on your desktop to open My Computer.

2. Select   **Favorites**   → **Subscriptions**   → **Manage Subscriptions** . The Subscriptions folder appears.

3. Right-click the icon in the upper-left corner of the Subscriptions folder Title bar and select `Create Shortcut` from the menu that opens. A message box will appear and tell you that the shortcut will be placed on the desktop.

4. Click OK. Now there's a shortcut on your desktop to make opening the Subscriptions folder easier. (Leave the Subscriptions folder open for the time being.)

The Subscriptions folder lists Active Desktop items, Web pages, and Channels that you have subscribed to. Each line in the folder lists a subscription and gives you information about it, including when it was last updated and the type of update schedule you gave it. Deleting, renaming, rescheduling, or changing the way an entry is received (that is, whether to receive a download of new content or just notification that the Channel has changed), is easy.

Follow these steps to delete or rename an entry in the Subscriptions folder:

1. Select an entry by resting the mouse pointer over it for a moment.

2. Click `File` in the menu bar to open the File menu. The File menu includes choices for renaming or deleting an entry.

3. Select `Delete` to delete the subscription, or `Rename` to rename the subscription's entry in the list. If you select `Delete`, a message box will ask you to confirm the deletion.

To edit an entry's update schedule or the way it's received, right-click an entry and select Properties from the shortcut menu that appears to open the entry's Properties dialog box (see Figure 4-16).

The Properties dialog box includes five tabs: General, Sharing, Subscription, Receiving, and Schedule. Click each tab in turn to bring it to the front and take a look at its contents. The Subscription, Receiving, and Schedule tabs include the options set up during the subscription process, and they can all be modified here using standard methods for interacting with dialog boxes.

Updating Channels Manually

If you select manual update when subscribing to a Channel, you have several options for updating it:

* With the Channel's button showing on the Channel bar, or in a category folder on the Channel bar, right-click the Channel and select Update Now from its shortcut menu.

* From within the Subscriptions folder, right-click an entry and select Update Now from its shortcut menu.

* From within any open folder, select Priorities→Subscriptions→Update All to update all of your subscriptions.

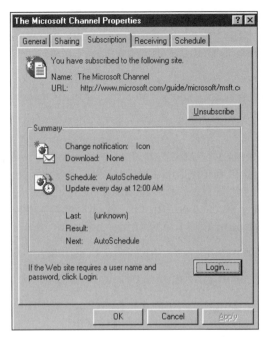

Figure 4-16 The Properties dialog box for a Channel subscription.

Customizing the Channel Bar

The Channel bar in the Channel viewer is the same as the Channel bar on your desktop. Both are created by the same file on your computer's hard disk. The Channel buttons listed on it can be dragged or cut-and-pasted into the category folders, copied into more than one category folder, or deleted. You can do this using the Channel bar in the viewer or the one on your desktop. Since they're both the result of the same file, any changes made to one are also made to the other.

The Channel bar comes with several sample Channel buttons that, if you choose not to subscribe to them, can be deleted. The category folders can be deleted as well, but they're so useful for sorting out Channels that we don't recommend that you do this.

Follow these steps to delete an unwanted Channel button:

1. Right-click the unwanted button to open its shortcut menu.

2. Select ⬚ **Delete** ⬚ . A message box asks you to confirm the deletion.

3. Click Yes. The button disappears.

As you add Channels, a button for each one added appears on the Channel bar. After a while you could have quite a crowd. The Channel bar also has built-in category folders (the dark blue buttons), and you can sort your Channels into these folders by dragging the Channel buttons to them. This is a simple drag-and-drop operation, so we won't list the steps. You can also drag buttons out of folders and onto the Channel bar, or from one folder to another.

TIP **If you accidentally delete the button for a Channel, it's easy to restore. Just open the Subscriptions folder (see Figure 4-15), right-click the Channel and select Copy from its shortcut menu. Then right-click a Channel category folder and select Paste from the folder's shortcut menu. You can't paste the button directly onto the Channel bar, but once it's in a folder you can drag it onto the bar or to another folder.**

BONUS

Using IE 4's Special Screen Savers

I E 4 adds two special screen savers to the screen saver list that appears in the Display Properties dialog box: the Active Desktop Screen Saver and the Channel Screen Saver. The Active Desktop Screen Saver lets you select Web pages that you have subscribed to or that you have visited recently, or both, to display in turn while the screen saver is activated. The Channel Screen Saver does the same sort of thing, but displays Channels instead of Web pages. Both of the screen savers are set up in much the same way.

Follow these steps to set up the Active Desktop Screen Saver:

1. Right-click the desktop and select Properties from the shortcut menu. The Display Properties dialog box appears.

2. Click the Screen Saver tab to bring it to the front.

3. Scroll down the list of screen savers and click Active Desktop Screen Saver to select it.

4. Click the Settings button. The Screen Saver Properties dialog box for the Active Desktop Screen Saver appears with the General tab at the front. The General tab lists Web pages that you're subscribed to, which can be included in the screen saver's presentation.

5. Click the Advanced tab to bring it to the front. The Advanced tab is where you select how to close the screen saver and choose to display Web pages that you're subscribed to (and/or Web pages that you've recently

visited). The default setting for closing the screen saver is to use the Close button (a new feature for a screen saver) that appears in the screen saver's upper-right corner. If you want to close it the usual way, select "Close the Screen Saver with mouse movement."

6. Click "Subscribed sites" to display the sites listed in the General tab while the screen saver is active. Then, click the most frequently visited Favorite sites option and set the number of sites. You can select one or the other, or both sets of Web pages.

7. Click OK in the Screen Saver Properties and Display Properties dialog boxes to save your choices and close the dialog boxes.

Follow these steps to set up the Channel Screen Saver:

1. Right-click the desktop and select 「 **Properties** 」 from the shortcut menu. The Display Properties dialog box appears.

2. Click the Screen Saver tab to bring it to the front.

3. Scroll down the list of screen savers and click Channel Screen Saver to select it.

4. Click the Settings button. The Screen Saver Properties dialog box for the Channel Screen Saver appears, with the General tab at the front (see Figure 4-17). The General tab lists the Channels that you're subscribed to, which can be included in the screen saver's presentation.

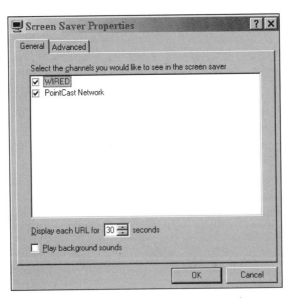

Figure 4-17 The General tab in the Channel Screen Saver's Properties dialog box.

5. Click the square next to each Channel that you want to include in the screen saver's presentation to place a ✓ in it.

6. Click the Advanced tab to bring it to the front. The Advanced tab is where you select how to close the screen saver. The default setting for closing the screen saver is to use the Close button that appears in the screen saver's upper-right corner. If you want to close it the usual way, select "Close the Screen Saver with mouse movement."

7. Click OK in the Screen Saver Properties and Display Properties dialog boxes to save your choices and close the dialog boxes.

Summary

The full potential of IE 4 is reflected in its Active Desktop features. Using an HTML background for virtually unlimited customization and Active Desktop items, you can seamlessly integrate your computer into the Internet. The most exciting new feature, Channels, takes advantage of the varied stream of data being "pushed" to your desktop by hundreds of information providers. Channels keep you on top of developments no matter what your range of business and personal interests may include.

EXPLORING THE INTERNET

In these chapters, you'll learn how to find useful information on the Web, how to create your own guide to the Web with Favorites, and how to download fun and useful software from Internet archives. We'll also show you *gophers*, a blast from the Internet's past that still has plenty to offer.

Internet Explorer also speeds up your access to information in another way. With Web page subscriptions you can keep up with the latest stock quotes, news that affects your business or organization, or developments relating to dozens of other subjects.

When you bought your computer you probably thought a lot about where to put it. Should it go in the family room, the spare bedroom, or even in one of the kids' bedrooms?

If you think that those issues are hard to deal with, can you imagine having to deal with a computer that is 51 feet long and weighs about 5 tons? That's like fitting a house inside your house! That's exactly what the first programmable computer looked like. It was built in 1943 by a team led by Howard H. Aiken at Harvard University in Cambridge, Massachusetts, with support from IBM. Not only was the machine absolutely gargantuan, it also had 750,000 parts. Try finding a computer technician to fix that baby! If you're a stickler for details, this machine isn't really considered to be a real computer. It was called an Automatic Sequence-Controlled Calculator Mark I.

In 1945, a team led by John W. Mauchly and J. Prosper Eckert, working at the Moore School of Electrical Engineering at the University of Pennsylvania in Philadelphia, created an electronic computer. And, picture this, it weighed 30 tons and took up about 1000 square feet of floor space! Not exactly something you can fit in the family room.

We've come a long way since the 1940s. Computers have shrunk in size but exploded in power. You can now do stuff with the computer on your desk that scientists of the 40s never even dreamed of.

For instance, the average desk used at home takes up between four and six feet of wall space. It's approximately three feet deep. By the time you add a chair, you're talking an additional three feet of space in front of the desk. All of this means that you're using about 36 square feet of space for your computer (give or take a few square feet depending on your house and your budget). And the computer itself takes up only a few square feet.

We now have laptop computers that take up less than 1 square foot of space. The laptop can do everything that your regular desktop computer can do.

If you think laptops are an amazing invention, you haven't seen the palmtop yet. It's a computer than fits in the palm of your hand! Palmtop users can check their e-mail, keep track of expenses, and access their regular desktop computer. Aiken, Mauchly, Eckert, and others, are probably grinning like Cheshire cats up there in that great computing lab in the sky.

If you're interested in the history of computers, check out Mark Brader's postings at alt.folklore.computers. Mark's articles are the source of the historical information above.

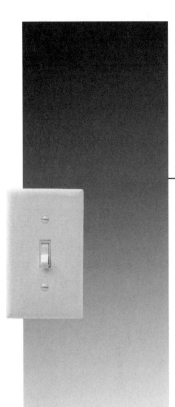

CHAPTER FIVE

CRUISING THE WEB

IN THIS CHAPTER YOU LEARN THESE KEY SKILLS

HOW TO USE LINKS   PAGE   104

HOW TO WORK WITH URLS   PAGE   106

HOW TO MOVE BACKWARD AND
   FORWARD   PAGE   109

HOW TO ADD A PAGE TO YOUR LINKS
   BAR   PAGE   112

HOW TO DEAL WITH FRAMES   PAGE   116

HOW TO CONTROL YOUR CHILDREN'S WEB
   VIEWING   PAGE   119

5

Robert Benchley, a famous humorist of the 1930s and 40s, said: "In America there are two classes of travel, first class and with children." Since neither the Internet nor the World Wide Web existed in Benchley's time, he certainly never browsed the Web. But *you* can travel all over the world, meet fascinating people, and learn more than you ever imagined possible without ever leaving your chair.

Internet Explorer's browser gives you a variety of ways to move around on the World Wide Web. At first, there may seem to be too many, but after using them all for a while you'll see that each one has advantages in certain situations. After we've shown you some of these techniques, we'll show you how you can print the pages that you find on the Web. We'll also show you how you can control what your kids see without it affecting what you can see, thanks to Internet Explorer's new Content Advisor.

Linking to the World

Links are what make the World Wide Web work. Click some underlined text or even a picture on your screen and in seconds you're connected to a computer halfway around the world. If you're relatively new to web browsing, you might want to put a timer on that roast in the oven or reschedule that appointment you have booked in the next hour. According to some people, browsing the Web is not only exciting, but also addictive. Be prepared to lose all track of time.

In the real world you go to a company's offices, pick up a catalog, or call on the telephone to find out what they have to offer. In the virtual world of the Internet, you connect to a Web site. Internet Explorer comes already set up with links to some really terrific and entertaining sites. The information on the Web changes constantly, and some sites are updated daily (and some many times during the day). This means that even if you follow our directions exactly, the pictures and information you see on your screen may not be the same as the examples we show. Don't worry. If you go back to the same site tomorrow it will probably be different from what you see today. Relax, have fun, and if you want to click a different link than we suggest, go for it!

Follow these steps to start your browsing adventure:

1. Click 🔵 on the taskbar to launch the Internet Explorer browser. If you are not already connected to your ISP, the Microsoft Connection Manager dialog box appears and makes the connection based on the settings you made during installation.

2. When you connect, you'll be at Microsoft's home page for Internet Explorer.

3. Move your mouse pointer slowly over the page. When it turns into a 🖑, as shown in Figure 5-1, it means it's over a link. Links can be icons, graphics, or text. When you click a link, it connects you to another Web site. While the pointer is over a link, the link's address, or URL, appears in the status bar at the bottom of the Internet Explorer window.

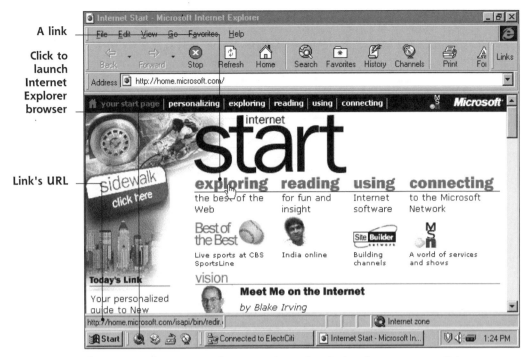

Figure 5-1 The mouse pointer turns into a hand when it passes over a link.
Screen shot reprinted by permission from Microsoft Corporation.

4. If you want to follow along with us, click the large red text that says "exploring the best of the Web." You'll connect to the screen you see in Figure 5-2. Use the scroll bar on the right of the site to see what's available. (A quick tip: The living section has some especially cool stuff.) Click any underlined text that piques your interest. You can move from site to site by clicking on links.

NOTE A *Web site* is the total collection of Web pages that an individual, company, or organization has on the Web. The *home page,* or first page you see when you visit a site, usually acts as an index to the rest of the Web pages at the site.

Figure 5-2 The Best of the Web is your link to exciting Web sites. Scroll through the site to see all the available links.

Screen shot reprinted by permission from Microsoft Corporation.

Connecting with U R Who?

You have undoubtedly noticed the ads on TV, in newspapers, and even on billboards that direct you to specific Web sites. These Web site addresses are officially called *Uniform Resource Locators,* or *URLs.* Every single Web site has a URL. In fact, individual pages and frames within a Web site have their own URLs. Use the URL to go directly to the Web site. It doesn't matter what Web page is on your screen when you type a URL. Just make sure the Address bar is showing. In this example, you'll visit the White House. Check it out and be sure to scroll through the site to see the links. We'd be very surprised if you didn't find several links that interest you.

Every single Web site has its own URL (Uniform Resource Locator).

Follow these steps to use the URL for the White House:

1. Click in the Address bar to highlight the URL that is currently there. See Figure 5-3 for the location of the Address bar.

Type URL here —

Figure 5-3 Leave a message for Bill and Hillary at www.whitehouse.gov.

2. Type the URL of the site you want to visit. It replaces the highlighted address. In this example, the URL is www.whitehouse.gov. (Don't type the final period.)

3. Press the Enter key on your keyboard. As the page, or Web site, loads onto your screen, notice that the URL adds "http://" to the beginning of the text you typed and "WH/Welcome.html" to the end.

4. If you want to speed up your browsing, click the "Text version" link in the upper-left corner of the page. If you select this option, the resulting page will retain a link for the "Graphics Version" in the same spot so you can get the images back. Try it for yourself.

You don't have to type the "http://" part of a URL when you're using the Address bar to go to a Web page. In fact, if you also leave out the "www." and "com" (or in this case "gov") parts of the URL, Explorer may still be able to locate the page for which you're looking. For example, to go to Microsoft's home page you only need to type "microsoft" in the Address bar and press Enter. However, this doesn't always work. To get to our Web page, the entire URL (`www.gbgroup.com/~gbgroup`) is needed. Abbreviating the name can cause a comedy of errors. Typing simply "whitehouse" will take you to WhiteHouse.com, which is a private site for commentary that parodies the White House and U.S. politics.

If you're not familiar with the symbols used in URLs, take a minute to examine your keyboard. Notice that there are two different slash marks, often in the bottom row of keys: a forward slash (/) and a backward slash (\). Don't confuse the two or the address won't be correct. The tilde (~), pronounced "*tild* eh," is not a hyphen that got smudged. On many keyboards it's the squiggle to the left of the number 1 key in the top row. Depending on the type of keyboard you have, however, it may be in a different spot or you may not have one at all. If you simply don't have a tilde on your keyboard (and some laptops or very compact keyboards may not), here's what you can do. Go to the Character Map in Accessories, select a font like Arial or Times New Roman, click the tilde in the Character Map, use the Copy button to copy it, and then paste it into the address. A pain-in-the-neck process, but it works.

SIDE TRIP

LEARNING TO TALK THE TALK

In online parlance, the periods in URLs such as www.whitehouse.gov are called *dots*. If you want to sound like one of the in-crowd, read the address as "www dot whitehouse dot gov." Reading URLs this way is called *dotspeak* in the online world. The "gov" in the URL means that this is a government site. There are six major categories, or domains, of Internet sites:

    com = commercial

    edu = educational

    gov = government

    mil = military

    net = networks (an Internet network, not a television network)

    org = organizations

Getting Back There Faster

It's very easy to follow one link to a second link to a third link and so forth and lose track of where you are (not to mention the time). Wouldn't you like to have the online equivalent of a "You are here" pointer in a mall directory map? Well, Internet Explorer has a couple of features to help you get around easily and figure out where you are and where you've been.

Going Backward and Forward

You can go back one page at a time by clicking the Back button in the toolbar. If you click the Back button repeatedly, you'll cycle through all the pages you visited until you get back to the Internet Explorer home page. When you go back to a page, notice that any underlined text links that you clicked will have changed color, indicating that you followed the link. Once you have gone backward, the Forward button becomes activated, and you can click the Forward button to revisit in sequence the pages you have already seen.

FEATURE FOCUS You don't even have to move your mouse to go backward or forward. IE 4 has added these commands to the shortcut menu. Simply right-click your mouse and then click Back to go to the previous Web site or Web page.

Internet Explorer has even thought about saving you the effort of multiple clicks to cycle through several Web pages. If you click the down arrow to the right of either the Back or Forward buttons, a list of pages you can go back or forward to appears. You can click a page in the list to go to it. This saves you the trouble of having to click either button repeatedly to reach a particular page. See Figure 5-4 for an example of the Forward button list.

Figure 5-4 Click the Back and Forward buttons to move through sites you've already visited. Click the down-arrow to the right of the Back and Forward buttons to see a list of sites.

Using the File Menu to Revisit Sites

When you're working in your word processing program, you're probably used to using the File menu to see the last few files you opened. Internet Explorer has incorporated this very convenient feature into its File menu. You'll see the pages or sites you last visited listed at the bottom of the File menu, with a checkmark beside the name of the site currently on your screen. This list is created every time you start Internet Explorer. Click a site to revisit it.

Reliving History

If you're like us, you probably don't remember what sites you visited *today* let alone three days ago. Fortunately, Internet Explorer's History list keeps a record of your browsing. This really comes in handy when you remember that you visited a terrific site but you can't for the life of you remember its address. You can even customize the extent of the record that Internet Explorer keeps.

FEATURE FOCUS Keeping a record of your browsing in the History list is a new feature of Internet Explorer. You can even specify how many pages are saved in the History list.

Follow these steps to see the History list:

1. Click the History button in the icon bar. The History list appears to the left of the current web page, with Today's list expanded (see Figure 5-5).

2. Click the appropriate folder and then click the Web icon to the left of the Web site you want to revisit. Figure 5-5 shows a link to the Welcome page of the IRS (http://www.irs.gov — another interesting site).

3. If you want to close an expanded folder, click the folder.

4. To scroll through a long list, click the down arrow at the bottom of the list.

5. To close the History list, click the History button again.

Additionally, you can customize the number of days that Internet Explorer keeps track of your pages. You can even clear the History list.

Follow these steps to customize the History list:

1. Click ▢ View ▢ in the menu bar and then click ▢ Options ▢ to open the Options dialog box.

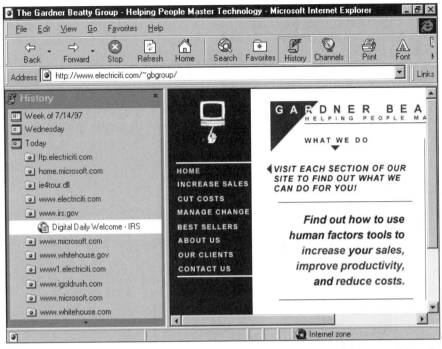

Figure 5-5 Click the History button and then click the appropriate folder to revisit a site.

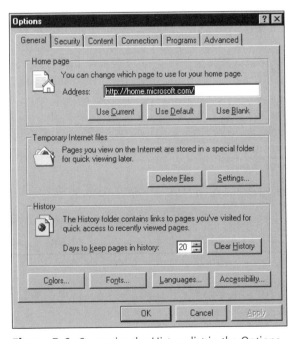

Figure 5-6 Customize the History list in the Options
dialog box.

2. Click the General Tab to bring it to the front.

3. In the History section, set the number of days that you want Internet Explorer to keep track of Web sites you visit.

4. If you want to clear the current list completely, click the Clear History button.

5. Click OK to make the changes and close the dialog box.

Love Those Links

If you thought the Back and Forward buttons, the File menu, and the History list discussed in the previous section were cool ways of getting back to a previously visited Web site, you'll get a kick out of adding a page to your Links bar. The Links bar is part of the customizable toolbars discussed in Chapter 3. We'll show you several ways to work with the Links bar.

Dragging and Dropping a Link

Figure 5-7 shows a closed Links bar at the far right of the Address bar. This is how IE 4 installed on one of our machines. It may have installed a little differently on yours and show only some of the items on the bar. Either way is OK. The steps we describe will work in either event. In Windows-based programs, you've undoubtedly learned that you can do the same task in several different ways. For example, to move text you can use the Cut and Paste buttons, you can drag and drop highlighted text, you can use the Cut and Paste command on the Edit menu, or you can use keyboard commands. It's sort of like, "You can call me Al or you can call me...." This multiplicity of methods is also true in Internet Explorer, but in spades. The Web metaphor has expanded the options you have for doing any task. We'll show you a couple of ways of dealing with links and trust that you'll discover more on your own.

Follow these steps to drag and drop a page to the Links bar:

1. The Web site that you'd like to revisit should be on your screen.

2. Drag the Web site icon in the Address bar over to the Links bar and drop it there. Notice that a shortcut arrow becomes attached to your mouse pointer as you drag. It doesn't matter whether the Links bar is closed (as it is in Figure 5-7) or open. We'll show you how to open the Links bar in the next section.

Web site icon ───

Links bar ───

Figure 5-7 Drag and drop a Web site icon onto the Links bar to create a quick connection tool.

Opening the Links Bar

You can expand the Links bar to a full open position or you can control the expansion manually. We suggest you play with the setting a little bit to find what suits you.

Follow these steps to expand and contract the Links bar:

1. Place your mouse pointer on top of the Links bar handle. It changes to a two-headed arrow, as shown in Figure 5-8.

Links handle ───

Figure 5-8 Double-click the Links handle to expand the Links bar completely.

2. Double-click the handle and the Links bar expands completely, as shown in Figure 5-9.

Click to scroll through links ───

Figure 5-9 A fully expanded Links bar.

3. Click ▶ at the right end of the Links bar to scroll through links that may not initially show on the expanded bar.

4. Double-click the handle again to close the Links bar.

When you double-click the Links bar handle, the Address bar is closed. It's a snap to manually adjust the size of the Links bar.

Follow these steps to adjust the size of the Links bar:

1. With your mouse pointer on top of the Links bar handle, press and hold your mouse button. The pointer changes shape, as shown in Figure 5-10.

Double-
headed
pointer

Figure 5-10 Drag the handle to manually control the size of the Links bar.

2. Holding your mouse button, drag the handle to the left or right to adjust the sizes of the Address bar and Links bar.

Launching a Web Page from the Links Bar

Once you've added a page to the Links bar, using it to launch a Web site is as easy as clicking your mouse on the link.

Adding a Link to the Favorites Menu

In addition to dragging and dropping a Web site icon onto the Links bar, you can add a Web site to your list of Favorites and tell Internet Explorer to add it to the Links bar.

Follow these steps to add a link to Favorites:

1. The Web site you want should be open on your screen.

2. Click ⎡ **Favorites** ⎤ on the menu bar, then click ⎡ **Add to Favorites** ⎤. The Add to Favorites dialog box shown in Figure 5-11 appears. It will be a smaller dialog box until you complete Step 3.

3. Click the Create in button. The dialog box expands as shown in Figure 5-11.

4. Click the Links folder to highlight it.

5. Click OK. The link shown in the Name box (in this example, Welcome to the White House) is added to your Links bar and to your Favorites folder.

 Favorites are discussed in more detail in Chapter 6, "Setting Up Web Page Subscriptions."

Deleting a Link

You can delete the pages that Microsoft preset on your Links bar if you don't want them. You may even find that you get tired of a link and want to replace it with something more exciting. As with everything else, there are several ways to do this. Deleting it directly from the Links bar is perhaps the easiest.

Follow these steps to delete a page from the Links bar:

1. Double-click the Links bar handle to open it fully, as shown in Figure 5-12.

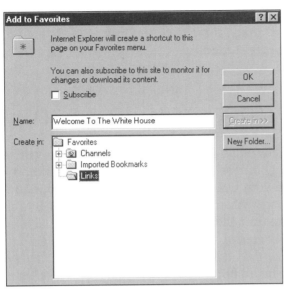

Figure 5-11 Click Favorites→Add to Favorites to add a page to the Links bar.

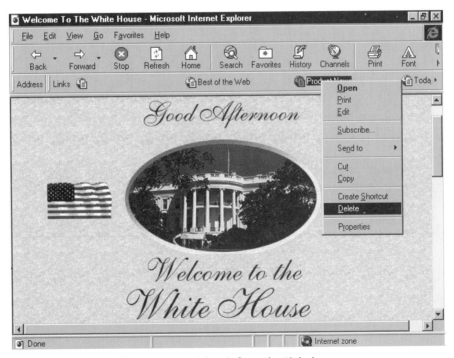

Figure 5-12 Right-click a page to delete it from the Links bar.

2. Right-click the "offending" link. A shortcut menu appears.

3. Click [Delete]. The page is gone.

TIP **You can delete pages from the Links bar through the Favorites menu. Click Favorites→Links. Right-click the link to be deleted and click Delete on the shortcut menu.**

What to Do When You've Been Framed

M any Web sites have pages that are divided into sections, called *frames*, that operate independently of one another. Frames work a little differently than your average Web page, so this section includes some tips and hints for working with frames. For our example of a Web site that uses frames, we chose one that every computer user should take a look at. The Year 2000 Information Center, a joint venture between Peter de Jager and the Tenagra Corporation, provides information and help on the "year 2000 problem." If you haven't heard about this, visit the site and check it out. The URL for the site is http://www.year2000.com. Type this URL into the Address bar and press the Enter key.

The most common use of frames in a Web site is to show an index or list of commands in one frame while showing you information in another frame. Use the scroll bars to see everything that's in a frame. The example in Figure 5-13 has three frames:

* The frame on the left side of the page acts as an index. The buttons at the top of the left frame lead to other pages at the site. The links in the lower part of the left frame lead to companies that offer products related to the year 2000 problem.

* The upper frame on the right side of the page contains a clock that counts down the time left until the year 2000.

* The lower frame on the right side has information about the Year 2000 Information Center.

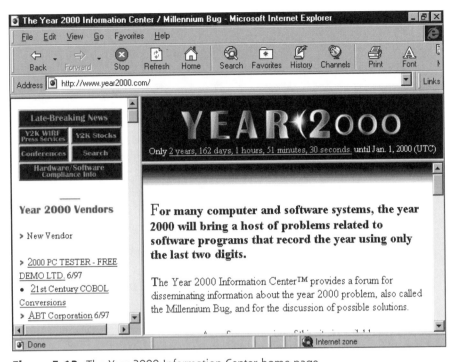

Figure 5-13 The Year 2000 Information Center home page.

Copyright 1996, 1997 The Tenagra Corporation (http://www.tenagra.com/) for the Year 2000 Information Center (http://www.year2000.com/). Used with permission.

Moving from Frame to Frame

When you're at a Web page that uses frames, and a link changes the contents of a specific frame but not the entire page, the Back and Forward buttons in the toolbar and the Back and Forward commands on the shortcut menu will not take you to the next or previous Web page you've visited. Instead, they'll take you to the next or previous frame within the Web page. What's a body to do? To get to the next or previous Web site, click the down arrow to the right of the Back or Forward button and use the list.

Printing a Frame (or a Page)

Frames can be printed just as whole pages can be.

Follow these steps to print frames:

1. Right-click inside the frame (or page) you want to print. (Make sure your pointer is not over a link when you do this.) A shortcut menu opens.

2. Click **Print** to open the Print dialog box you see in Figure 5-14.

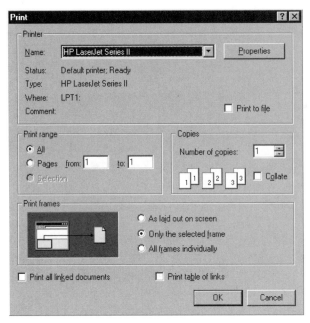

Figure 5-14 The Print dialog box lets you print an entire page or selected frames.

3. Within the Print frames section at the bottom of the dialog box, select the appropriate option:

* "As laid out on screen" prints the entire page.
* "Only the selected frame" prints only the frame in which your cursor is located.
* "All frames individually" prints the contents of each frame on separate pieces of paper.
* "Print all linked documents" prints all documents linked to the frame.
* "Print table of links" prints a table at the end of the document that lists all of the links in the document.

4. Click OK to print your selection.

TIP If the shortcut menu doesn't show the Print command, move your mouse pointer to another spot on the page, preferably onto some regular text.

Controlling What Your Kids See

I f you're a parent, you probably don't allow your children to wander unsupervised around town visiting any place that piques their interest. Like a real town, the virtual Internet community contains some places that are inappropriate for children or that you yourself may find personally offensive. Internet Explorer makes it very easy to block offensive or inappropriate material by letting you set up a rating system for language, nudity, sex, and violence, called the Content Advisor. You then create a "supervisor password" that absolutely blocks access to any site that does not match your ratings criteria. As the "supervisor," *you* can override the password, but your kids cannot. The glitch in this arrangement is that only about 25,000 sites have rated themselves. If you set up the password so that only rated sites can be viewed by your kids, they will be blocked from millions of unrated, but perfectly harmless, entertaining, and even educational, sites. It's your call.

FEATURE FOCUS You have control over what material reaches your kids with the new Content Advisor.

Enabling Ratings and Setting a Password

Internet Explorer gives you the option of setting ratings for what kind of language and how much nudity, sex, and violence you want your children to be able to see.

Follow these steps to enable the rating of Web sites and to establish a password:

1. Click View in the menu bar and then click Options to open the Internet Properties dialog box, as shown in Figure 5-15.

2. Click the Content tab to bring it to the front.

3. Click the Enable button. The Create Supervisor Password dialog box appears.

4. Type a password in the Password box, press the Tab key, and type the *same* password again in the Confirm password box. *Don't forget the password.* Write it down if you have to. If you forget it, the kids (and you) are forever locked into the settings you make the first time you do this.

5. Click the OK button. The Content Advisor dialog box shown in Figure 5-16 appears.

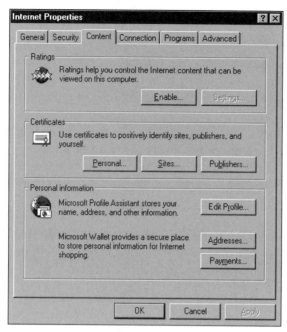

Figure 5-15 Ensure that inappropriate or offensive material cannot reach your kids.

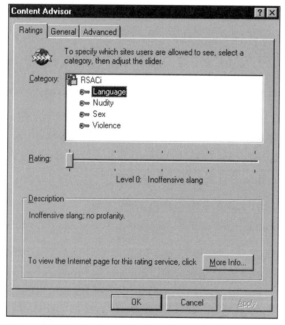

Figure 5-16 Set the rating levels you want for your kids.

Follow these steps to set rating levels for the categories you see in Figure 5-16:

1. If necessary, click the Ratings tab to bring it to the front of the Content Advisor dialog box.

2. Click Language, as shown in Figure 5-16. A Rating scale appears below the Category list.

3. Slide the bar on the Rating scale to a spot that reflects your preference. Notice that the rating level is defined just below the scale.

4. Repeat Steps 2 and 3 for Nudity, Sex, and Violence.

5. Click the General tab to bring it to the front of the dialog box, as shown in Figure 5-17.

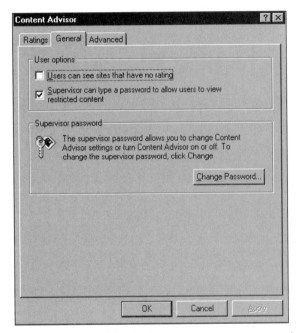

Figure 5-17 Decide whether users can see an unrated site or if it requires a password.

6. Select the appropriate user option:

   ✳ *"Users can see sites that have no rating:"* The vast majority of sites have not been rated. Selecting this option allows access to those sites, which means that some objectionable material may get through. However, leaving this option unchecked means that the user cannot view an unrated site no matter how safe it may be.

* *"Supervisor can type a password to allow user to view restricted content:"* Clicking this option will bring up a dialog box when an attempt is made to contact an unrated or objectionable site. It allows the supervisor to enter a password to override the block.

7. The Advanced tab contains settings that allow you to change the rating system and add ratings bureaus. We recommend you accept the default settings unless you have added specific software to your computer and want to use its rating system.

8. Click OK to apply the changes and close the Content Advisor dialog box.

9. Click OK in the Internet Properties dialog box to close it.

Overriding a Content Block with a Password

As owner of the password, you can bypass the Content Advisor. See Figure 5-18 for an example of the dialog box that comes up when you attempt to contact an unrated or objectionable site. (By the way, the block in Figure 5-18 was activated by Yahoo, a totally innocent search engine described in Chapter 7, because Yahoo is not a rated Web site.) Type in your supervisor password, click OK, and you'll be able to open the Web site.

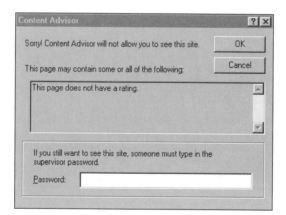

Figure 5-18 You can override the content block with a password.

Setting Up an Adult Browsing Session

It can be a real pain in the neck to enter your password every time you want to access a site that is unrated or objectionable by the standards you set for your six-year-old. Fortunately, you can disable the Content Advisor while you use the computer and then enable it again when you leave.

Follow these steps to turn off the Content Advisor:

1. In the Internet Properties dialog box, click the Content tab.

2. Click the Disable button. You're prompted to enter your password. The Content Advisor message box appears. Click the OK button. As the message indicates, make sure you turn the Content Advisor on again before you close out your session or your kids will get a big surprise the next time they sign on.

 WEB PATH **If parental supervision is a subject that interests you, check out the following Web site. It contains links to Internet Parental Control Web sites like those mentioned above.**

`http://www.worldvillage.com/wv/school/html/control.htm`

(No, there's no final "l" on "htm.")

BONUS

You Don't Have to Eat Cookies to Get Rid of Them

If you think of cookies as little treats you have with milk, you may be surprised to learn that in the virtual world of the Internet a *cookie* is actually an electronic spy. Cookies are small files sent to your computer by some Web sites. The cookie file may include such information as when you visited the site, what pages you looked at, and, at some commercial sites, your password and whether you ordered merchandise online. The next time you visit the site, it reads the cookie file to automatically enter your password or to see if you've been there before and to keep a record of your comings and goings. Generally, cookies are considered benign marketing tools (by marketing people needless to say), but some people consider the idea of another computer leaving files on *your* computer an invasion of privacy. If you visit a site that requires a password or a customer identification number, you may want to allow the cookie. It's your computer and your option!

The Advanced category in the Options dialog box gives you several options for cookies, including the options of prompting before accepting cookies or not accepting any ("Disable all cookie use").

Follow these steps to deal with cookies:

1. Click   **View**   in the menu bar, then click   **Options** . The Options dialog box opens.

2. Click the Advanced tab to bring it to the front, as shown in Figure 5-19.

3. Scroll through the list of options to Cookies. (It's toward the bottom of the list.)

4. Click the Cookie choice that makes you most comfortable. You can always change it down the road.

5. Click OK to close the Options dialog box.

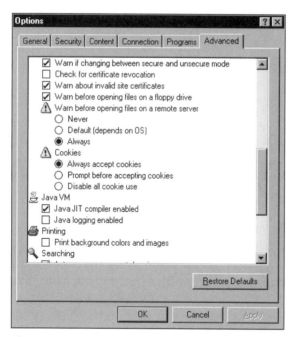

Figure 5-19 Whether you consider cookies to be electronic spies or benign marketing tools, you can choose to accept them or not.

TIP   If you set the option to be given a choice about accepting a cookie, you'll see a Security Alert dialog box. Depending on the originating Web site, it may say something like, "In order to provide a more personalized browsing experience, will you allow this Web site to put information on your computer? It goes on to say that if you click Yes, the Web site will put a file on your computer, but if you say No, the current Web page may not display properly. Ignore this statement completely. Saying No has *no effect* on how the Web pages displays. The Web page will work just fine.

WEB PATH   The following Web pages contain more information about cookies:

Malcolm's Guide to Persistent Cookies, by Malcolm Humes

`http://www.emf.net/~mal/cookiesinfo.html`

The Truth about Cookies, by Christopher Barr. Be sure to type the capital letters as they appear in the Web address.

`http://www.cnet.com/Content/Voices/Barr/042996/`

Summary

Robert Benchley would be green with envy if he knew how you travel around the world at the click of your mouse. You can cruise from link to link, or get right to the point and enter a URL for a direct connection to any Web site in the world. Internet Explorer provides some very cool ways to move around on the Web and, if you are a parent, gives you some comfort by providing a way for you to control the information that reaches your children.

SETTING UP WEB PAGE SUBSCRIPTIONS

IN THIS CHAPTER YOU LEARN THESE KEY SKILLS

HOW TO ADD FAVORITE WEB SITES TO YOUR FAVORITES FOLDER PAGE 127

HOW TO ORGANIZE YOUR FAVORITE FOLDERS PAGE 131

HOW TO SUBSCRIBE TO YOUR FAVORITE WEB SITES PAGE 137

HOW TO MANAGE YOUR SUBSCRIPTIONS PAGE 140

6

I n Chapter 5 you learned how to explore the Web and probably visited a number of sites that you would like to revisit often. The Web addresses of sites that you plan to revisit can be saved in the Favorites section of Internet Explorer so that you can get back to them easily. As you "adopt" more and more sites in your online travels, the need for organizing and updating your list of Favorites will increasingly become evident. Fortunately, you can "subscribe" to specific sites so that Internet Explorer can automatically update them for you.

Capturing Your Favorites

A s you continue to "surf" the web, you will probably find Web sites that you want to continue to visit. Once you see how easy it is to "capture" their addresses and add them to your Favorites list, you may find yourself becoming a connoisseur of Web pages. For example, you may end up collecting Web site addresses for cooking, worm farming, job opportunities, foreign embassies, travel agencies, and heaven knows what else!

Adding a Winner to Your List

As you become a connoisseur of Web sites, begin to think of your favorites as "winners," that is, sites you would share with your friends and business associates. Are you ready to start your collection?

If so, complete the following steps to add a Web site to your Favorites list:

1. Go online with Internet Explorer and surf to a Web site you want to add to your Favorites list.

TIP Do not click the Favorites button in the toolbar (see Figure 6-1). This is *not* where you add a Web site to your Favorites.

Click here ——

Do not
click here ——

Figure 6-1 Do not click the Favorites button.

2. Click [Favorites] → [Add to Favorites] as shown in Figure 6-2. An Add to Favorites dialog box appears.

3. Click the Create In button as shown in Figure 6-3. Another Add to Favorites dialog box appears showing a list of folders where you can store the Web address.

Figure 6-2 Adding a Web site to your Favorites list.

Don't click
here

Click here
to select a
Favorites
folder

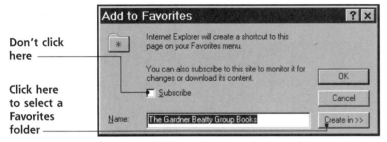

Figure 6-3 Completing the Add to Favorites process.

NOTE We'll discuss the Subscribe option shown in Figure 6-3 in the last section of this chapter.

4. The Favorites folder is highlighted as shown in Figure 6-4. If you click the OK button, the Web address will be stored at the bottom of the list. Or you can go onto the next section and create your own folder on the fly.

To view your favorites, click the Favorites button on the toolbar.

Adding a Folder on the Fly

If you are one of those people who can organize as you go along, you can take advantage of the option of creating folders for storing Web addresses as you add them to your Favorites.

Complete the following steps to create a Favorites folder as you add the Web site:

1. Click the New Folder button (see Figure 6-4). The Create New Folder dialog box appears.

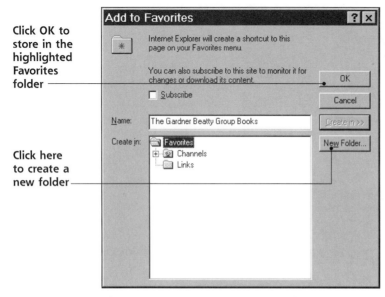

Click OK to store in the highlighted Favorites folder

Click here to create a new folder

Figure 6-4 Creating a new Favorites folder.

2. Type a name for the folder as shown in Figure 6-5.

3. Click OK. The Add to Favorites dialog box reappears.

Type a name here

Click OK

Figure 6-5 Naming the folder.

4. Click OK. The dialog box will close. Congratulations. You've created a Favorites folder on the fly!

5. Check out your new folder as illustrated in Figure 6-6 below. In our example, it's "Books."

6. Highlight the new folder and click OK to close the dialog box.

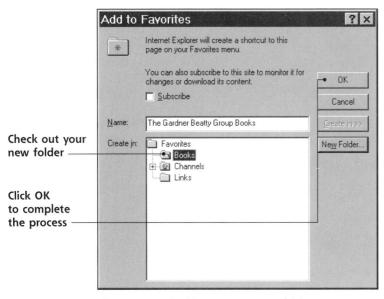

Check out your new folder ————

Click OK to complete the process ————

Figure 6-6 Checking out your new folder.

Organize, Organize

As you learned in the previous chapter, Internet Explorer comes equipped with an inventory of Web sites organized by topic that you can explore at your leisure. You can add your own faves (favorite sites) to the Favorites list at any time. However, a lot of people tend to go overboard in the excitement of the surfing moment, constantly adding Favorites (called bookmarks in Web parlance) to the point that keeping them organized becomes a major challenge. You can avoid this problem by simply organizing the Favorites folders in advance, rather than on the fly, as shown in the previous section.

You can create and organize your Favorites folders in advance.

Creating Your Own "Fave" Folder

We recommend you stop and think about the type of sites you want to collect and then create custom folders into which you can save them.

Complete the following steps to create your own Favorites folder:

1. Click ⬛ Favorites → ⬛ Organize Favorites (see Figure 6-7). The Organize Favorites dialog box appears.

Figure 6-7 Organizing Favorites

2. Click the ⬆ to create a new folder as shown in Figure 6-8.

Click here to create a new folder

Type a name for the new folder here

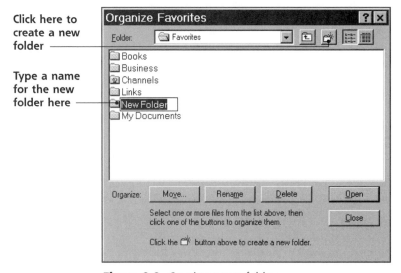

Figure 6-8 Creating a new folder.

3. Type a name for the new folder. As you can see in Figure 6-9, we typed "Fave" for "Favorites."

4. Click anywhere in the dialog box to complete the task.

5. Create a second folder if you like. We created a second one called "Technical," as shown in Figure 6-9.

A Folder by Any Other Name

Don't like the name "Fave?" Want to change it to another name? Renaming is easy.

Just complete the following steps to rename a folder:

1. Click the folder you want to rename to highlight it.

2. Click the Rename button. A text box appears with the current name highlighted, as shown in Figure 6-9.

Type a new name here ———

Click here to rename the highlighted folder ———

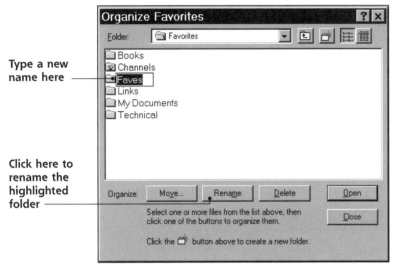

Figure 6-9 Renaming a Favorites folder.

3. Type a new name for the folder. In this example, we typed "Business" to replace "Fave."

4. Click anywhere inside the dialog box to complete the process.

Calling the Van Lines

Don't like the way the directory tree (folder tree) is organized after all this? Put a favorite site in the wrong folder? You can fix these problems easily by moving either the folder or the file(s) within a folder to another folder.

Complete the following steps to move a file to another folder:

1. Double-click the folder that contains the file you want to move, as shown in Figure 6-10. The contents of the folder will appear in a dialog box, as shown in Figure 6-11.

Double-click the folder —

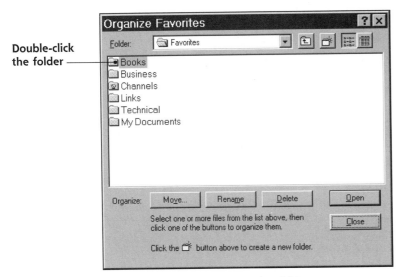

Figure 6-10 Opening a Favorites folder.

Click here to highlight the file —

Click here to move the file —

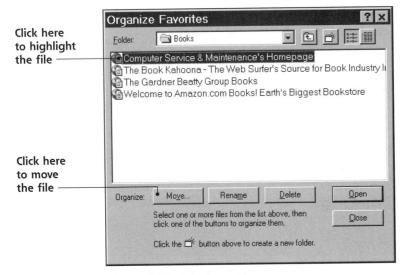

Figure 6-11 Selecting a file to move.

2. Click the folder to which you want to move the file to highlight it, as shown in Figure 6-12. In this example, we moved the Web site for Computer Service & Maintenance, Inc., our technical service suppliers, from the "Books" folder to the "Technical" folder.

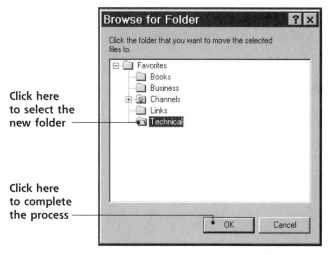

Click here to select the new folder

Click here to complete the process

Figure 6-12 Selecting the new folder.

3. Click OK. The Organize Favorites dialog box reappears as shown in Figure 6-13.

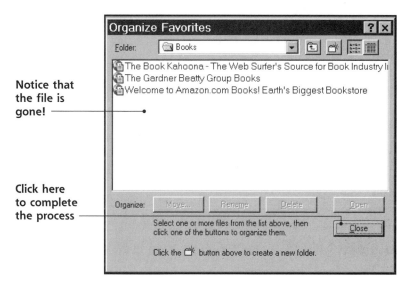

Notice that the file is gone!

Click here to complete the process

Figure 6-13 Finishing the move.

4. Click the Close button. All done!

Wasting a Folder or a File

Had an afterthought? Want to delete a folder? No problem.

Follow these steps to delete a folder:

1. Open the Organize Favorites dialog box and simply click the folder you want to delete to highlight it.

2. Next, click the Delete button, as shown in Figure 6-14.

Click the folder

Click Delete

Click Yes

Finally, click Close

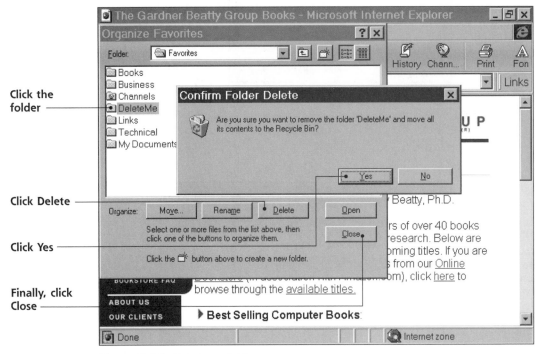

Figure 6-14 Deleting a folder.

3. Click Yes in the Confirm Folder Delete dialog box that appears.

4. Finally, click the Close button in the Organize Folders dialog box to complete the process.

You can "waste" a file in the same way. Simply open the folder where the file is located, click the file to highlight it, click the Delete button, click Yes to confirm, and then click the Close button.

Subscribing to Your Favorite Web Sites

I f you have stored a collection of Web sites that you visit often in your Favorites folder, you can look at them offline at any time. The problem is that if a Web site changes often, you will need to update it periodically. Internet Explorer 4 not only lets you subscribe to "Channels," as you did in Chapter 4, it also lets you "subscribe" to Web sites for updating purposes.

FEATURE FOCUS   **Web site subscriptions are a new feature of Internet Explorer 4.**

Signing Up Online

Becoming a subscriber online is easy.

Complete the following steps to subscribe to a Web site:

1. Go online to an awesome Web site that you want to add to your Favorites list.

2. Click `Favorites` → `Add to Favorites`, as shown in Figure 6-15. The Add to Favorites dialog box appears.

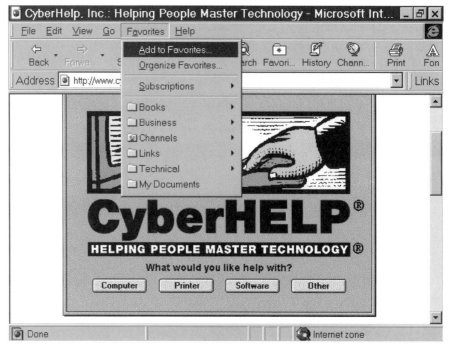

Figure 6-15 Adding a Web site to your favorites before subscribing.

3. Click Subscribe to put a ✔ in the box, as shown in Figure 6-16.

Click here to subscribe ——

Then, click here ——

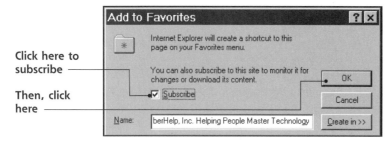

Figure 6-16 Subscribing to a Web site online.

4. Click OK. The Subscribe dialog box appears.

5. Click OK. All done (or go onto the next section to "customize" your subscription).

You can fine-tune the subscription (optional) by clicking the Customize button, as shown in Figure 6-17. A series of Web Site Subscription Wizards will guide you through a number of options. Unless you are a power user, we suggest you skip this for now.

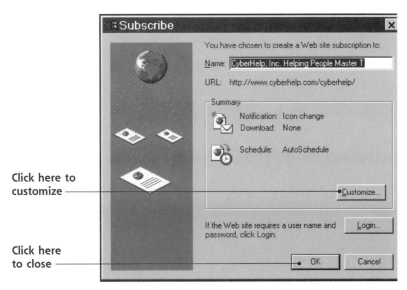

Click here to customize

Click here to close

Figure 6-17 Customizing the subscription.

Signing Up Offline

How do you subscribe to a Web site that you have already added to your list? Easy. And you can do it offline as well.

Complete the following steps to subscribe to a Web site that you have already added to your Favorites but have not made a subscription site:

1. Open My Computer and click to highlight your C: drive.

2. Click **Favorites** in the menu bar.

3. Click the folder containing the Web site you want to add to your subscription list.

4. Right-click the Web site in question. A menu appears, as shown in Figure 6-18.

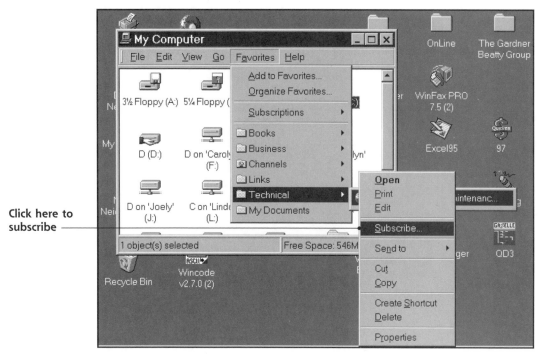

Click here to subscribe

Figure 6-18 Subscribing offline.

5. Click Subscribe. The Subscribe dialog box appears (not shown).

6. Click the OK button on the Subscribe dialog box. All done.

Control Yourself!

One of the problems with using the Internet is that each time you go online you get addicted to "collecting" Web sites. (David Gardner currently has 275 Web sites in his Favorites, and this is after thinning out 50 sites from his list!) The next thing you know you are addicted to subscribing to more and more Web sites. Followed to its logical conclusion, you could end up having your computer doing nothing but dialing 250 or more Web sites during the day to update them! Egad, what a depressing thought.

Updating in One Fell Swoop

You do not have to go online to manage your subscriptions.

Complete the following steps to update all of your subscriptions in one fell swoop:

1. Open My Computer.

2. Click [Favorites] → [Subscriptions] → [Update All]. The Download Progress dialog box appears. Internet Explorer 4 will go online and, even if you have 250 subscriptions (ugh), will update them all. Take a dinner break!

Managing Your Subscriptions

You can change your update schedule, manually update subscriptions one-at-time, delete subscriptions (if you have 250 subscriptions you may want to consider deleting a bunch to clear the field!), and rename them.

Complete the following steps to open the Manage Subscriptions dialog box:

1. Open My Computer.

2. Click [Favorites] → [Subscriptions] → [Manage Subscriptions] to open the C:\Windows\Subscriptions dialog box.

UPDATING A SINGLE SUBSCRIPTION

Follow these steps to update a single subscription:

1. Click the subscription you want to update to highlight it.

2. Click [File] → [Update Now]. Internet Explorer will go online and update this subscription.

CHANGING THE UPDATE SCHEDULE

If you have put a particular Web site on a schedule to automatically update itself while you sleep (quite frankly, we can't imagine why you would, but it takes all kinds), you can change the schedule in the Properties dialog box for the specific subscription.

Complete the following steps to change an update schedule:

1. Right-click the subscription whose update schedule you want to change.

2. Click [Properties] to open the Subscriptions dialog box.

3. Click the Schedule tab to bring it to the front, as shown in Figure 6-19. You can set it to update at 12:00 A.M. daily, weekly, or monthly, or set up a custom schedule of days and times.

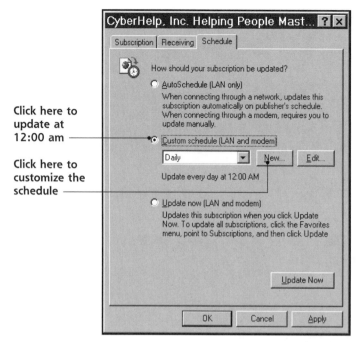

Click here to
update at
12:00 am

Click here to
customize the
schedule

Figure 6-19 Changing the update schedule.

WASTING A SUBSCRIPTION

You can get rid of a subscription in two ways. You can click the Unsubscribe button on the Subscription tab in the dialog box. You can also highlight the offending Web site in the dialog box, as shown in Figure 6-20 and then click File→Delete. Either way, you'll get a message box asking you if really mean it.

A ROSE BY ANY OTHER NAME?

You can rename any subscription quickly. Simply click the subscription you want to rename to highlight it. Next, click File→Rename. The current name becomes highlighted and surrounded by a text box, as shown in Figure 6-20. Type in a new name and then click anywhere in the dialog box to finish.

Type a new
name here

Figure 6-20 Renaming a subscription.

BONUS

Gourmet Subscriptions

Now that you know how to add Web sites to your Favorites list and keep them up-to-date, there is nothing stopping you from making a folder called FOOD or COOKING and filling it with mouthwatering gourmet cooking and recipe sites. We asked our friend Ursula St. Louis, who is not only an avid Web surfer for her business, but also a great cook who collects cooking and food Web sites, to recommend some of her favorites. Here are just a few of them.

The Good Cooking Web site is a great place to begin your journey into the world of gastronomic delights. This is a Web site that will appeal to almost anyone, from people who want to become chefs to your average cook looking for ideas for a party to food and beverage professionals. In 1996, *Internet World* called it "a mouthwatering site on the Internet." Leave your Fen-Phen at home and click your way to:

    http://www.goodcooking.com/

The Diabetic Gourmet Magazine Web site is *not* just for diabetics. Part of the "hard copy" *Diabetic Gourmet Magazine,* it has some great recipes and healthy living ideas that both diabetics and nondiabetics can sink their teeth into with gusto! You may want to subscribe not only to the Web site, but also to the hard copy version:

    http://gourmetconnection.com/diabetic/

Into TV cooking shows? The CyberKitchen Web site carries recipes from 19 TV shows on cooking. The recipes from specific shows are kept on the site for 14 days after the show airs.

To find a recipe from a particular show, complete the following steps:

1. Go to the CyberKitchen Web site (address shown below).

2. Click the Recipes link.

3. Click the TV show in question (e.g., "Cooking Monday to Friday."). You will be linked to the recipe list for that show. It takes a minute to download the list.

4. Scroll down the list until you find your recipe. Voilà. You are an instant chef!

The CyberKitchen Web site is definitely a candidate for a subscription:

`http://www.foodtv.com/`

WEB PATH **Other sites Ursula recommends you explore:**

Yahoo! - Cook Books

`http://www.yahoo.com/Business_and_Economy/Companies/Books/`
`Cookbooks/Titles/`

Chefs Corner!

`http://www.chefscorner.com/framemain.html`

thrive@eats: The Healthy Living Experience

`http://www.thriveonline.com/@@5Jh7FgcAOPTshbbu/thrive/eats/`
`pyramid/`

The Low-Fat Vegetarian Archive (over 2000 recipes!)

`http://www.fatfree.com/`

Summary

In this chapter you learned how to save your favorite Web sites to Internet Explorer 4's Favorites list. You also had the opportunity to creatively organize your favorite folders, including moving and deleting favorite folders and the files within them. In addition, you learned how to subscribe to specific Web sites so that IE 4 could update them for you. Lastly, you learned how to cancel a subscription.

W ithin its short history, the Internet has grown to include millions of Web sites, each of which contains information. In addition to Web sites, there are an untold number of gopher sites. (No, not the kind you have in your front lawn. These gophers are "libraries" of information available on the Internet. You'll learn more about gophers in Chapter 8, "Finding Free and Not-So-Free Stuff.") In order to find a specific item of interest on the Internet, are you supposed to spend your entire life linking from one Web site to another and then to another until you're old and gray? Or are you supposed to have an uncle in the business who'll give you the inside scoop on a specific Web address? The answer to both questions is a resounding No.

Nowadays, there are things called *search engines*. A search engine is like a very knowledgeable librarian. Tell the search engine what you need and it will help you find it. Search engines look for Internet resources that have information on topics that you specify. The resources it looks through can be Web sites, newsgroups and their own privately maintained directories, or other directories.

Directories are maintained by entities such as universities and private companies. They organize Internet sites by subject. Using an Internet directory is much like using your local phone company's Yellow Pages. You go to the topic you're interested in and browse through the sites that are listed under it. Each directory has its own organization scheme, so one may work better for you than another.

The slightly confusing thing about all this is that most companies with search engines also manage directories. Yahoo!, for example, has a search engine that will search the Internet, specific parts of the Internet, or its own directories. Or, you can go directly to one of Yahoo's directories and search it yourself. In this chapter we'll look at both ways of searching for Internet resources: search engines and directories.

Setting Up Your Search Pane

Search engines operate on the basis of links. And just like browsing the Web, it's easy to jump from link to link and lose sight of where you started from. Internet Explorer has solved that problem and set up a brand-new way of searching. The Search button on the toolbar opens a special pane that shows the search engine on the left side of your screen and the results of a search on the right.

FEATURE FOCUS IE 4 contains a split browser pane that shows the search engine on the left and the results of a search on the right.

Follow these steps to open the Search pane:

1. Go online and open the browser.

2. Click the Search button in the toolbar. The Search pane opens, as shown in Figure 7-1. Whatever was on your screen when you opened the Search pane will be on the right side of your screen.

3. Notice the following:

   ✳ The search engine that appears in the Search pane is the "Pick of the day." In this example, it's HotBot. Your screen may show a different Pick of the day.

   ✳ Each pane has its own scroll bars so you can scroll through the site on the right independently of the Search pane.

✻ The Search button in the toolbar works like a light switch. Click it to open the Search pane; click again to close it. (Or, you can click the little x in the Search pane titlebar.) Click a third time to open the Search pane again.

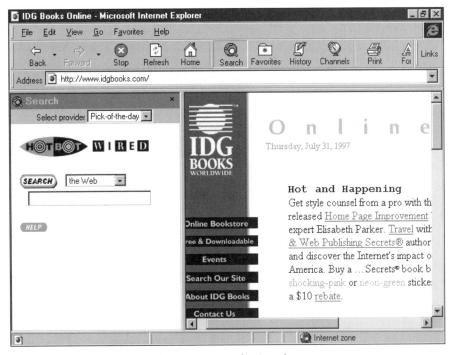

Figure 7-1 Click the Search button to open the Search pane.

4. Click the down arrow to the right of the Pick of the day to open the list of available search engines.

5. Click Excite. The search engine in the left pane changes to Excite.

It's Elementary, My Dear Watson

What exactly *are* search engines and how do you use them to find stuff? Search engines are programs provided by various service companies that have been set up to search the Internet for you. They are supported by the advertising that appears on their Web pages. Each search engine works just a little differently, and after you've tried a few of them, you'll probably find one that works best for you. For future convenience, you can make it a "favorite" (see Chapter 6) or even make it your home page.

Follow these steps to start your search:

1. Type the name of the topic in which you're interested in the search box and then click the Search button. A list of matches appears in the Search pane. If you want to follow along with the example you see in Figure 7-2, type **jobs**.

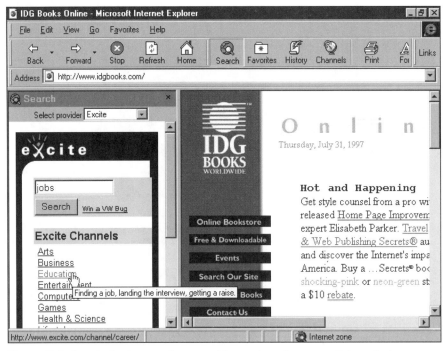

Figure 7-2 Search the Internet for a specific word or phrase, or click an Excite category to search it.

 TIP Entering a word or phrase in the search box will start a search of the Internet. Most search engines also give you the opportunity to search within categories they have set up, such as "Computers and Internet," or "Lifestyle." The Excite search screens gives you channels to explore. Rest your mouse pointer over the links shown under "Excite Channels." A pop-up label appears giving you more information about this category. Sometimes a scrolling marquee appears. Click an area of interest to start narrowing your search. It appears in the right panel. You can then switch to the left panel to continue to refine your search. If you already typed "jobs" and pressed Enter, there's no easy way to get back to the initial Excite search screen other than choosing another "Pick of the day" and then returning to Excite.

2. When the search results appear, as shown in Figure 7-3, notice the following details:

* When it says that the search returned the top 100 of 607,290 documents about jobs, it means that in its search of the Internet, Excite found over 600,000 documents that contain the word "jobs."

* Excite shows you ten matches at a time in order of decreasing relevance. The relevance rating to the left of each match shows you how confident Excite is that this site matches your search criteria. There's a button at the bottom of the list that will bring up the next set of ten matches, but don't bother with that right now.

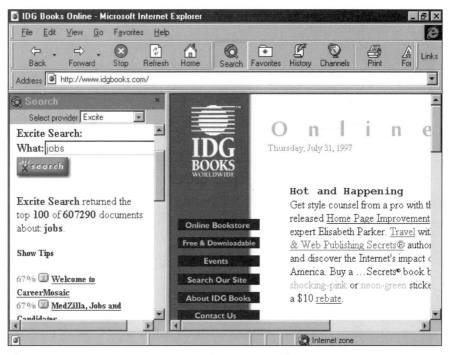

Figure 7-3 An Excite search shows a relevancy rating for matches.

3. Click the icon to the left of the first match. This opens a description of the site. If this description seems to be right on target, look for the link at the bottom of the description that says [More Like This] to bring up more choices in the Search pane like this one.

4. Click the icon again to close the description.

TIP You can see all ten descriptions by scrolling to the bottom of the left pane and clicking the link to View Summaries. All ten descriptions appear in the right pane.

Thus far, you've been dealing only with the left Search pane. Notice that the right pane has remained the same. Now you're ready to use it:

1. Click a link in the Search pane. In this example it's <u>Welcome to CareerMosaic</u>. The browser pane on the right brings up that Web site.

2. Scroll through the pane on the right as you would any other Web site.

3. If you find the smaller browsing space a little claustrophobic, place your mouse pointer on the dividing line between the panes, as you see in Figure 7-4. It turns into a two-headed arrow. You can drag the dividing line to the left or right to change the size of either pane.

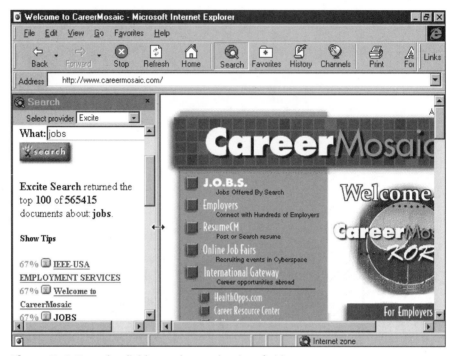

Figure 7-4 Drag the divider to change the size of either pane.
Copyright© Career Mosaic® 1997.

4. As you scroll through the right pane, notice that the Back button affects only this pane.

NOTE Once you're in a Web site, you can click the Search button to close the left pane. However, this will close the list of matches as well. If you think you'll go back to the search results in the left pane, drag the dividing line back and forth. This will keep both panes open but give you more room to browse when you need it.

Finding a Needle in a Haystack

Today's search engines are pretty sophisticated. They can search phrases as well as single words. Some of them, such as Excite, will look for words related to your original request. But computers are rather literal, and sometimes they come up with some pretty weird results. For example, entering Chicago Bulls will retrieve documents containing one or both words, so you'll end up with articles about Chicago, articles about bulls, and also articles about the Chicago Bulls. Each search engine has a Help file that will give you tips about conducting an effective search. Look for a Help link or a Tips link. You can refine your search using AND, OR, AND NOT, quotation marks, and parentheses. Please notice, by the way, that the words are typed in solid capitals with a space before and after the words when you use them in a search. Table 7-1 shows the most common examples of how to refine a search.

TABLE 7-1 Refining your search

Use	To look for:	Example
AND	All words joined by AND	Chicago AND Bulls
		wizard AND oz AND movie
OR	At least one of the words joined by OR	kitten OR kitty
AND NOT	The first word but not the second	China AND NOT Taiwan
parentheses	Specific categories within the first word	jobs (technology OR software)
" "	All of the words in the quotation marks in the order in which they appear	"Boston Red Sox"

Getting It from the Horse's Mouth

If you find that you don't like the split window, you can go directly to a search engine. The opening page of the search engine provides more choices than the same search engine shown in the Search pane in Internet Explorer. Following are the URLs of the search engines included in Internet Explorer. The search engines listed in Pick-of-the-day are subject to change, so your list may be different. All of the search engines search the Web and USENET (newsgroups).

You can search for people, companies, and maps, as well as Web sites, newsgroup articles, and online magazine articles. Each of these search engines goes through millions and millions of resources looking for just what you want, but because each organizes itself a little differently, if you can't find something in one try another. Check out AOL's NetFind Kids Only if you'd like your kids to learn about searching. If you want to search databases in other languages, see AltaVista. As you use each of the different engines, you'll find you develop a preference for one presentation over another.

ALTAVISTA	http://www.altavista.digital.com
AOL NETFIND	http://www.aol.com/netfind
EXCITE	http://www.excite.com
HOTBOT	http://www.hotbot.com
INFOSEEK	http://www.infoseek.com
LYCOS	http://www.lycos.com
YAHOO!	http://www.yahoo.com

Using Internet Directories

Internet directories list resources by subject, like your phone company's Yellow Pages. They work similarly to gophers (see Chapter 8) and other menu systems. On a page that lists general subjects, you choose a link that leads to a page where the subject is broken down into more detail. The links on the more detailed page may lead to an even more detailed breakdown of the subject, or to a list of links to resources from which you can choose.

Use Internet directories to find resources by subject, like your phone company's Yellow Pages.

We'll show you exactly what we mean by using Yahoo!, an extremely popular directory. Type the URL for Yahoo in the Address bar.

Yahoo!'s URL is:

http://www.yahoo.com

Yahoo!'s home page, like those for other directories, includes a search box that you can use to search within the directory. This is helpful if you don't see a subject listing that you think would include the topic for which you're looking.

Directly below the search box (see Figure 7-5) are links to specialized information services offered by Yahoo!. Most Internet directory providers are expanding their services to include similar offerings, as well as directories of local information developed for specific cities. Below those links are links to the general subject areas of the directory. Each general subject has a few more specific subjects listed just below it. For our example, we'll click one of the more specific links under Computers and Internet.

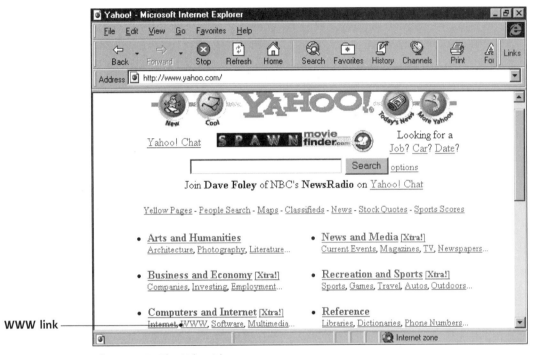

WWW link

Figure 7-5 The Yahoo! home page.

Text and art copyright©1996 by Yahoo! Inc. All rights reserved. Yahoo! and the Yahoo! logo are trademarks of Yahoo! Inc.

Follow these steps to use Internet directories:

1. Click the WWW link under Computers and Internet. The Yahoo! Computers and Internet: Internet: World Wide Web page appears (see Figure 7-6).

   Notice that the Computers and Internet page also has a search box near its top. However, this one lets you select whether to search all of the Yahoo! directory, or only the Computers and Internet section. The lower part of the page lists more specific topics having to do with computers and the Internet.

2. Scroll down the Computers and Internet page to see how this subject is subdivided in the directory.

Internet directories have a structure similar to that of a tree. You start at the trunk (the Yahoo! home page), then go down a major branch, then down a smaller branch, and so forth. But the subject breakdowns contain more than links to smaller branches. The ones that end with an @ sign take you to a completely different branch in the directory. However, since they're related to the main subject of the page, they're listed here as well as elsewhere in the directory.

3. Click <u>Sub Category Listing</u> at the top half of the page to see an expanded version of the categories at the bottom of the page. By following the branching links of the directory you will eventually reach a page of specific resources. Many of the links to specific pages include a short description to help you with your choice.

Click to see more detail

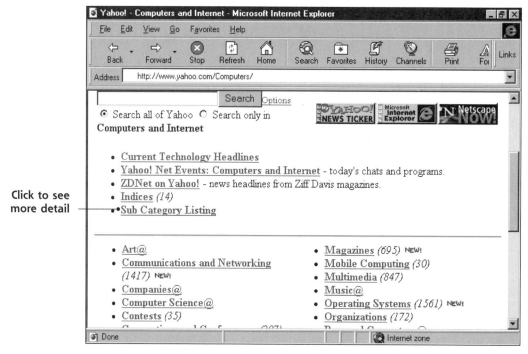

Figure 7-6 Click Sub Category Listing to see an expanded version of the categories listed below.

You can create your own, personal directory to Internet resources using what are called *favorites* (discussed in Chapter 6). Favorites let you return to a Web page quickly without having to remember its URL or use a directory. If you find a favorite page in an Internet directory such as Yahoo!, you can mark it so that the next time you want to use it, you won't have to go through all of the pages that originally led you to it.

When Searching for Your Heart's Desire, There's No Place Like Home

Y ou don't have to go farther than the Microsoft home page to do some first-class searching. Microsoft has done a great job of including resources on all sorts of useful subjects. Take a look at the following topics.

What's Aunt Tilly's Zip Code?

Check out the bottom of the Internet Explorer home page, shown in Figure 7-7. Talk about convenience. Now you have no excuse not to send Aunt Tilly that birthday card! You can even find her area code and give her a call. Or, better yet, set up a NetMeeting (see Chapter 15).

Figure 7-7 Scroll to the bottom of Microsoft's home page to find useful links to commonly needed information.

Screen shot reprinted by permission from Microsoft Corporation.

Yours for the Asking

Would you like to get a map to somebody's house? Or maybe you want to get the Internet address of a publicly traded company so you can invest the millions that Aunt Tilly will leave you? From Internet Explorer's home page, link to "exploring the best of the Web." On the right side of the exploring page you'll find links to some great search places. Figure 7-8 shows Search the Web, which links you into a goldmine of information. It's anybody's guess what you'll see when you go to this spot because the content changes frequently.

Follow these steps to Search the Web:

1. Click the Home button in the toolbar to go back to the Internet Explorer home page. (If you changed your "Home" page, type **http://home.microsoft.com** in the Address bar.)

2. Click the link to exploring the best of the web.

3. The search categories are on the right side of the Best of the Web page. See Figure 7-8.

Figure 7-8 Use Search the Web to link into an impressive library of resources.
Screen shot reprinted by permission from Microsoft Corporation.

4. Click to check out a specific category. Great maps are available toward the bottom of the Specialty screen.

Pass Go, Collect $200 Worth of Information

Internet Explorer has added a very cool Autosearch feature. Type "go" followed by any word or phrase in the Address bar, press the Enter key, and IE will initiate a Yahoo! search of the Internet for you. See Figure 7-9 for an example of the Address bar. Figure 7-10 shows the results.

Figure 7-9 Type "go" and a topic to make Internet Explorer start a Yahoo! search for you.

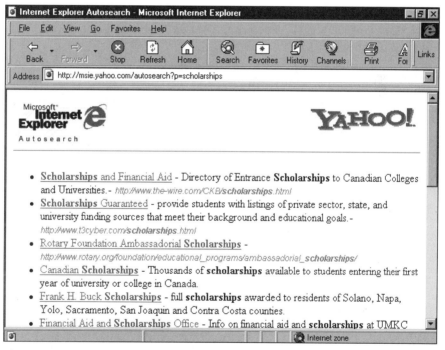

Figure 7-10 Results of the "go scholarships" search.

Text and art copyright©1996 by Yahoo! Inc. All rights reserved. Yahoo! and the Yahoo! logo are trademarks of Yahoo! Inc.

BONUS

Citing Internet Resources

Information and graphics that you find on the Internet are most probably covered by copyright. If you plan to use these things in your own work, you may have to contact the copyright holder for permission, and at the very least you will have to give proper credit for their origin. In academic circles, this is called *citing* the source of your information. If you're citing Internet sources for a school project, make sure that your instructor approves of the method of citing sources that you select before you turn in your work.

One handbook containing guidelines that we have used is *Electronic Styles: A Handbook for Citing Electronic Information* by Xia Li and Nancy B. Crane (published by *Information Today, Inc.,* 1996).

In addition to books on this subject, several Web sites contain helpful information. You may find differences between the guidelines offered from one such page to the next. Some of these sites and their authors are listed below:

The Copyright Website (Benedict O'Mahoney)
`http://www.benedict.com/`

U.S. Copyright Office Home Page
`http://www.lcweb.loc.gov/copyright/`

10 Big Myths About Copyright Explained (Brad Templeton)
`http://www.clari.net/brad/copymyths.html`

Wired Style: Intro Essay (HardWired, Inc.)
`http://www.hotwired.com/hardwired/wiredstyle/toc/index.html`

MLA-Style Citations of Electronic Sources (Janice R. Walker)
`http://www.cas.usf.edu/english/walker/mla.html`

Web Extension to American Psychological Association Style (T. Land)
`http://www.beadsland.com/weapas/`

Summary

In spite of its great size and the fact that it's constantly growing, the Internet can be tamed to some extent by using directories and search engines. Many different search engines and directories exist, though all of them work in more or less the same way. By trying several you can find the one that works best for you.

CHAPTER EIGHT

FINDING FREE AND NOT-SO-FREE STUFF

IN THIS CHAPTER YOU LEARN THESE KEY SKILLS

HOW TO SET UP MICROSOFT WALLET FOR ONLINE PURCHASING PAGE 160

HOW TO SHOP ON THE WEB PAGE 164

HOW TO FIND SOFTWARE ARCHIVES AND DOWNLOAD PAGE 166

HOW TO DIG UP INFORMATION WITH GOPHER PAGE 170

T he Internet is a treasure house of free software and information that you can get using IE 4. In addition, there's lots of not-so-free stuff available, ranging from software that you can download to every consumer item imaginable.

First, we'll show you Microsoft Wallet, the latest tool for secure, convenient online money transactions. From there we'll go on to give you some tips on how to shop online for anything, from a house to a mouse (for your computer). Next, we'll take you to our favorite software outlet, where you can download "shareware" programs, whose publishers let you use their software for a while before you buy it. And finally, we'll demonstrate gopher, an online information locator from the "old days" of the Internet that still has a lot to offer.

8

Get Out Your Wallet

Spending money over the World Wide Web isn't new. From the start, the possibilities for commercial applications on the Web were obvious. Online stores and catalogs sprang up quickly, but didn't take off at first. The biggest reason people were reluctant to buy things on the Web was that they couldn't be sure that their credit card numbers, which had to be sent over lines that anyone could tap into, were safe. But with the potential for untold millions in profits looming, it wasn't long before methods for making online transactions secure came along.

First, encryption methods were developed that allowed retailers to have "secure" Web pages that, when viewed with browsers that could interact with them, significantly reduced the risk of sending confidential information over the Internet. Most browsers in use today can do this. But for IE 4, Microsoft carried the idea one step further and created Wallet. Wallet lets you store credit card information safely on your computer, send it over the Internet securely, and shop with it online at WWW stores that support Wallet.

With Wallet, you can store credit card information safely on your computer, send it over the Internet securely, and shop online at stores that support Wallet.

Finding Your Wallet

Wallet is a set of folders and files on your computer that store information about your credit cards. (At the time this was written, Wallet supported four major types of credit cards.) Setting up these files is a simple, straightforward process that starts with finding your Wallet.

Follow these steps to open Wallet:

1. Right-click the desktop icon named The Internet and select **Properties** from its shortcut menu to open the Internet Properties dialog box.

   or

   With IE 4 open, select **View** → **Options** to open the Options dialog box (which is the same as the Internet Properties dialog box).

2. Click the Content tab to bring it to the front. Notice that there are two buttons in the lowest part of the tab, named Addresses and Payments (see Figure 8-1).

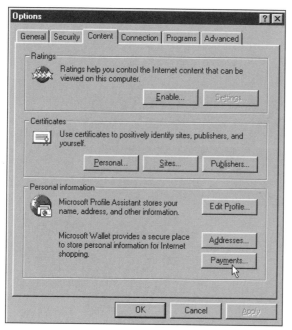

Figure 8-1 Open your Wallet by clicking Payments on the Content tab of IE 4's Options or Internet Properties dialog box.

3. Click Payments. The Payment Options dialog box appears (see Figure 8-2).

NOTE Two other things may occur after you click the Payments button:

* If you have a Windows password that you use to log on to your computer when it boots up, a Protected Storage dialog box may appear and prompt you for a password. Type the password and click OK. The Payment Options dialog box appears.

* If you have updated your IE 4 files online and a payment method for a new type of card was included in the update, a dialog box appears saying that Wallet is trying to install the update. Click Install. The new type is added and the Payment Options dialog box appears.

Setting Up Wallet

You can have information about several different cards and several different billing addresses in your Wallet. If more than one person uses your computer, each user can have his or her own password-protected files stored in Wallet.

Follow these steps to set up your Wallet:

1. Follow Steps 1–3 in the previous section to open Wallet's Payment Options dialog box (see Figure 8-2).

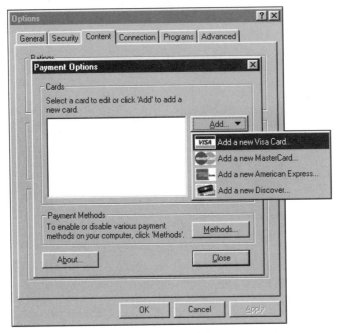

Figure 8-2 The Payment Options dialog box showing a list of credit cards you can use.

2. Click Add. A list of credit card types appears.

3. Click a card type. A License Agreement dialog box appears.

4. Read the agreement and click I Agree (if you click I Disagree, you won't be able to proceed with the setup). The first Add a New Credit Card Wizard dialog box appears.

5. Read the information in the dialog box and click Next. The Credit Card Information dialog box appears (see Figure 8-3).

6. You have the option of making up a name for this data in the Display name box, or you can accept the one that the wizard provides. Type the information called for into the boxes and click Next. The Credit Card Billing Address dialog box appears. After you have set up one card, you can select the billing address you set up for it from the drop-down list in the Credit Card Billing Address dialog box when you add other cards.

7. Click the New address button in the Credit Card Billing Address dialog box. The Add a New Address dialog box appears.

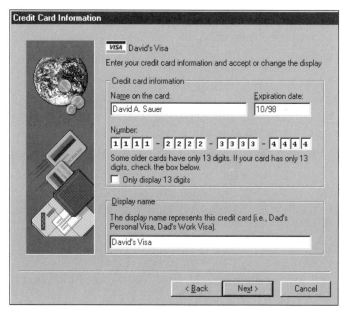

Figure 8-3 The Credit Card Information dialog box in Wallet.

8. You have the option of making up a name for this address in the Display name box, or you can accept the one that the wizard provides. Type the information called for into the boxes and click OK. The Credit Card Billing Address dialog box reappears.

9. Click Next. The Credit Card Password dialog box appears.

10. Make up a password, make a note of it (remember to put the note in a safe place), type it into the Password box and the Confirm password box, and click Finish. The Payment Options dialog box reappears, with the credit card listed in it.

11. Click Close in the Payment Options dialog box to close it, and then click OK in the Internet Properties (or Options) dialog box to close it. Now you're ready to shop!

Managing Credit Card Information

Once information for a card and billing address is entered into Wallet, you can edit or delete it. You will have to edit card information every time a new card is issued, to update its expiration date.

Follow these steps to edit or delete information in the Wallet:

1. Follow Steps 1 and 2 in the "Finding Your Wallet" section to open the Content tab in the Internet Properties (or Options) dialog box.

2. Click Addresses to edit or delete addresses, or click Payments to edit or delete credit card information. The Address Options or Payment Options dialog box will appear (see Figure 8-2).

3. In the Address Options or Payment Options dialog box, click the card you want to edit or delete, and then click Delete to delete the information, or click Edit to edit it. If you click Edit in the Payment Options dialog box, you will be prompted for your credit card password. (Enter the password and click OK to proceed.)

4. If you click Delete, a dialog box will ask you to confirm the deletion. Click Yes to delete the information, and then click Close in the Address Options or Payment Options dialog box and OK in the Internet Properties (or Options) dialog box.

   or

   If you click Edit, the Edit Address or Edit Card dialog box appears (similar to Figure 8-3). Edit the information that you want to change, and then click OK.

5. Click Close in the Address Options or Payment Options dialog box to close it, and click OK in the Internet Properties (or Options) dialog box to close it.

Hanging Out at the Online Mall

New Web stores and catalogs seem to appear every day. Some sites also offer links to a number of WWW shops on one page, a virtual online Mall. We'll show you how to find some here.

Follow these steps to quickly locate some examples of online shops:

1. Open Internet Explorer and click the Best of the Web link in the links section of the toolbar. If your links don't include Best of the Web, type **home.microsoft.com/best/best.asp** into the Address box and press Enter. Microsoft's Best of the Web page appears (see Figure 8-4).

Figure 8-4   The Best of the Web page has links that lead to several online stores.
Screen shot reprinted by permission from Microsoft Corporation.

2. Click the "living" link. The living page appears.

3. Scroll down the page until you see the link for The Plaza and click it. The Plaza page appears, offering links to several stores for you to choose from. If the Plaza is no longer linked on the living page, look for another link to online shopping and click it.

Most online stores generally work in the same way. You use the browser to go through the store or online catalog and if you see something that you want to buy, you click a link that says something like "add to shopping basket." When you're done shopping, a page will appear that summarizes what you've selected and how much it will cost. Then you will be presented with various payment and delivery options and forms that you have to fill out. Web stores that support the Microsoft Wallet make online shopping easy for you because you don't have to type in all of the credit card and shipping information. (Perhaps they're making it a little too easy?)

 Try these other Web pages for more online shopping adventures.

Amazon Books (a frequent recipient of our business):

`http://www.amazon.com`

CDworld (videos & music, from Tupac to Tchaikovsky):

`http://www.cdworld.com`

Yahoo!'s list of directories to online shopping malls:

`http://www.yahoo.com/Business_and_Economy/Companies/`
`Shopping_Centers/Online_Shopping/Directories/`

Try Before You Buy

Software archives store large numbers of programs and other electronic files for public distribution. In most cases, these programs fall into one of three categories: *public domain,* meaning that anyone who wants the program can copy and distribute it freely; *freeware,* which may have restrictions on how the program is used, copied or distributed; or *shareware,* which can be sampled without cost for a short time (usually 30 days) before it has to be registered. Software in all three categories can be copyrighted, and usually comes with a document file (often named "readme.txt") that you should read to see what rules apply to the software's use.

Any of the search engines and directories shown in Chapter 7, "Becoming an Expert Explorer," can be used to locate software archives. Just look for links to software. You can also use the search engines and directories to locate updates and "fixes" for programs that you already own by searching for the Web site of the program's publisher. Many software publishers prefer to distribute updates this way to get them to their customers quickly and save on shipping expenses.

NOTE Most programs that you find in archives are compressed so that they take up less space on the archive's computers and can be downloaded more quickly. The most popular form of file compression is called *zipping,* after one of the first compression programs, PKZip. Files compressed in this way are called *zip* or *zipped* files. Our example in the next section shows where you can locate a program that both zips (compresses) normal files and unzips (expands) compressed files.

Finding the Programs

In the examples illustrated here, we'll show you one of our favorite archives, Jumbo. In addition to a wide selection of software for a variety of computers and operating systems, Jumbo features great graphics. Jumbo's URL is `http://www.jumbo.com`. We'll demonstrate how to locate and download a shareware copy of a program called WinZip.

Follow these steps to go to the Jumbo archive:

1. Open IE 4.

2. Type **www.jumbo.com** into the Address box and press Enter. The Jumbo home page appears (see Figure 8-5).

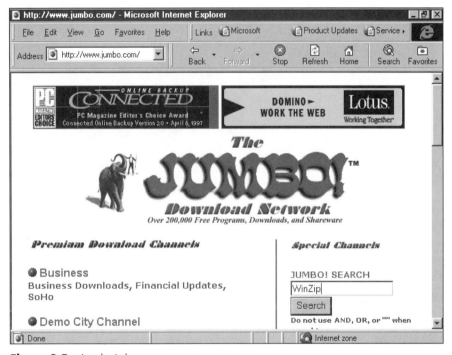

Figure 8-5 Jumbo's home page.

© 1995-7 JUMBO! Inc. (www.jumbo.com)

CHECKING WINDOWS 95 SETTINGS FOR DOWNLOADING

Before starting to download files, you should check two things in your Windows 95 Control Panel. One has to do with the Internet settings, the other with call waiting.

1. Open the Control Panel window and click the Internet icon. The Internet Properties dialog box will appear.

2. Click the Connection tab to bring it to the front.

3. Notice the setting "Disconnect if idle for __ minutes." If this setting is checked and the download takes longer than the number of minutes listed, your computer will be disconnected automatically before the download is completed. Either uncheck this setting or adjust the time limit accordingly.

4. Click OK to close the Internet Properties dialog box.

5. If you have call waiting, double click the Modems icon. The Modems Properties dialog box will appear.

6. Click the Dialing Properties button. The Dialing Properties dialog box will appear.

7. Notice the setting "This location has call waiting. To disable it, dial __." If you have call waiting and receive a call on your modem's line while downloading, the call waiting signal may disconnect your modem. Check this setting and fill in the disable code (available in your local phone directory) if appropriate.

Most software archives let you search their files, and Jumbo's no exception. The search feature is on their home page.

Follow these steps to search for a program in a software archive:

1. Type the name of a file or program into the search box and click Search. In our example, we typed WinZip. If you receive a Security Alert dialog box asking if you want to continue, click Yes. A page with search results appears.

2. Scroll down the page to see what you've found. You may also have to click a link with a name such as "Next Page" if several pages of files were found. When you see a link to the program you want, click it. In our example, we located "WinZip 6.2 for Windows 95" and clicked it. A page listing download sites appears (see Figure 8-6).

Figure 8-6 Jumbo's page showing download sites for WinZip.
© 1995-7 JUMBO! Inc. (www.jumbo.com)

Downloading

After you locate a program you want, retrieving it is a snap. The process is called *downloading,* as if you were receiving the program's file from a computer hovering in the air over your location. Similarly, transferring a file from your computer to another is called *uploading.*

Follow these steps to download a file:

1. Follow the steps in "Finding the Programs," to locate the file you want to download.

2. Click the link for a download site that's near you. In our example, we clicked a link named "United States (California)." A File Download dialog box appears.

3. Click OK. A Save As dialog box appears.

4. Browse to the folder where you want to save the file and click Save. A message box appears and keeps track of the download's progress.

Most software archives screen the programs that they contain for viruses. However, it's a good idea to be careful of any file that you download from the Internet. We suggest that you download files to a folder that you create just for this purpose, and then scan the files with a virus-detection program before you use them. Jumbo includes several virus scanning programs that you can download.

Using "Old-Fashioned" FTP Sites

When searching for downloadable files, you may come across archives that don't have their file lists presented with graphics on Web pages. They simply present you with a screen full of text. These are standard FTP sites that will give you a taste of what the entire Internet used to be like. In such a case, the screen is showing you a directory (or folder list, in Windows 95 terms) of what's on the computer you have connected to. Underlined text on the screen is a link, either to another directory or to an individual file that you can download.

The first screen you encounter at an FTP site may have a list with names in it such as "bin," "incoming," and "pub." Generally, the files available to the public for downloading are in the pub directory. If you click the pub link, you'll be taken to another directory listing subjects or operating systems. Eventually, you'll reach a screen with a list of filenames and sizes, which may or may not include short descriptions of what's in the files.

If there are no file descriptions, look for a file named "index" near the top of the list. Download that file first and open it with Notepad or a word processor to see descriptions of the files at the site. At FTP sites, the filenames themselves are links. If you click one, you'll receive the File Download dialog box, and you can proceed with the download from there.

Tunneling Around with Gopher

B efore the Web was developed, much of the information on it was available in text-only format through Internet programs called *gophers*. The original gopher program was developed at the University of Minnesota and named after the school's team, the Golden Gophers. Gopher programs run on computers called *gopher servers* that are linked to the Internet. Gophers organize links to documents on the servers into menus. Just as you can go from Web page to Web page by clicking on graphic links, you can go from gopher menu to gopher menu by clicking text links.

All of the gopher servers on the Internet are sometimes referred to collectively as *gopherspace*. There are still thousands of gophers on the Internet offering a wealth of useful data, although many have been converted to Web sites. One of our favorite directories, Yahoo!, is a great place to go gopher hunting.

Follow these steps to find some gophers:

1. Open Internet Explorer.

2. Type **www.yahoo.com/Computers_and_Internet/Internet/ Gopher/** in the Address box and press the Enter key. The Yahoo! Computers and Internet: Internet: Gopher page appears (see Figure 8-7).

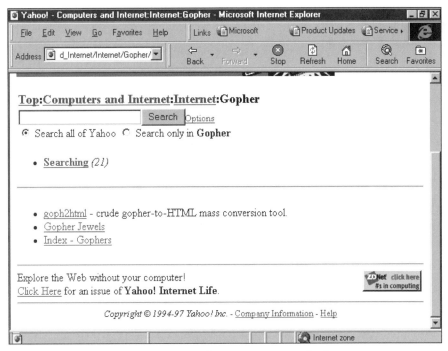

Figure 8-7 The Yahoo! Computers and Internet: Internet: Gopher page (scrolled down).

Text and art copyright © 1996 by YAHOO! INC. All rights reserved. YAHOO! and the YAHOO! logo are trademarks of YAHOO! INC.

The Yahoo! Computers and Internet: Internet: Gopher page has several links on it, including: Searching, Gopher Jewels, and Index-Gophers. Gopher Jewels is a collection of links to gopher resources that have been labeled *jewels* because of their value. They represent some of the best information resources you can find in gopherspace. Index - Gophers leads to a page that lists gopher servers.

The Searching link leads to a page with two links: Jughead and Veronica. These aren't comic book characters, but computer programs that search gopherspace much like the search engines discussed in Chapter 7. The Veronica program's name is supposed to be an acronym for "Very Easy Rodent-oriented Net-wide Index of Computerized Archives." Jughead, developed by a programmer named Jonzy, is an acronym for "Jonzy's Universal Gopher Hierarchy Excavation And Display." Jughead searches through the titles of gopher menus on specific gopher servers. Veronica, on the other hand, searches the titles on all of the gopher servers in gopherspace.

Try the link to Gopher Jewels. If you've only explored the Internet's fun side up to now, you may be surprised at the extent of "serious," useful information you can find by searching through the gopher menus this leads to.

BONUS

Internet Hoaxes

As is the case in any lively community, the Internet has its share of hoaxes. One, for example, tells about people who unsuspectingly downloaded a file that somehow took control of their computers. Others deal with plots to use the Net to control the world, how you can save someone who's dying, or how to rescue an organization that's going broke just by sending them e-mail, and similar silliness. Below are URLs for several sites that keep up-to-date information on Internet and other hoaxes:

Don't Spread That Hoax! by Charles Hymes
`http://www.nonprofit.net/hoax/hoax.html`

The AFU and Urban Legends Archive (AFU stands for alt.folklore.urban, an Internet newsgroup; see Chapters 12 and 13 for more information on newsgroups.)
`http://www.urbanlegends.com/`

Internet Hoaxes (one of the best sources from the U.S. Department of Energy Computer Incident Advisory Capability)
`http://ciac.llnl.gov/ciac/CIACHoaxes.html`

Patrick Crispen's Roadmap 96: Map09 - Spamming and Urban Legends
`http://www.mobiusweb.com/~mobius/Roadmap/map09.html`

Computer Virus Myths by Rob Rosenberger
`http://kumite.com/myths/`

The Symantec Corporation's AntiVirus Research Center site
`http://www.symantec.com/avcenter/index.html`

And for more information on real viruses, check this Yahoo! page:
`http://www.yahoo.com/Computers_and_Internet/Security_and_Encryption/Viruses/`

Summary

Shopping sites on the Internet offer you a wealth of goods and services that you can locate using the directories and search engines shown in Chapter 7. Explorer simplifies finding and downloading programs that you can use on your computer from software archive sites. Be sure to check programs that you download for copyright and registration restrictions, and to scan the files that you download for viruses. Gophers, developed to organize Internet information before the World Wide Web existed, still offer text resources that can be extremely useful for schoolwork and business. Locating information using a gopher's text-based format is much faster than doing so by browsing slow-loading Web pages.

PART THREE

COMMUNICATING WITH EXPLORER

THIS PART CONTAINS THE FOLLOWING CHAPTERS

E-mail is such a pervasive part of today's culture that you are out of the loop if you don't have an e-mail address. We know people who haven't used e-mail in years. You may not have gotten to that point in your life, but Outlook Express will help move you closer. E-mail is an incredibly convenient way to keep in touch with friends and family and is fast becoming the standard way to do business. If you're comfortable with e-mail, you're ready to get involved with newsgroups, the oldest and one of the most popular features of the Internet. Newsgroups are worldwide public discussion groups. Join a newsgroup and you can discuss your favorite hobby with enthusiasts around the world, get advice on a particularly burning issue in your profession, or even get help with your love life!

Five years ago, most people communicated by telephone. Does this ring a bell with you? (Sorry, the pun was just too good to put on hold.) Because you've bought this book on Internet Explorer, we think that you'll fit into the next statistic as well. There are currently close to 50 million e-mail users. We'll bet you're on the phone less and writing e-mail more. Shakespeare (and your eighth-grade English teacher) would be proud!

Now that you're busily writing e-mail to family, friends, and business associates, how long do you think it would take to write a 200-page book? Well, *every day* participants in newsgroups write the equivalent of 2,000 200-page books, according to Phil Trubey, president of NetPartners Internet Solutions, Inc., in San Diego, California. And Phil should know. He's been working in the Usenet world since the early 1980s and his company produces products that help individuals and businesses deal with the overwhelming amount of data that comes from newsgroups.

Usenet, which is the loose network of sites that carry newsgroups, has been in existence as a service since the Internet began. It started as a way for technical experts to exchange ideas and discuss projects. In recent years, it has become the world's largest information forum, where millions of people can participate in discussions on every imaginable topic. And, like the Internet, no one owns or manages Usenet.

Over 20,000 newsgroups are currently in existence and some estimates put it at over 22,000. According to records kept by The UseNet Calculator, a NetPartners product, each newsgroup receives an average of 50 e-mail messages a day. This equals *1 million messages each day* wending their way through cyberspace for newsgroups alone.

To put the volume of newsgroup correspondence in different terms, newsgroups generate the equivalent of 730,000 books every year. If the library in your town is like 50 percent of all libraries in the United States, it contains between 10,000 and 50,000 volumes (according to the National Center for Education Statistics). If the mail in newsgroups were housed in your town's library, you would have to build a brand-new library building every six to 30 days! Just imagine what that would do to your taxes.

Some newsgroups are moderated, which means there is someone who reviews messages, or postings, sent to the newsgroup to make sure they are in keeping with the topic under discussion. Most newsgroups, however, are not censored in any way. Newsgroups are filled with a mind-boggling amount of informative, useful, profound, useless, silly, heartwarming, plain dumb and engaging communications.

CHAPTER NINE

SETTING UP E-MAIL

IN THIS CHAPTER YOU LEARN THESE KEY SKILLS

E lectronic mail can save you lots of time. Just think. No more envelopes and stamps and last-minute trips to the post office—you can do it all on your computer instead. However, before you can jump into this fascinating way of communicating with business associates, friends and loved ones, you have to tell your Internet Explorer program

* who you are
* where to find your incoming electronic mail so it can be delivered to your computer, and
* where to send your outgoing mail so that it will be delivered properly to your correspondents

Read on for more information about how to set up and use Outlook Express, the e-mail program that comes with Internet Explorer.

Setting Up Internet Explorer to Send and Receive Mail

Before getting yourself organized to send and receive mail, it's a good idea to set up Internet Explorer to work offline in order to avoid "time and charges," or tying up your phone line. You can work offline for most of your mail and newsgroup activities.

Setting Internet Explorer to Work Offline

To set up Internet Explorer to work offline, start the Internet Web browser.

Then, complete these steps:

1. Click the Internet Explorer icon on the Quick Launch toolbar just to the right of the Start button on the taskbar to connect to your ISP.

2. Once online, click **File** in the menu bar, as shown in Figure 9-1.

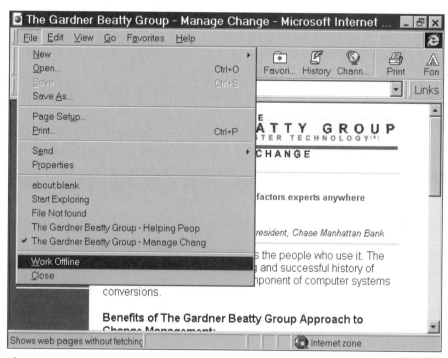

Figure 9-1 Setting Internet Explorer to work offline.

3. Click [**Work Offline**] to put a ✓ to the left of Work Offline. The [**File**] menu closes.

4. Click [**x**] to close Internet Explorer. Now you can open Internet Explorer's mail program, called Outlook Express, and work offline. This works with some machines and not with others. One of our machines insists on dialing every time we open Outlook Express. If it does, just keeping clicking on Cancel buttons to prevent your computer from going online.

Opening Outlook Express

Once you get Outlook Express customized to your needs, you are going to love it. So let's open it and get down to work.

To open Outlook Express, complete the following steps:

1. Click the Outlook Express icon on the Quick Launch toolbar to the right of the Start button on the taskbar to open Outlook Express, as shown in Figure 9-2.

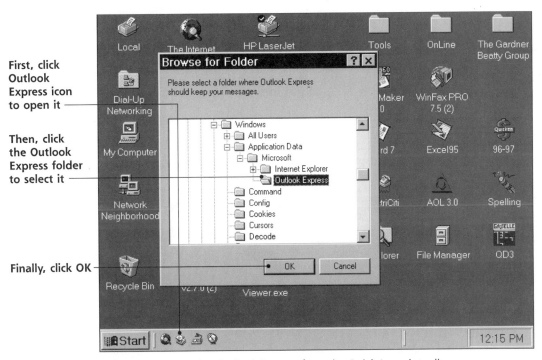

Figure 9-2 Opening Outlook Express from the Quick Launch toolbar.

NOTE The first time you open Outlook Express from the Quick Launch toolbar, you will be asked to select a folder where Outlook Express should keep your messages. We recommend that you accept the default folder, Outlook Express, as shown in Figure 9-2.

2. Click OK. Outlook Express is now open.

Setting Mail Preferences

Outlook Express walks you through the process of telling it where to send and receive your mail. If you have difficulty answering some of the questions on the various screens involved in the mail setup process, check with your ISP technical staff. It's a one-time but necessary process. If your computer acts differently from the example shown in this book, don't panic; you'll still be able to set your preferences correctly. Computers tend to react differently to the same software installation. For example, on one of our machines, the Wizard screens described below showed up the first time we opened Outlook. On two of our other machines, Outlook went right to the Outlook Express window as shown here. Oh well, nothing is easy these days.

Complete the following steps to set your mail preferences:

1. Click **Tools** in the menu bar. The Tools menu appears.

2. Click **Accounts** to open the Internet Accounts dialog box, as shown in Figure 9-3.

3. Click the Mail tab to bring it to the front.

4. Click the Add button. A small menu appears as shown in Figure 9-3.

Click here to start the e-mail setup process —

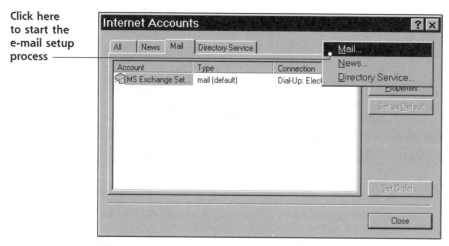

Figure 9-3 Starting the Internet Wizard Mail Setup Process.

5. Click Mail on the small menu. A series of Internet Wizard setup screens will appear.

6. You will have to fill in the following information as each Internet Connection Wizard dialog box appears:

✶ *Your Name* — Type your own name or any name (e.g., Joely Beatty) where it says Display name and click the Next button to continue.

✶ *Internet E-Mail Address* — Type your e-mail address and click the Next button to continue.

✶ *E-mail Server Names* — Type your Incoming (SMTP) and Outgoing Mail server (POP3) names, as shown in Figure 9-4. You can get this information from your ISP. Click the Next button to continue.

Type the name of your incoming mail server here ——

Type the name of your outgoing mail server here ——

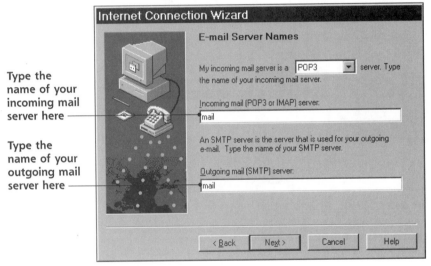

Figure 9-4 Entering e-mail server names.

NOTE **Do not change the type of server shown on the dialog box (e.g., POP3). Internet Explorer enters this automatically.**

✶ *Internet Mail Logon* — Type your POP account name and password here. You can get this information from your ISP. Your ISP will help you if they require you to use the Secure Password Authentication option. Click the Next button to continue.

✶ *Friendly Name* — Type any name to identify the connection that you are setting up. It will appear as the account name of this mail connection setup in the Internet Accounts dialog box when you have finished the process. Click the Next button to continue.

✳ *Choose Connection Type* — We recommend you click "Connect using my phone line" to put a dot in the circle if it is not already there. Otherwise, check with your system administrator or technical service person. Click the Next button to continue.

✳ *Dial-Up Connection* — We recommend that you click your standard ISP connection and click the Next button to continue. If you have any doubts about what to do here, check with your ISP or your technical advisor. In the example in Figure 9-5, we chose our standard ISP connection service, ElectriCiti.

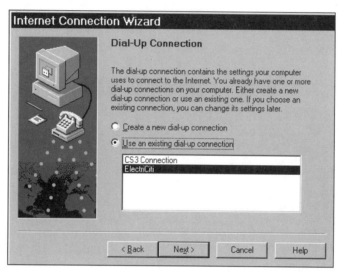

Figure 9-5 Selecting your Dial-Up Connection.

7. Click the Finish button. All done.

Exercising Your Options

Outlook Express is a very sophisticated program. The Options dialog box contains seven tabs. Each tab has from five to nine optional settings. In all, there are over 50 options for you to consider. If this boggles your mind, just follow our suggestion that in general you accept the default options that Outlook Express set for you automatically when you installed it. There are, of course, exceptions to our general rule. These are discussed in Table 9-1. But first, let's take a look at the Options dialog box.

FEATURE FOCUS The Options dialog box, with over 50 choices, is a new feature in Internet Explorer 4.

Opening the Options Dialog Box

To exercise all of your options, you must open the Options dialog box and check them out.

Click **Tools** → **Options** to open the Options dialog box, as shown in Figure 9-6.

Click any tab to bring it to the front

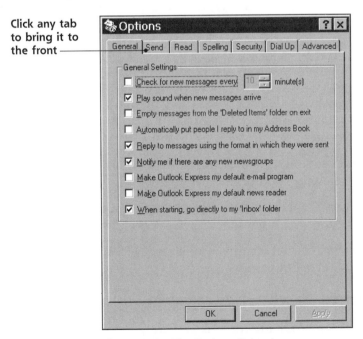

Figure 9-6 The Options dialog box.

Fine-Tuning Your Options

The suggestions and comments in Table 9-1 can help you get past all the choices in the Options dialog box.

TABLE 9-1 Fine-Tuning Outlook Express Options

Tab	Comments and Suggestions
GENERAL	Up for grabs is whether or not you want Outlook Express as your default e-mail and/or news reader.
	For heaven's sake, don't select "Check for new messages every... " unless you want your computer to continuously dial in to your ISP, making you stop what you're doing till it's done.
	We highly recommend you select "When starting, go directly to my Inbox folder."
SEND	Check "Plain Text" as your outgoing message format for both mail and newsgroups. People who do not have the same e-mail program as you do really get annoyed getting HTML text. In some cases, they can't decipher your HTML message at all!
SEND	Nice options on quotes. If you don't care, stick with the indented angle bracket (>) Also, remove the check mark from "Include message in reply." It makes your messages much too long and annoys people who pay for download time. See Chapter 11 for tips on quoting relevant portions of the original message.
READ	You may want to change the five-second setting on marking a message "as read." Otherwise, for now, stick with the default options. Later on, after you get the hang of Outlook Express, you may want to play around with fonts. For more discussion about this options tab, see Chapter 14, "Participating in Newsgroups."
SPELLING	Some of the options are similar to those in Word. We really like the option to ignore quoted text and/or Internet addresses.
DIAL UP	The key selection here is "to dial or not dial" automatically when opening Outlook Express. It's a question of your personal work style.
SECURITY	The default setting for Internet security is Medium. We recommend you set it to High. It's a jungle out there!
	If you do a lot of shopping online (or you are slightly paranoid), you may want to get a Digital ID. It can help protect you from some hacker using your name to send mail and/or make purchases in your name.

Digital IDs also make it easy for vendors to verify who you are when shopping online. Simply click the Get Digital ID button. Explorer will hook you up to the appropriate Web pages for getting a Digital ID.

ADVANCED   See Table 13-1 in Chapter 13 for more information about this tab.

Customizing Your Style

Assuming you are corresponding with people who have *compatible* e-mail programs, you can go way beyond the standard text e-mail format for your letters. To change the look and feel of your outgoing messages, you must open the Stationery dialog box.

Complete the following steps to open the Stationery dialog box:

1. Click ▐ **Tools** ▐ in the menu bar. A menu appears.

2. Click ▐ **Stationery** ▐. The Stationery dialog box appears, as shown in Figure 9-7.

Click here to customize your fonts

Click here to add artwork to your outgoing messages

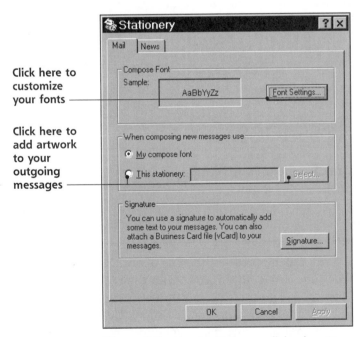

Figure 9-7   Use the Stationery dialog box to customize your outgoing e-mail.

To customize how your e-mail messages look, complete the following steps:

1. Click the Font Settings button to open the Font dialog box. You can select any font, size and style from the list of available fonts. Once you have selected your new font look, click the OK button to return to the Stationery dialog box.

2. Click This Stationery to put a dot in the circle. The Select button is now active.

3. Click the Select button. The Select Stationery dialog box will appear. Once you have selected the background artwork you want to use, click the OK button to return to the Stationery dialog box.

4. Click the News tab to bring it to the front. This tab has options identical to the Mail tab options.

5. Repeat Steps 1–3 to select the Font and Stationery for your outgoing newsgroup messages.

SIDE TRIP

DOING YOUR OWN THING

You can click Browse in the Select Stationery dialog box to select another file with an .htm or .html extension on your computer, and add it to your stationery background. See Chapter 19, "Creating and Publishing Your Web Page" to create a "stationery" page for your e-mail or newsgroup messages.

Signing Your Messages

You can create a signature file for your e-mail messages in the Stationery dialog box. The options are as follows:

* You can click the Text option, as shown in Figure 9-8, and type any text message in the text box.

* You can skip the text approach and select the File option instead. The Browse button will become active. In this case, click the Browse button to select a customized text file of your creation. Whatever text is in this file will be added to the bottom of your outgoing messages. Use Windows Notepad to set up a personal signature file in advance. Frankly, unless you want a "fancy" signature, use the Text option illustrated in Figure 9-8.

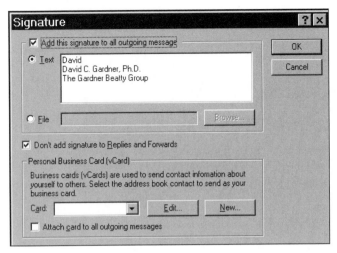

Figure 9-8 Signature options.

✴ If this isn't enough, you can also add a "business card" to your outgoing mail. See Chapter 10, "Setting Up Your Address Book," for instructions on how to make a business card.

Customizing Outlook's Look and Feel

You can customize Outlook's appearance on your screen by fiddling with a number of options from the Window Layout Properties dialog box, as shown in Figure 9-9. Click View and then Layout to open the dialog box. Once it is open, here's what you can do:

✴ You can add or delete buttons from the toolbar, change its location (top, bottom, right, left), and show text on its buttons.

✴ You can change the buttons on the toolbar to your heart's content.

✴ You can add or remove not only the Outlook bar, but also the Folder bar, the Folder List, and the Tip of the Day.

✴ Finally, you can customize the preview pane to show messages in a pane below the list of messages or to the right of a list of messages.

Play around with the possibilities! Have fun!

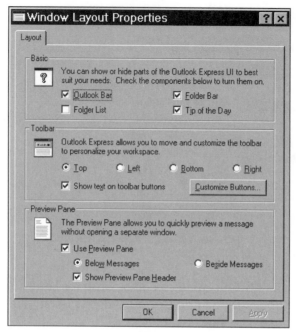

Figure 9-9 You can customize your Outlook Express screen in the Window Layout Properties dialog box.

 TIP If you want more "window space," remove the text from the toolbar, remove the Folder bar and the Tip of the Day, and do not select the Folder List.

BONUS

Showing Your Emotions

What are those funny-looking things you encounter in e-mail correspondence? They are called Smileys, or Emoticons. Smileys are little symbols that people use in e-mail to express emotions. Table 9-2 illustrates just a few of the ones in current use.

TABLE 9-2 Sample Smileys

Smiley	Emotion	Smiley	Emotion
:-)	Happy	:-*	Kiss
:-(	Sad	X-(	Brain dead
:-D	Laughing	:-\	Undecided

WEB PATH ➡ If you would like to see lots more Smileys, explore the following "smiley" Web sites:

http://www.atcom.co.at/atcom/smileys/

http://members.aol.com/bearpage/smileys.htm

http://www.cg.tuwien.ac.at/~helwig/smileys.html

This one is rather unpredictable. It generates smileys for you at random:

http://www.goldendome.net/Tools/cgi-bin/smiley.cgi

Summary

In this chapter, you set up Outlook Express to send and receive mail from your Internet Service Provider. You set up the way Outlook Express handles your mail once the connection is made. You added a signature file and customized your stationery and outgoing mail fonts. Finally, you customized the way Outlook Express appears on your screen.

CHAPTER TEN

SETTING UP YOUR ADDRESS BOOK

10

IN THIS CHAPTER YOU LEARN THESE KEY SKILLS

U sing Internet Outlook Express's Address Book makes sending e-mail a much simpler task because once you have entered an Internet e-mail address, you don't have to remember it again or run the risk of a typing error. Since many Internet e-mail addresses are long and complicated, you have a tremendous incentive to use this time-saving feature!

Understanding Internet Addresses

The bottom line before sending e-mail is that you must ask the person to whom you wish to send e-mail to give you his or her Internet address. There is no really easy way to look up someone's e-mail address because there is no comprehensive directory of Internet names and addresses.

Following are the Web addresses of five popular online directories. You can search them automatically in Outlook Express or from any Web browser:

The Bigfoot Directory: `http://www.bigfoot.com/`

The Four 11 Directory: `http://www.four11.com/`

The InfoSpace Directory: `http://www.infospace.com`

The Switchboard Directory: `http://www.switchboard.com/`

The WhoWhere Directory: `http://www.whowhere.com`

Combined, these directories cannot compete with Ma Bell's telephone directory system! Ergo, finding a person's Internet address can be daunting.

Internet addresses can be confusing at first glance but there is a logical format behind them. A simple Internet address usually consists of three parts: (For example, one of David Gardner's Internet addresses is `gbgroup@msn.com`)

* The first part of an address is usually the person's name or some other name (gbgroup)
* The person's name is always followed by @ (the "at" sign)
* The last part is called the domain name (msn.com)

Typically, a domain name consists of two parts.

* The first part of the domain name is either a special domain name that the person (or company) registered with the government, such as "cyberhelp," or the domain name of the person's Internet service provider (e.g., ElectriCiti, AOL, or MSN). Special registered domain names have to be renewed once a year for a fee.
* The second part of a domain name always follows a period (called a dot in online talk) and indicates the type of domain. Table 10-1 shows the most common domains:

TABLE 10-1 Types of Domains

Domain Extension	Type of Domain
COM	Commercial
·EDU	Education
GOV	Government
MIL	Military
NET	Networks
ORG	Organizations

NOTE You may also see two-letter country codes in Internet addresses, such as US for United States, UK for United Kingdom, etc.

There are, of course, more complicated addresses. Some addresses contain an underscore, such as David_Gardner@domain.com. Moreover, if an organization has more than one computer connected to the Internet to serve various staff members, it will have a different domain address for each computer. For example, at Boston University, your e-mail address could be assigned to one of several computers, e.g., name@acs.bu.edu or name@crsa.bu.edu., where *bu* stands for Boston University, *edu* stands for Educational and *acs* or *crsa* stand for specific computers, called *servers,* hooked to the Internet.

For people who belong to online services such as America Online or CompuServe, here's a simple formula for converting their online service e-mail addresses to Internet addresses:

1. Type the person's **screen name** (or identification number or user id)

2. Type **@** after the name or id (no space)

3. Type the **name** of the online service (e.g., CompuServe)

4. Type a **.** (a period or "dot")

5. Type **com** to identify it as a commercial service.

Table 10-2 shows what two online service e-mail addresses look like after conversion to Internet addresses.

TABLE 10-2 Sample Online Service Addresses Converted to Internet Addresses

Online Service	Online E-Mail Addresses	Converted to Internet Addresses
AMERICA ONLINE	Write Bks	writebks@aol.com
COMPUSERVE	73540,675	73540.675@compuserve.com (It doesn't matter whether you use uppercase letters, lowercase letters, or a combination of letters and numbers.)

In the case of CompuServe addresses, the comma (,) should be changed to a dot. CompuServe now offers members the option of changing their addresses from numbers to names, like AOL does. You may begin to see them more often in the future (e.g., gbgroup@compuserve.com).

In the case of AOL addresses, a space should be eliminated.

Enough already on Internet addresses! Let's start adding names to your Address Book. You will probably run into problems with Internet addresses, but they usually work themselves out simply because they get returned to you as undeliverable and you then have to figure out what you did wrong or call the person to get the correct address!

 Watch what you're typing. Typing commas instead of periods or putting space between words and numbers are common errors.

Opening the Little Black Book

When working with your Address Book, you will find that it makes a lot of sense to open Outlook Express and set it up to work offline. No point in paying for online time if you have a limited time arrangement with your ISP.

 Follow the steps in the sections of Chapter 9 entitled "Setting Up Outlook Express to Send and Receive Mail" and "Fine-Tune Outlook Express Options" to set Outlook Express to work offline.

To open the Address Book, complete the following steps:

1. Click the Address Book icon in the toolbar. The Windows Address Book dialog box appears. As you can see from Figure 10-1, it is too small to work with, so go on to Step 2.

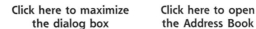

Click here to maximize
the dialog box

Click here to open
the Address Book

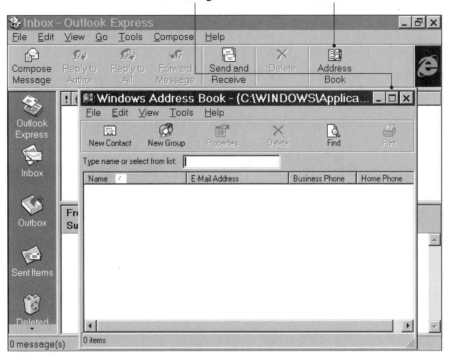

Figure 10-1 Opening and maximizing the Windows Address Book dialog box.

2. Click the ▢ to maximize the window. Now you are ready to fill in your Address Book.

Populating Your Address Book

The Windows Address Book will keep you organized with contact information and make addressing your e-mail a snap.

To add a name to the Address Book, you must first open a blank Properties dialog box for each new person. Click the New Contact button on the toolbar to open a blank Properties dialog box (see Figure 10-2).

**Click here to add a
new contact to your
address book**

Figure 10-2 Opening a new contact Properties dialog box.

You do not have to fill in all of the information in every tab in the individual contact's Properties dialog box in order to use the Address Book just for e-mail. In fact, if you have your Address Book information stored somewhere else, say in Sidekick or ACT, you may want to use this Address Book in a limited way, just for sending e-mail.

To use the Address Book strictly for e-mail, complete the following steps in the Properties dialog box to add a name to the Address Book:

1. Type the person's first name in the First box, as shown in Figure 10-3.

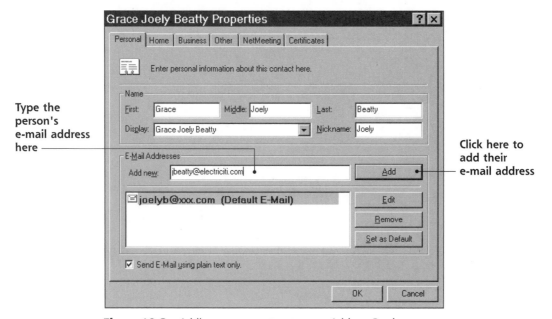

Figure 10-3 Adding a new contact to your Address Book.

2. Click the Middle box to set the cursor.

3. Type the person's middle name in the Middle box.

4. Press the Tab key to move to the next box or continue to click each box to set the cursor. As you fill in the First, Middle, and Last boxes, the person's name appears in the Display box and on the Properties title bar.

5. Continue filling in the remaining fields: Last, E-Mail Addresses, Nickname.

6. Click OK to close the person's Properties dialog box when you have finished.

We suggest that you click the "Send E-mail using plain text only" box to put a ✓ there unless you know for certain that the person wants HTML mail. HTML is short for "HyperText Markup Language." It's a way to format text, fonts, and graphics so that they can be viewed like a formatted word processing document on the Web. (In Chapter 19, you will learn how to produce an HTML document in FrontPage Express). Most people prefer plain-text e-mail. It has lots of advantages, not the least of which are that it can be opened in any word processing program and can be read by all e-mail programs.

NOTE You can continue to add additional e-mail addresses for a specific individual by typing in a new address and clicking the Add button. Make sure you select the e-mail address you want to use most of the time for this person. Simply highlight the address and click the Set as Default button, as shown in Figure 10-3.

You can select to have a person's nickname, rather than their complete name, displayed in the Address Book list. Simply click the ▼ to the right of the Display box. A drop-down list appears. Click the person's nickname. Voilà. Their nickname will appear in the Address Book Name column when you close the dialog box and in the To: text box when you address a message.

Editing a Name in Your Black Book

To edit an address, you have to open the Address Book and then the Properties dialog box for the addressee.

X-REF Follow the steps under "Opening the Little Black Book" in this chapter to open the Address Book if it is not already open.

Complete the following steps to open the Properties dialog box for the person whose address you want to edit:

1. Click the name of the addressee that needs editing to highlight it.

2. Click the Properties button on the toolbar. The Properties dialog box for that person appears.

3. Click the Edit button to change or update the e-mail address. The person's e-mail address appears surrounded by a box, as shown in Figure 10-4.

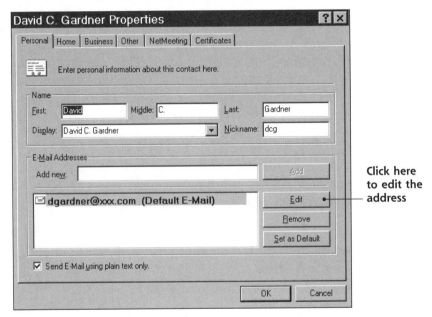

Figure 10-4   Click the Edit button to edit the e-mail address.

4. Type the new text for the e-mail address.

5. Click the OK button to complete the process.

NOTE   Remember the old days when you wanted to edit something in Windows? All you did was click an item in the Edit menu. For some unknown reason, that logical path of using the Edit menu to edit has been replaced by the not-so-intuitive "Properties path." Do you suppose today's programmers are part-time real estate agents?

Filling in All the Blanks

Once you have filled in the Personal tab information above, you can e-mail to your heart's content. However, if you want to store additional information about a person, there are five additional tabs you can fill in with tons of stuff. Table 10-3 covers the basics of each tab.

TABLE 10-3 Adding other information into the address book

Tab	Comments
HOME	Type in the person's home address, home phone, and fax numbers. Note that you can also put in their personal Web site address.
BUSINESS	Type in the person's business address, business phone, and fax numbers. Note that you can also put in their business Web address.
OTHER	A very optional tab.
NETMEETING	If you are into "online conferencing" you can fill this tab in later in Chapter 15. Otherwise, ignore it.
CERTIFICATES	If you are worried about the security of your messages, you may want to get a digital ID. This way you can attach it to your address entry and/or the address entries of other addressees who require it.

In the e-mail world, a Business Card consists of your own contact information, which you have entered into the Address Book converted to vCard format. VCard is a digital way of sending your vital statistics to your correspondents. (How secure vCards and Certificates truly are, as well as other information on the net, is up for grabs. We know of at least one large firm that does not permit any company business to be conducted over the Internet except at the "see you at the volleyball game" level.

You can create and attach your "business card" to all of your e-mail very easily by completing the following steps:

1. Create an address card for yourself. Enter your own address and additional information into the Address Book the same way you did in the section entitled "Populating Your Address Book."

2. Click your name in the Address Book list to highlight it.

3. Click File → Export → Business Card (vCard)

4. Save the Card to the Windows folder (or any folder).

5. Choose **Tools** → **Stationery** to open the Stationery dialog box. Click the Signature button. The Signature dialog box appears, as shown in Figure 10-5.

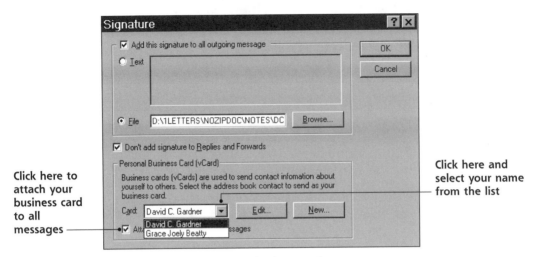

Click here to attach your business card to all messages

Click here and select your name from the list

Figure 10-5 Attaching your business card to your messages.

 X-REF See "Create a Signature File for E-mail and News Mail" in Chapter 9.

6. Click "Attach card to all outgoing messages" to put a ✓ in the box.

7. Click the ▼ to the right of the Card box. A drop-down list appears. Click your name.

8. Click OK, then OK again. Your "business card" will now be attached to your outgoing messages!

Importing Another Black Book

You can import Address Books from other programs such as Eudora or Netscape or previous versions of Internet Explorer. You can also import address lists which you've already formatted into comma-separated text files.

To import an address book from another program complete the following steps from the Address Book window:

1. Click **File** → **Import** → **Address Book**. A dialog box appears, as shown in Figure 10-6.

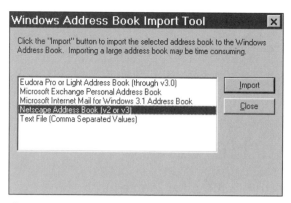

Figure 10-6 Importing an address book.

2. Click the name of the Address Book you want to import. Outlook Express will find the Address Book on your computer and import it instantly.

3. Click the Close button to complete the importing process.

Seek and Ye Shall Find

Searching for someone's e-mail address is a snap in Outlook Express.

To find an e-mail address, simply complete the following steps:

1. Click **Edit** → **Find** . The Find People dialog box appears, as shown in Figure 10-7.

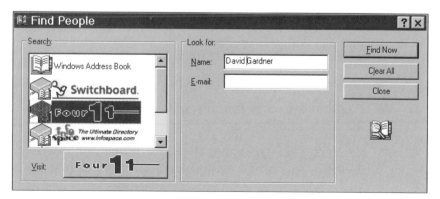

Figure 10-7 Searching for an address online.

2. Click the directory you want to search.

3. Type the person's name in the Name box.

4. Cross your fingers and click the Find Now button. Good Luck!

5. Repeat the process with each online directory until you find the elusive person's e-mail address.

The Gang's All Here!

Sending a lot of stuff to the same people all the time (e.g., recipes, jokes, family updates, etc.)? Tired of separately entering their names into the "To:" box? Problem solved, because one of the nice features of the Outlook Express Address Book is that you can create mailing lists for specific groups of people. Once you have created the list and added names to it, you can send the same message to all of the people on the list without having to enter their Internet addresses individually. You simply type in the name of the group mailing list, and Outlook Express automatically sends the message to everyone on the list.

You can create mailing lists in the Address Book for specific groups of people.

To set up a group mailing list, complete the following steps:

1. Click the New Group icon on the Address Book toolbar. A Properties dialog box appears, as shown in Figure 10-8.

2. Type a name for the group mailing list. This can be any name that broadly describes the recipients or purpose of this mailing list.

3. Click the Select Members button to open the Select Group Members dialog box.

4. Click a name from the list to highlight it.

5. Click the Select button. The person will be added to the group list.

6. Continue the process until you have selected all the names you want in the group mailing list.

7. Click OK. Click OK again. The group name will appear in the Address Book list. Your group mailing list is ready for its first mailing!

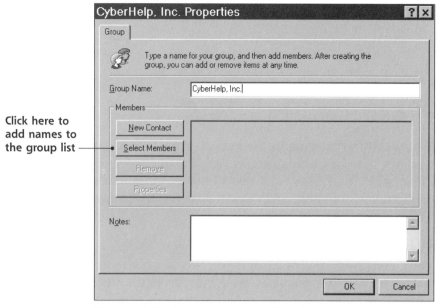

Click here to add names to the group list ——•

Figure 10-8 Creating a group mailing list.

NOTE You can edit the group list and/or add or remove names by highlighting the list name and clicking on the Properties icon on the toolbar. When you want to send the same message to all the people in the group, simply click the group name instead of individual names and Outlook Express will send the message to everyone on the group list at one time.

Changing the Way Things Are

D on't like the Address Book look? Don't like the layout? Problem solved in this versatile data storage unit.

You can do something about it right now by completing the following steps:

1. Click **View** on the menu bar. A menu chock-full of view options appears.

2. Click any of the menu items and see what happens.

3. Have fun!

BONUS

You Ought to Be in Pictures

The next best thing to being in the movies or on TV yourself is keeping up with what's hot with a favorite television or movie celebrity and corresponding with them. We've got two Web sites for you to visit where you can get e-mail and/or snail mail addresses of your favorite stars and shows.

Checking out the Mr. Showbiz Site

Like to express your opinions? The Mr. Showbiz Web site has a great forum where you can chat online with like-minded celebrity watchers. You can also sign up for updates of *e-mail movie reviews*, Hollywood headlines, and much more.

To visit the Web site and sign up (it's free), follow these steps:

1. Connect to http://www.mrshowbiz.com

2. Click Sign me up!

3. Fill in the blanks on the two-page registration form, including signing up for e-mail movie reviews, etc.

4. Enter a "code word" in the Type of word box. Click the ▾ to see a list of code word choices. Like Groucho, we chose a "Secret word" instead of one of the other choices (e.g., Mother's maiden name). You may need this code word for customer service or if you forget or lose your password.

5. Click Complete Registration and wait 15–60 seconds. You're now a registered member.

Tracking Celebrities on CelebSite

At http://www.celebsite.com/index.html, you can track celebrities who are currently in the news, check out "Today's celeb birthdays," or find links to your favorite celebrities' Web sites quickly, where, in many cases, you can find the e-mail address of the star and/or the show. In addition, you can join the Celeb Club (it's free) and receive access to members-only information. Snail mail addresses of several hundred celebrities will be at your disposal. Complete the short online registration form and a password will be sent to your e-mail address in a day or so.

To visit Celeb Site, follow these steps:

1. Connect to the Celeb Site home page at
   `http://www.celebsite.com/index.html`

2. Click JOIN The Club, which is at the lower right of the page. The Join CelebSite page will appear.

3. Click the ▼ in the lower-right corner of the page to scroll down to the membership form.

4. Fill out the form and click the Complete Registration button. A confirmation page will appear. On this page you can go directly to the members-only premium area by clicking the <u>Go to our premium area now</u> link at the bottom of the confirmation page.

5. Once your official ID and password are sent to you, you can log on at any time.

Have fun!

Summary

Now that you understand the key components of Internet addresses, addressing and handling e-mail will be a breeze. Setting up your Address Book may initially take a few minutes depending on the number of entries, but using the Address Book is a valuable time-saver each time you want to send a message. In addition, you can even add a mail listing for specific groups of people to your Address Book for handy reference.

WRITING AN E-MAIL LETTER

Just think. You can send an electronic letter to anyone anywhere in the world without leaving your house or office with Outlook Express's mail program (as long as they have an e-mail address). In fact, the unparalleled growth of the Internet in recent years has spawned a revival of correspondence between friends, family, and business associates not seen since the invention of the telephone. However, there is one difference: Today's correspondence (e-mail messages) tends to be shorter and to be sent more frequently than in the pre-telephone era.

Composing an E-Mail Message

If you have a time-limited service, we recommend that you compose all of your outgoing messages offline in order to save money. Moreover, if you only have one phone line, why tie it up? If you have been following along in this section of the book, you have already set up Outlook Express to open in the offline mode in the Inbox window.

X-REF See "Setting Internet Explorer to Work Offline" in Chapter 9 to learn how to work offline.

Opening a New Message Dialog Box

You can start composing a message in just a few clicks!

Complete the following steps to compose a new message:

1. Click  to open Outlook Express.

2. Click the Compose Message button on the toolbar (see Figure 11-1). A New Message dialog box will appear.

Click here to start a new message

Figure 11-1 Opening a new message dialog box.

Send to Whom?

There are several ways to address a message in Outlook. In one fell swoop you can address a message with carbon copies and blind carbon copies with just a few mouse clicks.

METHOD#1: CLICK, CLICK

To address a new message, complete the following steps:

1. Click the 🔳 to the immediate right of "To:" to open the Select Recipients dialog box (another view of the Address Book) or click the Address Book button on the toolbar (see Figure 11-2). Either way, the Select Recipients dialog box appears.

2. Click the name of the person to whom you want to send a message to highlight it.

 NOTE You can also double-click a name to move it to the Message Recipients To: section.

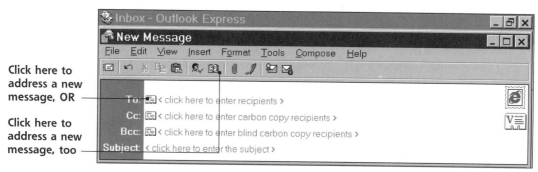

Click here to address a new message, OR

Click here to address a new message, too

Figure 11-2 Addressing the message.

3. Click the To: button. The addressee's name moves to the Message Recipients To: section, as shown in Figure 11-3.

Click here to add a highlighted name to the To: section

Click here to add a highlighted name to the Cc section

Click here to add a highlighted name to the Bcc section

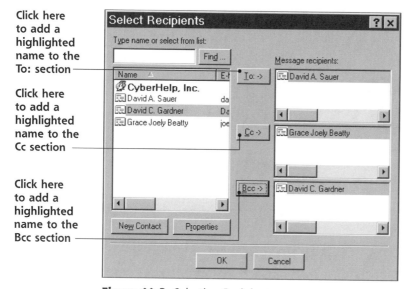

Figure 11-3 Selecting Recipients.

4. Click the name of the person to whom you want to send a carbon copy to highlight it.

5. Click the Cc: button. The addressee's name moves to the Message Recipients Cc: section.

6. Click the name of the person to whom you want to send a blind carbon copy to highlight it.

7. Click the Bcc: button. The addressee's name moves to the Message Recipients Bcc: section.

NOTE When you address a copy of the message to a person in the Bcc: ("blind carbon copy") text box, Outlook sends a copy of the message to the person named in the To: row (the primary recipient) but conceals the name of the Bcc: recipient.

8. Click the OK button. All Done!

METHOD #2: TYPE, TYPE, TYPE

To address a message without using the Address Book complete the following steps:

1. Click the <click here to enter recipients> line. A text box window opens and the cursor flashes in the box, as shown in Figure 11-4.

2. Type an e-mail address in the box.

3. Repeat Steps 1 and 2 to fill in the Cc: and Bcc: fields if appropriate.

Click here and begin typing the e-mail address ——

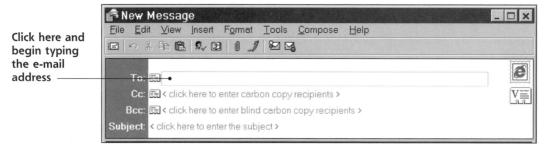

Figure 11-4 Typing an e-mail address.

Rules for Successful E-Mail

Before you fill in the Subject line and type your message, here are our two major rules for how to be a successful e-mailer. Keep them in mind when composing a message:

RULE NUMBER 1: SELL, SELL, SELL

When you put an attention-getting message title in the Subject box, you increase the chances of it being read by the recipients. This is increasingly important if you are conducting business on the Internet because most e-mail users are being buried in unsolicited commercial messages. People are getting very annoyed—to the point that they are deleting messages without reading them. Case in point: Several weeks ago the three of us were scheduled to give a seminar to a local computer users group. We sent some confirming information (as requested) to the host, who promptly (and accidentally) deleted the message while in a fit of annoyance at all of the advertising junk in his inbox!

Use an attention-getting message title and increase the chances of your message being read. In the example in Figure 11-5, we chose Pacifica Del Mar as the subject because the recipients *love* that restaurant. It is unlikely they will forget the business meeting time and date!

RULE NUMBER 2: USE THE KISS METHOD FOR COMPOSING MESSAGES

E-mail is a great way to do business and to keep in touch with family and friends. However, most people who have computers lead hectic and crazy lives (at least the ones we know)! This means that they like things short, simple, and to the point, as the example in Figure 11-5 illustrates. Always remember KISS (Keep It Simple, Stupid).

Follow the two preceding rules, and you will enjoy keeping in touch!

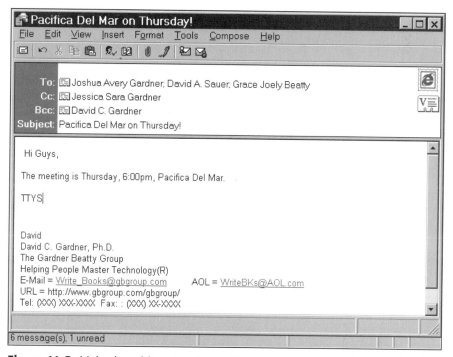

Figure 11-5 Make the subject attention-getting, and the message short and simple.

WHAT DO ALL THOSE FUNNY ACRONYMS MEAN?

Notice in Figure 11-5 that we used "TTYS" as our closing. TTYS is one of many acronyms that you will see floating around in Internet correspondence. Table 11-1 lists some of them.

TABLE 11-1 Selected Acronyms

Acronym	Expression
BTW	By the way
FWIW	For what it's worth
FYI	For your information
GD&R	Grinning, ducking, and running
GMTA	Great minds think alike
IMHO	In my humble opinion
OBTW	Oh, by the way
TNX	Thanks
TTFN	Ta-ta for now
TTYS	Talk to you soon
WB	Welcome back
WTG	WAY TO GO

WEB
PATH For more e-mail tips, advice, and information on e-mail personal and business etiquette, we suggest you visit these five Web sites:

A Beginner's Guide to Effective E-Mail

http://www.webfoot.com/advice/email.top.html

E-Mail Etiquette

http://www.augsburg.edu/library/aib/mailmanners.html

http://www.albury.net.au/new-users/netiquet.htm

```
http://www.netpath.net/~gwicker/email.htm
```

International Business E-Mail Etiquette

```
http://www.wp.com/fredfish/Netiq.html
```

Visits to these sites will ensure that you're e-mail smart.

Check Your Spelling Now!

You can write a great, on-target message and then negate the whole thing because you forget to check your spelling. No "execuses" with Outlook Express. Spelling checking is just a couple of clicks away. Simply click Tools→Spelling to open the spell check program.

 FEATURE FOCUS   Spell checking is a new feature in IE 4.

Attaching a File to an E-Mail Message

Sometimes a text e-mail message isn't able to convey all the information you'd like. Maybe you need to send along a spreadsheet to show off the latest sales figures. Or perhaps you have a great piece of artwork you want to share. Attaching a document or graphic file to an e-mail message in Outlook Express is a piece of cake.

Complete the following steps to attach a file to your message:

1. Click `Insert` → `File Attachment`. The Insert Attachment dialog box will appear. (You can also click the "paper clip" on the toolbar.)

2. Type the file name and click the Attach button. Alternately, you can browse to the file you want to attach and click it to highlight it. Its name will appear in the File name box, as shown in Figure 11-6.

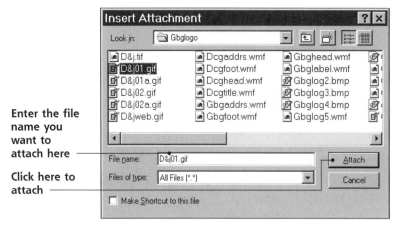

Enter the file name you want to attach here

Click here to attach

Figure 11-6 Attaching a file to an e-mail message.

Saving an E-Mail Message to the Draft Folder

If you are composing a very important e-mail message, you may want to save it to the Draft folder. You can go back to it later to make your changes. You can even save the message's e-mail attachment to the Draft folder as shown in Figure 11-7.

To save your e-mail message to the Draft folder, follow these steps:

1. Click **File** → **Save** . A message box appears.

2. Click the OK button. This message is now located in the Outlook Express Draft folder.

TIP Continue to compose as many messages as you like and send them to the Draft folder. When you finish, you can click the Drafts Icon in the Outlook bar to edit, review, and send each message one at a time. You can get your incoming mail and send all of the messages in the Draft folder in one operation. In the Draft folder, click the Send and Receive button on the toolbar and away you go!

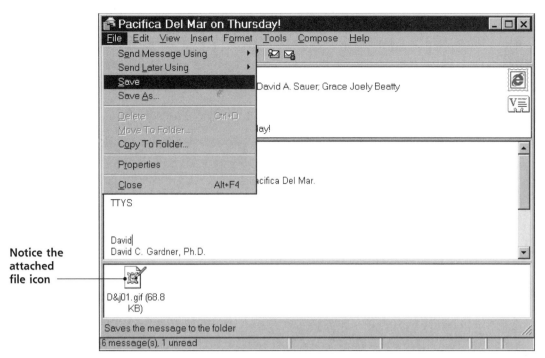

Figure 11-7 Sending a message to the Draft folder.

Sending an E-Mail Message Now

Sending a single e-mail message from the window is a very simple process.

To send an e-mail message, follow these steps:

1. Click the Send button in the far left corner of the toolbar as shown in Figure 11-8.

2. Cool it and wait while your message is sent. If you have graphic files attached to the message, it may take a while. If there are messages in your Outbox, they will also be sent in the same operation.

3. Don't forget to close your connection if you haven't set Outlook to close down automatically after sending and receiving mail. Just click the Disconnect button on the Connected dialog box and you're offline again, as shown in Figure 11-9.

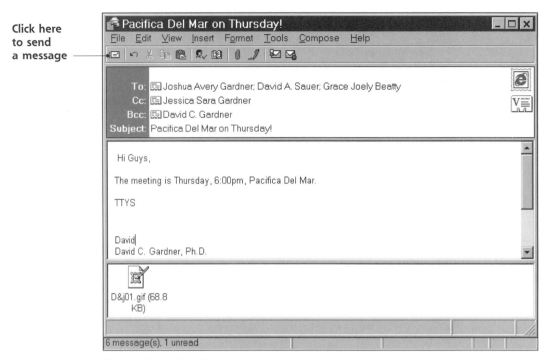

**Click here
to send
a message**

Figure 11-8 Sending a message.

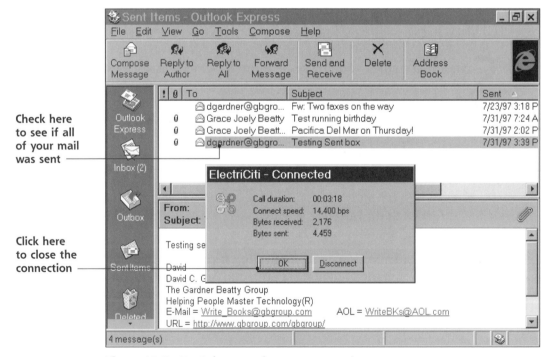

**Check here
to see if all
of your mail
was sent**

**Click here
to close the
connection**

Figure 11-9 Don't forget to close your connection.

BONUS

Get Online Worldwide with the Powers That Be

Today, with a computer and a modem, staying in touch with our government is only a few keystrokes away. This Web address

```
http://www.law.vill.edu/fed-agency/fedwebloc.html
```

will help you contact Washington, D.C., without leaving your house or making a phone call. Simply type this URL in the Web browser location address box and press Enter; the Federal Web Locator page will appear. By using the site's search feature and typing "Congress," you will get links to the Library of Congress and to representatives' and senators' e-mail addresses. Similarly, you can find many more government links, including the White House, the FBI, and the State Department.

Want to contact government officials in far-away and not-so-far-away lands? Clicking the Web site addresses below will a get you a list of Web links to the home pages of foreign embassies and consulates based in Washington, D.C. Some embassy sites allow you to download travel visas. You can also get Washington telephone and fax numbers and street addresses. E-mail addresses are few and far between in the sites we checked out, but several of them have a visitor's book or a contact screen set up for you to ask questions or make comments online.

Complete the following steps to get to your favorite embassy or consulate home page:

1. Connect to `http://www.yahoo.com`.

2. Type **Embassies** in the Search text box.

3. Click the Search button.

4. Scroll down the list of embassy sites (links).

5. For foreign embassies in Washington, D.C., click <u>Regional: U.S. States: Washington, D.C.: Government: Foreign Embassies.</u>

   or

   for consulates in other parts of the U.S.A., click <u>Government: Embassies and Consulates: United States: Foreign Embassies and Consulates in the United States.</u>

Summary

n this chapter you learned about Outlook Express's basic features. In the process, you discovered some of the rules of the road in composing e-mail, such as, two basic rules for effective e-mail communication, and, BTW, a list of common Internet e-mail acronyms. Moreover, you were able to send a message and to save a draft letter for later editing. You are well on your way to becoming a successful e-mail aficionado. The next chapter will hone your e-mail skills even more!

ANSWERING YOUR E-MAIL

IN THIS CHAPTER YOU LEARN THESE KEY SKILLS

12

Now that you've sent e-mail to the immediate world, your mailbox will be flooded with enthusiastic replies. Although computers have simplified the process of sending mail, you still have to read through it, sort it, save it, or delete it. If you expect to get mail from a specific person or source, you can set up a mail filter (sort of like an electronic traffic cop) to send it to a specific folder. And when you want to reply, it's as easy as clicking your mouse.

Responding to e-mail messages is the same process as responding to newsgroup messages, so you may also want to read through Chapter 14, "Participating in Newsgroups." Some of the issues discussed in that chapter apply to regular mail.

Reading Your Mail

Before you can read your mail, you have to get it. You have to be online to get mail, but exactly how this happens depends on how you set up Internet Explorer. You may have to go online first and then open Outlook Express. Or, you may be able to go to Outlook Express and log on to your ISP when you get your mail. Once you're in Outlook Express, getting to the Inbox also depends on the setup you chose. Outlook Express is set up so that the Outlook Express window is the first thing you see. Click the Inbox icon in the Outlook bar.

Getting Your Mail

The Send and Receive button you use to *get* your mail also *sends* any mail you may have in your Outbox.

Follow these steps to get your mail:

1. Open Outlook Express and go to the Inbox (however that happens for you). Notice the letter from Microsoft Outlook Express waiting in your Inbox.

2. Click the Send and Receive button in the toolbar (see Figure 12-1).

Figure 12-1 Click the Send and Receive button to get new mail.

3. If you're already online when you click the Send and Receive button, you see a screen like the one in Figure 12-2. If you're set up to have Outlook Express ask if you want to log on, a Logon dialog box appears on top of the screen shown in Figure 12-2, which lets you enter your user name and password and then gets your mail. Figure 12-2 shows the Details section of the dialog box expanded.

4. If you want to go offline when you have your mail, click the box to the left of Hang up when finished. Or, you can choose to stay online.

5. When you have your mail, click the ☒ if necessary to close this dialog box and see your mail.

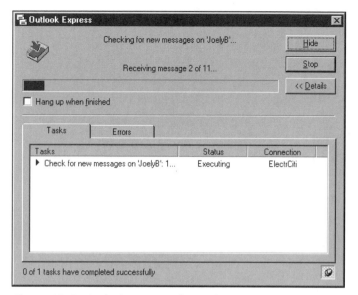

Figure 12-2 Outlook Express tells you how many messages you have and its progress as it downloads them.

Changing the View

Outlook Express is set up to show two panes in the Inbox window (unless, of course, you changed that on the Read tab in the Options dialog box). The top pane shows your messages and the preview pane at the bottom shows the high-lighted message. As you click a new message, it appears in the bottom pane.

 TIP **Double-click a message listing (officially called a *header*) in the top pane to open the letter in its own window.**

You can change the size of either pane by dragging the divider up or down. You can also change the width of any column in the top pane by dragging the column dividers to the left or right. You can even change the size of the print in which the message appears on your screen and in which it will print.

Follow these steps to change the view in the Inbox:

1. To change the size of the top or bottom pane, place your mouse pointer on the divider; it changes shape as you see in Figure 12-3. Press and hold the mouse button and drag the divider up or down to increase the size of either pane.

2. To change the width of a column, place your mouse pointer on a column divider. In Figure 12-3, it's on the Subject column divider. The mouse pointer changes shape. Drag the column divider to the right or left to change the column width.

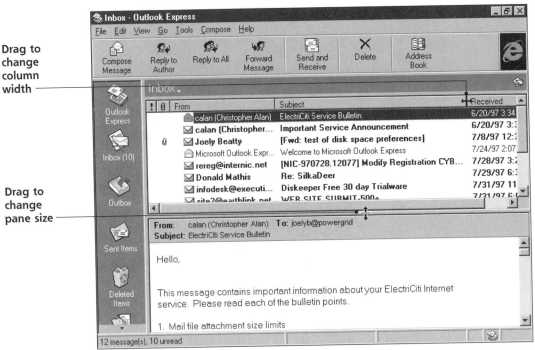

Drag to change column width ————

Drag to change pane size ————

Figure 12-3 Change the size of the preview pane or columns by dragging the dividers.

3. To change the size of the print that you see on your screen, click ⟨View⟩ in the menu bar, and then click ⟨Font⟩. A second menu with font sizes appears. Click the appropriate size. The size of the message font in the preview pane changes. It's kind of cool that the size of the font in the printed message also reflects the choice you make here.

Figuring Out What You've Got

The icons, or little pictures, you see in the Inbox are pretty easy to understand, but just for the sake of clarification, Table 12-1 shows a summary.

TABLE 12-1 Inbox icons

Icon	Indicates
!	The message has been marked high priority by the sender.
↓	The message has been marked low priority by the sender.
0	The message has an attachment.

Icon	Indicates
✉	This message has not been read. The message listing appears in bold type.
✉	This message has been read. The message listing appears in light type.

Sorting Messages

When your snail mail (mail sent through the post office) is delivered, you sort through it to see if you got that refund from the IRS or, if you're like us, how many bills came today. You can sort your e-mail too. There are two ways to sort your mail:

* Method #1: Click a column heading to sort by that item. For example, click the Received column heading to sort by date, as shown in Figure 12-4. Click until you see a ▲ to show the earliest date at the top of the list and the most recent date at the bottom. Or click until you see a ▼ to show the most recent date at the top of the list.

Figure 12-4 Click the Received column heading to sort by date.

* Method #2: Click **View** → **Sort By** and then choose how you want your messages arranged.

"Yes, I Accept the $10,000,000"

When Ed McMahon sends you e-mail saying you've won the $10,000,000 sweepstakes prize if you send your response in by April 10, you certainly want to respond as quickly as possible. Fortunately, responding to e-mail is a piece of cake. Outlook Express even addresses the letter for you.

Follow these steps to respond to an e-mail letter:

1. Click to highlight the letter.

2. Click the Reply to Author button in the toolbar. A Compose Message window, shown in Figure 12-5, opens with the To: line and the Subject: line already filled in.

3. Remember the following:

* Add names to the To: line or the Cc: line by clicking the card file icon. The Select Recipients dialog box appears and you can select names, as you learned in Chapter 10, "Setting Up Your Address Book."

* If appropriate, choose a priority rating for this letter by clicking the e-stamp icon in the right corner of your response letter.

* You can also see a vCard icon in Figure 12-5, which you learned how to create and include with your e-mail in Chapter 10. Click the vCard icon to delete it. Or, you can open it if you don't remember what information you included in it.

* Figure 12-5 also shows an icon in a bottom pane of the letter. This is what you'll see if you chose the option *not* to include the original letter in your response, which we recommend. Since the recipient doesn't see this icon and there are 0 bytes (meaning there is nothing attached or associated with it), it makes no sense to us that it's there. Just ignore it.

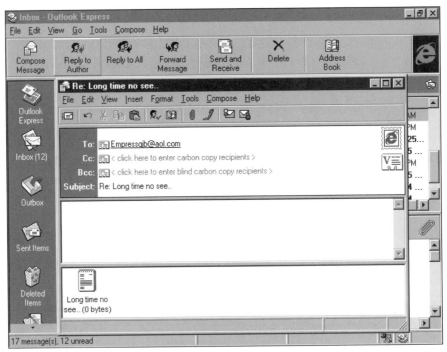

Figure 12-5 Click Reply to Author to respond to an e-mail letter.

4. Complete the letter and send it now or later (as discussed in Chapter 11, "Writing an E-Mail Letter.") If you chose the option to always spellcheck your letters, that will happen before it gets sent or put in the Outbox.

NOTE If the original message was sent to you and several other people, you can respond to all of them at once by clicking the Reply to All button. This will put all the original recipients in your To: line and all the original Cc recipients in your Cc: line. This way, everyone is kept in the loop.

To Quote or Not to Quote, That Is the Question

We recommend that you *don't* include the original message in your e-mail. It adds unnecessary length to your mail, takes longer to upload and download, and doesn't necessarily contribute to the exchange. Quoting can be helpful when you want to refer to a specific part of the original message. It's very effective to quote a specific comment and respond to it, then quote another comment and respond—much more effective than showing the whole letter at the end of yours. Unfortunately, Outlook Express doesn't let you quote a portion of the original letter but we'll show you how to work around that.

12

Don't include the entire text of the original message when you reply to e-mail. Instead, quote selected lines.

Follow these steps to quote just a piece of the original letter:

1. With the original letter open, drag your mouse pointer over the text you want to highlight, just as you would do in your word processing program (see Figure 12-6).

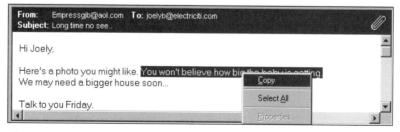

Figure 12-6 Copy relevant text instead of including the entire original letter in your response.

2. Right-click the highlighted text and click `Copy` on the shortcut menu.

3. Click Reply to Author to open the response.

4. Right-click your mouse pointer in the message section and then click `Paste` on the shortcut menu.

5. Insert the > by hand to the left of each line, as shown in Figure 12-7. If you're quoting several lines of text, try putting a line of asterisks above and below the quoted text instead of adding the > in front of each line.

Sharon, you said

> You won't believe how big the baby is getting.

No kidding! What are you feeding that child?

Figure 12-7 Type a > in front of each line of quoted text.

6. To quote another section of the original letter, minimize your response letter by clicking ▬. Highlight another phrase or sentence in the original letter and copy it. Then enlarge your response letter and copy the new material into it.

"See, Mom, I Won $10,000,000!"

When you get that letter from Ed McMahon, you can forward it to your mother so she can see it. When you forward a letter, it is included in your response. You type your comments above it.

Follow these steps to forward a letter to another person:

1. With the original letter open on your screen, click the Forward Message button on the toolbar. A Compose Message window appears with the subject line filled in and the original message in the bottom pane of your response (see Figure 12-8).

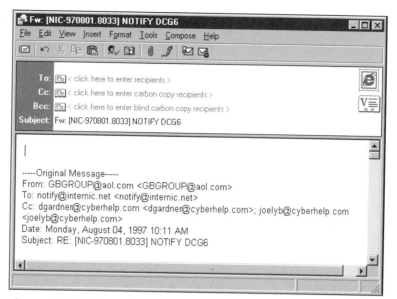

Figure 12-8 A forwarded message includes the complete text of the original.

2. Complete the address portion of the letter as you normally do. You can even edit the subject line by clicking it and then using regular editing procedures to revise it.

3. Type your message above the "Original Message," and then send it as you normally do. If the original message includes an attachment, the attachment will appear in a third pane (as in Figure 12-5). The new recipient will receive the attachment along with your letter.

Saving a Letter

Outlook Express lets you get as organized as you want to be. You can copy mail to a special folder or even move it to the folder.

Follow these steps to move a letter to a special folder:

1. Right-click the message listing in the top pane, and then click Move to on the shortcut menu. The Move dialog box appears as shown in Figure 12-9.

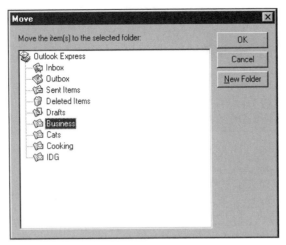

Figure 12-9 Move (or copy) a letter to a special folder.

2. Click the folder where you want to send the letter, and then click OK. The letter is moved to that folder.

NOTE While you are in the Move or Copy dialog box shown in Figure 12-9, you can create special folders as you need them. The process is much like creating a folder in Explorer. If you want to make the folder a main folder, click Outlook Express to highlight it. If you want to make the new folder a subfolder of another topic, click the folder you want it to go under. Now click the New Folder button and type the name of the new folder in the New Folder dialog box that appears.

Dealing with Attachments

A paper clip to the left of a letter means that there is an attachment to the letter. The attachment can be a file, such as a word processing document or a spreadsheet, or it can be a graphic. If the attachment is a graphic, Outlook Express displays it within the letter, which is very cool. If it's a file, you have to open it to see it.

Follow these steps to view and save attachments:

1. Click the message header in the top pane to open the letter in the preview pane.

2. Click the paper-clip icon on the right of the header bar (see Figure 12-10). A label appears with the name of the file and its type. The attachment in Figure 12-10 is a graphic file (.gif) and has a picture icon to the left of the name. If this were a document, you'd see an open-envelope icon.

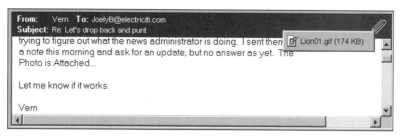

Figure 12-10 Click the paper clip, and then click the label to show or save the attachment.

3. Click the label. An Open Attachment Warning appears. Notice that "Save it to disk" is already selected.

4. Click OK. A Save As dialog box appears. Before you save the file, be sure to choose the appropriate file type in the lower part of the Save As dialog box if it is not already selected.

X-REF See the Bonus in Chapter 14, "Displaying and Saving Graphics in Newsgroups," to learn more about working with graphic files.

Writing Richly

You can write your letters in "rich text," or HTML-formatted text. This means that you can make your text bold, underlined, or in color. You can make numbered or bulleted lists and even add a picture or an active link to a Web site that will take your reader directly to the site. That's the good news. The bad news is that not everyone is able to read rich text, so all your efforts will be wasted if your reader can't see the formatting. Frankly, we recommend that you *not* send e-mail in HTML-formatted text unless you know for a fact that the recipient can read it. Check the Send tab in the View→Options dialog box to see if you selected HTML or plain text for your mail sending option. If you select plain text, you can still create an HTML letter. We'll show you how.

TIP The General tab in the Options dialog box has another option you might want to check. In the middle of the list is the option to "Reply to messages using the format in which they were sent." If you leave this option selected and you receive a message formatted in HTML, you'll automatically open a reply window set up to create rich text. A rich-text message can be three or four times the size of the same message in plain text. If you file copies of your letters, you'll use up a lot more disk space with an HTML message than with a plain-text message. If you leave this option unchecked, you can still choose to create an HTML message when appropriate.

Follow these steps to compose a message in rich text:

1. Click Reply to Author (or the Compose Message button). These steps work in any of the Compose Message windows.

2. Click **Format** in the menu bar, and then click **Rich Text (HTML)**. The window changes to show a formatting toolbar, as shown in Figure 12-11. If you maximize the window, you'll be able to see the entire formatting toolbar. We won't show you how to use these formatting tools here because you'll learn about them in more detail in Chapter 19, "Creating and Publishing Your Web Page."

Figure 12-11 The formatting toolbar for HTML messages.

Cleaning House

Unless you're a compulsive pack rat, you don't need to save every piece of mail you receive. In fact, you'll probably receive your fair share of junk e-mail and want to dump it as quickly as possible.

Follow these steps to delete messages:

1. Highlight the message(s) you want to delete.

2. Right-click a highlighted message, and then click **Delete**. The message is sent to the Deleted Items trash bin.

3. Right-click the Delete Items icon on the Outlook bar and click **Empty Folder**. If you want to check what's in the folder before you empty it, click the folder to display the contents. Then you can decide to empty the folder or move a specific letter back to another folder.

I Don't Want to See Mail From *Him*!

Although it's easy enough to move mail from one folder to another, you can set up a filter that will inspect the mail as you receive it and automatically file it in the folder of your choice. Or, if you get nuisance mail from a specific source, you can send it to the trash can without ever having to see it. You can even elect to delete it off the server.

Setting Up the Filter

Think of the filter it as an electronic traffic cop and you get to set up the traffic rules! Use the Inbox Assistant to create the rules.

Follow these steps to set up filters for your incoming mail:

1. Click <kbd>Tools</kbd> → <kbd>Inbox Assistant</kbd> to open the Inbox Assistant dialog box.

2. The very first time you open the Inbox Assistant, the only button that is activated is the Add button. Click the Add button. The Properties dialog box shown in Figure 12-12 appears.

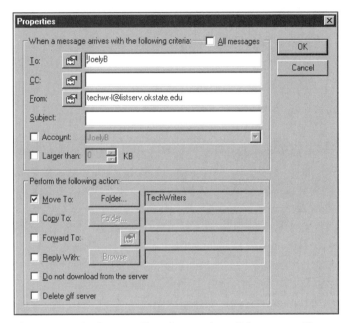

Figure 12-12 Create a filter that sends mail from a specific source to a specific folder.

3. This filter was created to identify mail sent to JoelyB from a mailing list (Tech Writers) and put it in the TechWriters folder. Notice that you can use your Address Book to enter a name in the From: box. Or, you can type in the name of someone new, a spammer or junk e-mailer, for example. Select the elements of the filter you want to create.

4. Click OK.

Applying the Filter

Now that you've created your filter, you can apply it to the mail already in your Inbox.

Follow these steps to apply a filter:

1. Highlight the filter you want to apply.

2. Click **Apply To**. The Select Folder dialog box appears.

3. Click the Inbox icon to apply this rule to all of the mail in the Inbox.

4. Click OK.

Did It Work?

Now you get to check the results of the filter. Pick one of these methods to switch to another folder (see Figure 12-13).

✳ Click the folder icon in the Outlook bar.

   or

✳ Click the Inbox button to open a list of folders and then click the appropriate folder.

Figure 12-13 Switch to another folder by clicking its icon in the Outlook bar or selecting the folder from the menu.

BONUS

Two for the Price of One

Y ou can set up Outlook Express for more than one mail or news account. For example, if you have a personal account and a business account, you can set up Outlook Express to get mail for both accounts and then set up a filter to sort them into separate folders.

Follow these steps to set up a second mail account:

1. Open Outlook Express.

2. Click **Tools** in the menu bar and then click **Accounts**. The Internet Accounts dialog box appears (see Figure 12-14).

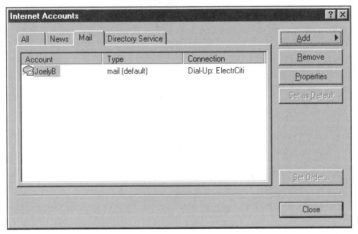

Figure 12-14 Click Tools→Accounts to set up multiple mail accounts.

3. Click the Mail tab (to add a mail account).

4. Click the Add button and then click Mail. The Internet Connection Wizard appears. Follow the Wizard through the process of setting up a second mail account.

Summary

I f you don't have an e-mail account these days, you're definitely out of the loop. More and more business is being done online, and having an e-mail account lets you keep in touch with friends and family all over the world. E-mail has brought back the art of letter writing, with a new electronic flavor. You don't have to wait days for snail mail to be delivered to your home. You can send and receive e-mail in seconds. You can, with a click of your mouse, reply to a message, forward a message, and send a reply to all recipients of a message. Filing messages is a snap and you can even have your mail sorted as you receive it.

SUBSCRIBING TO NEWSGROUPS

13

Newsgroups are among the most interesting and popular options on the Internet. In addition to being called newsgroups, they are also referred to as discussion groups, Usenet news, Net news, and Internet news.

If the concept of newsgroups is new to you, you may be surprised to discover that they do not contain "news," although there are newsgroups that discuss current events. They can best be described as worldwide discussion groups or bulletin boards in which people post and read messages on specific topics. It's impossible to get an accurate count of newsgroups because new ones come into existence every day, but as of this writing it's safe to say there are more than 22,000 newsgroups worldwide. Newsgroups are organized by subject and there is probably at least one newsgroup for any topic you can imagine.

You can add a newsgroup to your reading list if you know the address (name) of the newsgroup. Or, you can search for a newsgroup by topic and then add it to your list. In addition to walking you through the search capabilities within Internet Explorer, we'll introduce you to a Web site that will search through over 15,000 newsgroups, show you those that match a topic of your choosing, and give you the opportunity to check out the messages.

X-REF If you haven't already done so, read the section in Chapter 9 on setting up e-mail. The processes described in the e-mail chapters also apply to newsgroup mail, so you may want to read Chapters 10 and 11 as well.

Getting Ready to Subscribe to a Newsgroup

Before you can subscribe to a newsgroup you have to let Outlook Express know where to get your newsgroup messages. In other words, you have to set up a news server. This is the same process you did in Chapter 9, "Setting Up E-mail," when you set up your mail server.

You Say Potayto and I Say Potahto

You should be online and in Outlook Express, so if you're not already there click the Launch Outlook Express icon in the Quick Launch toolbar. As you've discovered, Internet Explorer is completely customizable. What happens when you open Outlook Express depends on whether you're already online or not. It also depends on whether you have it set up to dial automatically or to ask if you want to dial into your ISP. You can also set up Outlook Express itself to look exactly the way you want; consequently, your opening screen for Outlook Express may look different from the example we show.

Setting Up Your News Server

Outlook Express has a wizard that will walk you through the process of setting up your news server, but there's one detail you need to have handy before you start the process. You need the exact name of the Internet news (NNTP) server that your ISP uses. Check the materials from your ISP or call them for the name. Once you have that information, you're all set to go.

Follow these steps to set up your news server:

1. Click Tools in the menu bar and then click Accounts . The Internet Accounts dialog box appears.

2. Click the News tab to bring it to the front of the dialog box.

3. Click the Add button and then click News on the menu that appears. See Figure 13-1. The Internet Connection Wizard appears.

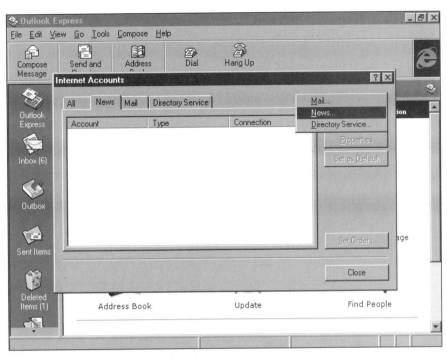

Figure 13-1 Before you can subscribe to a newsgroup, you must set up a news server.

4. As each Internet Connection Wizard dialog box appears, fill in the following information then click the Next button to go to the next screen.

* Your Name-Enter your real name or an online "handle."

* Internet News E-mail Address-Enter your regular e-mail address.

* Internet News Server Name-Enter the exact name of the news server. With our ISP, it's simply called "news," but your ISP may use something else. If your news server requires you to log on, your ISP will give you an NNTP acount name and password.

* Friendly Name-This is a name you choose to identify this particular news server. This name will also appear under the icon for newsgroups in the Outlook bar, so don't make it very long. We suggest "Newsgroups" or "News."

* Choose Connection Type-Click the appropriate choice. If you're using your home computer, click "Connect using my phone line" if it's not already selected. If you're at work, check with your LAN administator.

* Dial-Up Connection-Your ISP should already be listed, so click "Use an existing dial-up connection." Your ISP's name is highlighted. Click Next to go on.

* Congratulations-You're done! Click the Finish button.

5. When the Wizard closes, you go back to the Internet Accounts dialog box. Your news server shows on the News tab. Click the Close button.

6. When you close the Internet Accounts dialog box, the Outlook Express message shown in Figure 13-2 appears. Click Yes to download a list of available newsgroups.

TIP   Downloading the list of available newsgroups takes a few minutes, so if you don't want to take the time right now, click No. When you're ready, come back to Outlook Express and click Go in the menu bar and then click News. You see a message box asking if you want to view a list of available newsgroups. Click Yes. This brings you right back to the results of step 6 above. Carry on with "So Many Newsgroups to Choose From . . . So Little Time" below.

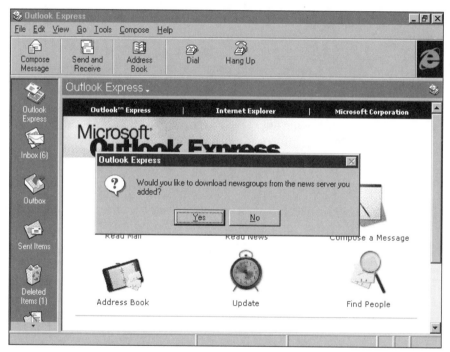

Figure 13-2   After you set up your news server, you can see the list of available newsgroups.

You're almost ready to embark on your newsgroup adventure. There's just one thing more you need to know—proper etiquette on the Net, or *netiquette* as it's called online.

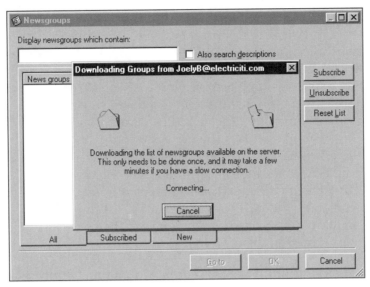

Figure 13-3 Downloading available newsgroups.

So Many Newsgroups to Choose From . . . So Little Time

Thousands of sites, or servers, around the world carry newsgroups. They range from individual computers that may host a single newsgroup to universities that may carry a few dozen newsgroups to commercial services that list thousands of newsgroups. The newsgroups to which you have access are determined by your ISP because the ISP links to, or hosts, the servers. With over 22,000 newsgroups in existence and new ones being added every day, no one news host can list all newsgroups, but your ISP probably provides a connection to many of them.

There are over 22,000 newsgroups in existence.

As the news server downloads the list of available newsgroups, your computer screen should look like the one in Figure 13-3. As the message says, this only needs to be done once, but may take a few minutes depending on the speed of your modem. If you're easily amused, you can watch the flying pages. We suggest you take a stretch break. In fact, drink a glass of water; it's good for you. When you come back, the Newsgroups window will be filled with names. Scroll through the list to see what they look like. Our news server downloaded close to 7,000 newsgroup names. If your server is similar, the list will be quite long. Don't think you have to scroll through the whole thing to find a newsgroup. We'll show you how to subscribe to one in the next section.

The mail for newsgroups is located in Outlook Express along with other e-mail because newsgroup members use e-mail to communicate. There is a big difference between regular e-mail and newsgroup mail, however. Regular e-mail is like a letter sent from one person to another. Newsgroup mail is like a notice posted to a "bulletin board" where, quite literally, *anyone* can read it.

You can go to Outlook Express from anywhere in Internet Explorer; it doesn't matter what's on your screen when you click the Launch Outlook Express icon on the Quick Launch toolbar.

NOTE You should be online if you're following along with this chapter on your computer. If you're not already online, when you do Step 1 below you may see a Connection dialog box or an Outlook Express dialog box asking if you want to connect to the server. Do whatever it takes to connect.

Follow these steps to open Outlook Express if it's not already on your screen:

1. Click 🎴 in the taskbar to launch Outlook Express.

2. When Outlook Express opens, you have two ways to get to newsgroups, as shown in Figure 13-4.

   ✳ Click the icon for newsgroups in the Outlook bar. You may have to scroll down the list in the Outlook bar before you see the Newsgroup icon. In this example, it is named "Newsgroups." You selected the name for this icon back in Chapter 9 when you set up your news server.

   ✳ Click   Go   in the menu bar, and then click   News .

Use the
Go menu

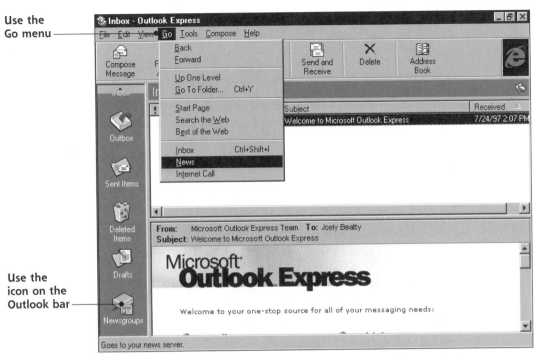

Use the
icon on the
Outlook bar

Figure 13-4 You have two ways of getting to newsgroups from Outlook Express.

Outlook Express, being the very smart critter that it is, knows that you're not subscribed to (signed up for) any newsgroups and will ask you the question shown in Figure 13-5. Choose Yes.

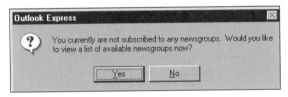

Figure 13-5 Choose Yes.

When You Know What You Want

With over 22,000 newsgroups worldwide, there's probably one for almost any interest you can name. Your news server, however, won't carry all of them so you may not be able to find something if it's especially esoteric or, let's be frank, weird. If you're new to newsgroups, you probably don't have a clue what newsgroups you want to join, so we'll show you how to search for one.

If you know the address of a newsgroup, subscribing is incredibly easy. By the way, if you like animals, check out the newsgroup shown in this example (alt.binaries.pictures.animals). Contributors send in some beautiful pictures.

Follow these steps to subscribe to a newsgroup when you know its name:

1. Enter the address of the newsgroup in the "Display newsgroups which contain" text box, as shown in Figure 13-6. After a brief pause, the name of the newsgroup will appear in the bottom part of the dialog box.

2. Click the name of the newsgroup to highlight it.

3. Click the Subscribe button to subscribe. Notice the little newspaper icon that appears to the left of the name. That's it! What could be easier?

4. If you want to search for a newsgroup by subject (covered in the next section), highlight the newsgroup title in the upper text box and delete it.

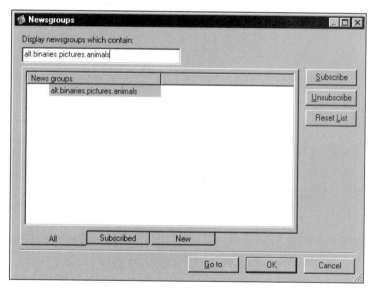

Figure 13-6 Type the newsgroup address and click the Subscribe button.

Searching for a Newsgroup By Subject

If you took the opportunity to scroll through the list of newsgroups, you noticed that the subjects are divided into major headings such as "alt" for alternative, "comp" for computer, "rec" for recreation, and "soc" for sociology and psychology. It's often pretty hard to tell much about a newsgroup from its name. If you don't know a newsgroup you'd like to join, you can search for one by subject.

Follow these steps to search by newsgroup subject:

1. Click the All tab at the bottom of the dialog box if it isn't already in front.

2. Type a subject in the "Display newsgroups which contain" text box, as shown in Figure 13-7. After a brief pause, a list of newsgroups will appear in the lower part of the dialog box.

3. Click a newsgroup that interests you and then click the Subscribe button. You can subscribe to as many newsgroups as interest you, but from a practical perspective don't go crazy and subscribe to lots of newsgroups in the same subject category because you'll have tons of messages to go through. If you don't like a newsgroup, you can always unsubscribe and try another one.

4. If you want to check out more subjects, delete the original subject and repeat the process.

5. Click the Subscribed tab at the bottom of the dialog box. You'll see a list of newsgroups to which you've subscribed.

6. When you've subscribed to the newsgroups you want, click the OK button to close the newsgroup dialog box. The Newsgroups folder is open on your screen and the newsgroups to which you subscribed are listed.

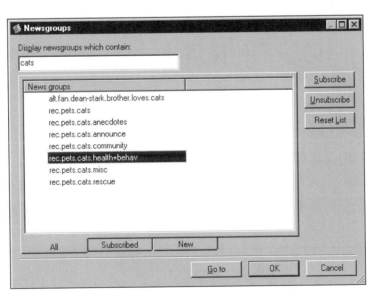

Figure 13-7 You can search for newsgroups by subject.

Look Before You Leap

If you already know how to read newsgroups, you'll like the handy Go to button at the bottom of the Newsgroups dialog box. After you've searched for a newsgroup by subject, click an interesting newsgroup in the resulting list and then click the Go to button. The messages will be displayed as shown in the figure below.

If, after browsing through the messages, you want to subscribe to the newsgroup you can do it directly from the list:

1. Right-click the newsgroup icon on the right of the Folder bar.

2. Click   Subscribe to this Group . (If you hid the Folder bar back in Chapter 9, use   Tools → Subscribe to this newsgroup   to subscribe.)

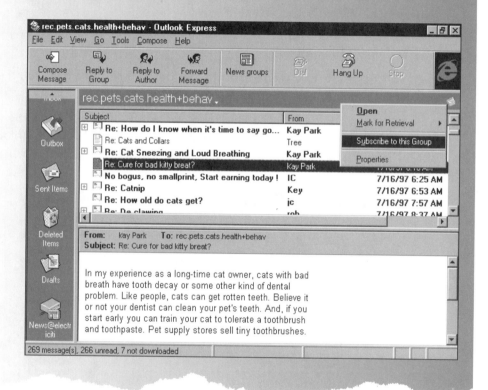

Deleting a Newsgroup

I f you're new to newsgroups, you may want to skip ahead to Chapter 14, "Participating in Newsgroups," to learn how one works before you worry about unsubscribing. Presuming you've checked out the newsgroup and decided you don't like it or for some other reason don't want it on your list, unsubscribing is a piece of cake. Just follow the steps in any of the three methods described below.

Method #1:

1. If the Newsgroups folder is not already on your screen, click the Newsgroups button in the Outlook bar or click `Go` → `News`.

2. Right-click the newsgroup listing, as shown in Figure 13-8, and then click `Unsubscribe from this newsgroup`.

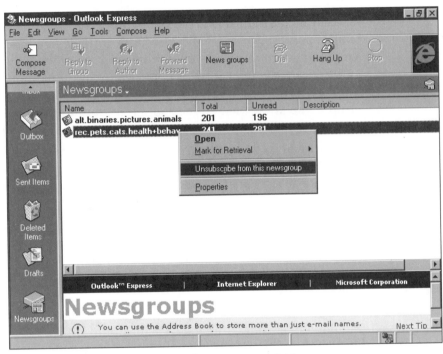

Figure 13-8 Unsubscribe while in the Newsgroups folder.

Method #2:

1. You can unsubscribe from within the newsgroup. After you've opened the newsgroup, right-click the Newsgroups icon on the right of the Folder bar. See the figure in the Side Trip for the location of the Newsgroups icon.

2. Now click `Unsubscribe from this newsgroup` on the shortcut menu.

Method #3:

1. Click the Newsgroups icon in the toolbar to open the Newsgroups list.

2. Click the Subscribed tab to bring it to the front.

3. Click the name of the newsgroup you want to delete and then click `Unsubscribe`.

Netiquette Is More Than a Weird Word

With today's technology, the phrase "when in Rome" is more appropriately rephrased "when in cyberspace." To be a good citizen of cyberspace, or a *netizen,* you need to know the rules. If you violate the rules, you're likely to get *flamed,* which means you get messages from people who are unhappy with you and the content of your e-mail. Flames are more than polite disagreement. They contain pointed criticism and on occasion can be downright nasty. Here is some food for thought on netiquette:

* There is no guarantee that regular e-mail is private, and newsgroup mail is purposely very public. Don't say *anything* in e-mail or newsgroup correspondence that you wouldn't say to someone's face with a roomful of witnesses listening. Some people seem to feel that anonymity comes with a screen name and behave in ways they would never consider with people who know them. Cyberspace is a community. If you want to be welcomed, behave as you would with your coworkers and friends.

* Be concise and to the point. Stream of consciousness may have sold the works of James Joyce, but online readers don't appreciate it. Include a very clear subject line to give readers a good idea of what your message is about.

* Although IE 4 allows you to format e-mail with hypertext (see Part 5: Creating HTML Documents with Composer), newsgroups are text-based. Therefore, readers won't be able to see bold type, italics, color, large fonts, etc. Use keyboard symbols, such as the asterisk, to *emphasize* specific words.

* Typing a SINGLE word in capital letters can be used to add emphasis, but don't type your entire message in capital letters. TYPING IN CAPITALS IS CONSIDERED TO BE THE SAME AS YELLING AND IS RUDE!

* In a personal conversation, your tone of voice and body language give as much meaning to your statements as do the words themselves. In e-mail, your reader doesn't have anything other than the words to convey meaning. Use humor judiciously because, without the nonverbal cues of tone of voice and body language, humor can be interpreted as sarcasm. Many people use smileys, also called emoticons (pronounced ee *mo* tih cons), to add the smile or shrug that would be part of a personal conversation. Instead of a smiley, you can include words such as *smile, wink,* and *sigh* in parentheses after a statement to convey feelings. Not that WE have any problems being perfectly clear in our written communications (just kidding).

 X-REF See the Bonus in Chapter 9, "Showing Your Emotions" for more details on smileys.

* If you quote someone directly, use the person's name. For example, "In his post of March 24, John Smith said:" Use the quoting feature contained in IE 4 to quote only a small portion of the original post. Many people consider quoting (including) the entire original post in your response to be in bad form because it takes up bandwidth (space on the airwaves) and crowds people's mailboxes with unnecessarily long letters.

* End your post with your real name. It makes the communication much more of a "letter from a friend."

* Include your e-mail address at the end of your message. Some ISPs don't always relay the personal address in addition to the address of the newsgroup itself, making it difficult for someone to send you a personal reply. See Chapter 9 to learn how to create a signature file that automatically includes your name and e-mail address.

BONUS

Getting Around Your News Server

If you didn't find what you wanted in the Subscribe to Discussion Groups dialog box, you'll love this bonus section! The list of newsgroups that appears in the Newsgroups dialog box depends on those carried by your ISP. If your ISP doesn't carry a particular newsgroup, call them and ask about it. However, they have to pay for the servers they host and may be unwilling to add more servers. You can add a server to the one you already have, but you too have to pay for it so we don't recommend that unless you're a newsgroup addict.

Several Web sites allow you to search for a newsgroup by subject. You can't subscribe to the newsgroup if it's not on your server, but you can check out the messages. AltaVista, shown in Figure 13-9, is a great place to start. The topic "organic gardening" didn't produce any results when we looked for it in the Outlook Express newsgroups list, but there were several matches in AltaVista.

Follow these steps to search for a newsgroup by subject:

1. Click the Launch Internet Explorer Browser icon on the Quick Launch toolbar to open the browser.

2. Click the Search button in the toolbar. The Search pane shown in Figure 13-7 appears on the left of your screen.

3. Click the down arrow to the right of the Select provider box and click AltaVista.

4. Click Usenet in the Search line.

5. Type a subject in the Search box.

6. Click **Submit**. A list of articles that contain your search word appears.

7. Hold the mouse pointer over an article name. (Newsgroup messages are also called *articles* or *posts*.) A pop-up label appears with the name of the newsgroup and the full name of the article. See Figure 13-10 for an example.

8. If the article interests you, click the name. The article appears in the right pane. Expand the pane if you want more space in which to read.

9. Click the link for the newsgroup name in the article to go back to the Newsgroup window in Outlook Express. If your server actually does carry it, the newsgroup will appear. If your ISP does not carry it, you'll get a message to that effect. It's worth a try.

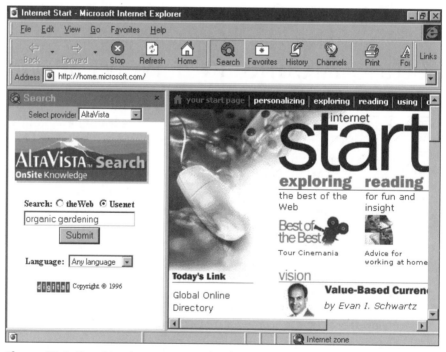

Figure 13-9 Searching for newsgroups in AltaVista.

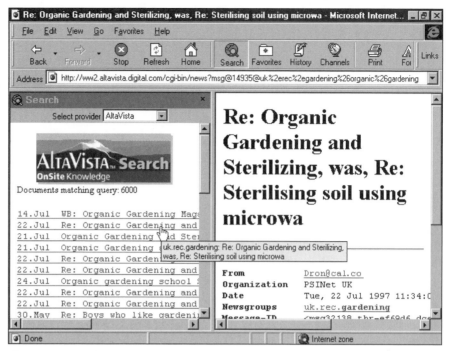

Figure 13-10 The pop-up label helps when you read newsgroup articles in AltaVista.

Summary

I n this chapter you've learned how to subscribe to a newsgroup when you know the address. You've also learned how to search for a newsgroup in Internet Explorer and how to use Web pages to search by subject.

If you decide that reading a particular newsgroup is not a worthwhile use of your time, you can delete it easily.

If you subscribed to a couple of newsgroups and you're really looking forward to reading all your messages, go right on to Chapter 14, "Participating in Newsgroups." There you learn all about threads, how to send your response to the entire newsgroup (so it can be read by the whole world) or just to the original author of the message, and how to download interesting graphics from newsgroups.

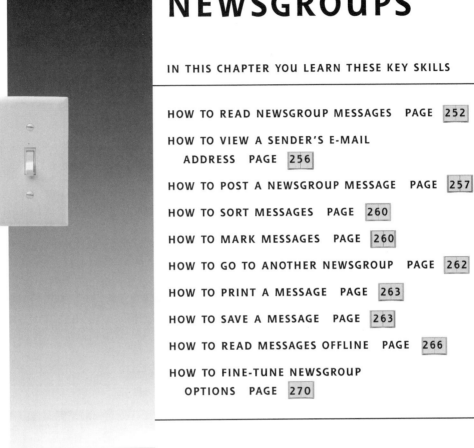

CHAPTER FOURTEEN

PARTICIPATING IN NEWSGROUPS

IN THIS CHAPTER YOU LEARN THESE KEY SKILLS

14

Some newsgroups have thousands of messages and there's little likelihood that you'll want to or have the time to read them all. And, let's face it, some newsgroup messages and threads are total drivel. (Not mine or yours, of course!) Internet Explorer gives you lots of options for making the number of messages more manageable. You can sort messages by subject or sender, for example. You can mark messages and entire threads as read so that they won't keep showing up. This chapter will introduce you to some of the ways to manage the messages in your newsgroups.

Getting the Latest News

I f you're following along with the chapters in this book, you've subscribed to some newsgroups. Here's your chance to check them out.

If you imagine a tree with large branches leading to small branches and then even smaller branches, you already understand how newsgroups are structured. Except that in newsgroups, the branches are called *threads*. One person sends in a message on a specific topic. Other people respond to the message or article, creating a thread or conversation. Sometimes people respond to the responses, creating the third level of the thread.

Follow these steps to open a newsgroup (you should be in Outlook Express, so if you're not, click the Launch Outlook Express icon on the Quick Launch toolbar):

1. If the list of newsgroups is not already on your screen, click the Newsgroups button on the Outlook bar. The Newsgroups folder appears on your screen, with your newsgroups listed as shown in Figure 14-1. Notice the number of total and unread messages to the right of the newsgroup name.

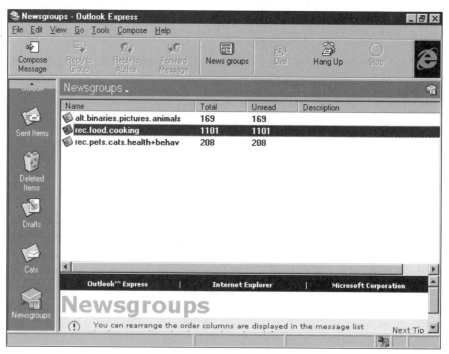

Figure 14-1 Go to the Newsgroups folder, and then double-click the newsgroup you want to read.

2. Double-click the newsgroup you want to read. Depending on the number of messages, it may take a little while to download the messages the very first time you open a newsgroup.

A Split Personality

When you open the newsgroup, the top pane shows the various messages within the newsgroup and the bottom pane, or preview pane, shows the highlighted message. You can expand either pane by dragging the divider up or down. If a message has responses, meaning it is part of a thread, you'll see a + sign to the left of the subject. Notice that the sender, newsgroup, and subject are shown in the bottom pane.

Follow these steps to read a message:

1. Scroll through the list of messages in the top portion of the screen as shown in Figure 14-2. When you find a subject that interests you, click the message subject. The message appears in the bottom portion of the window.

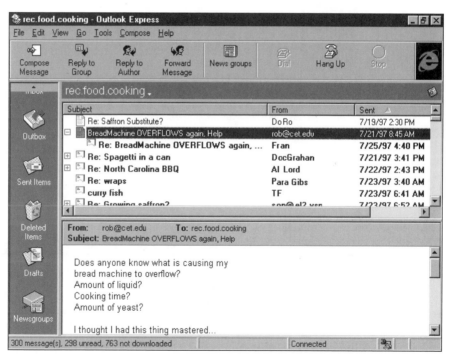

Figure 14-2 Click a newsgroup message in the top pane and read it in the bottom pane.

2. A + sign to the left of the message means there are responses to this message. Click the + sign to open the list of responses, and then click a response to read it.

NOTE Notice that unread messages appear in bold, or darker, type. When a message is read, the type becomes lighter. Also, the icon to the left of an unread message is a partial page. When you read the message, the icon becomes a full page.

Reading a Message in Its Own Window

If you get tired of having to scroll through the message in the bottom pane, you can make the message appear in its own window.

Follow these steps to read a message in its own window:

1. Double-click the listing in the top pane. The message appears in its own window, as shown in Figure 14-3.

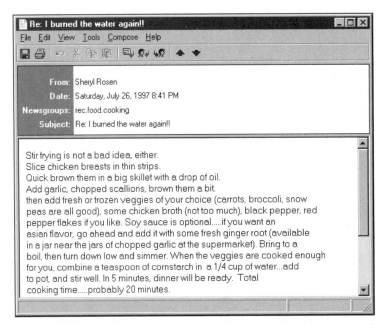

Figure 14-3 Double-click a message listing to open it in its own window.

2. Click ⬜ to see the window full screen.

3. When you're through with the message, click ⌧. You are back at the newsgroup listing.

SEEING THE BIG PICTURE

If you find you like reading your messages in the full-screen view, you don't have to close the window to see the next message. Use View→Next to select the next message to appear in the window. You can also use the up arrow on the toolbar to see previous messages, and the down arrow to see the next message, or use the keyboard commands shown in Table 14-1.

TABLE 14-1 Use keyboard commands to see messages in a maximized window

To see	Use this keyboard command
NEXT MESSAGE	Ctrl+>
PREVIOUS MESSAGE	Ctrl+<
NEXT UNREAD MESSAGE	Ctrl+U
NEXT UNREAD THREAD	Ctrl+Shift+U

Time Runneth Out

News servers don't carry articles forever. Each one has its own policy about how long an individual message remains on the server. If you try to read a message that has expired, you'll see the message shown in Figure 14-4. Simply click OK and go on to the next message you want to read.

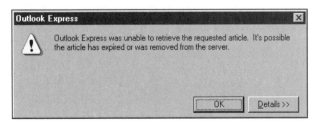

Figure 14-4 Each server has its own policy about how long individual messages are kept.

Who Is That Masked Man?

Sometimes a sender has set up his newsgroup server account so that it doesn't show his real name or e-mail address. If you see only a nickname, there's no simple way to get the e-mail address. Even if you click Reply to Author, the Compose Message dialog box lists only the person's nickname (such as Fearless Fred) as opposed to his or her e-mail address (such as F_Doe@myisp.com). There is a way you can see it, however.

Follow these steps to see the sender's e-mail address:

1. Right-click a message listing and then click Properties on the shortcut menu.

2. Click the Details tab in the dialog box that appears. The author's e-mail address is in the From: line unless, of course, he set up his news server to give a false name to foil the spammers.

See the following Side Trip for some tips on protecting your privacy and/or foiling spammers.

SIDE TRIP

"CURSES, FOILED AGAIN!"

Are you old enough to remember when the villian used to say that after being outwitted by Dudley Do-Right? Well, here's a way to outwit villianous spammers. Spammers are people who use specialized software to search through newsgroup messages, chat rooms, and membership directories for e-mail addresses. They then send you *spam* e-mail. If you've been online for even a few weeks, you've undoubtedly experienced the barrage of letters claiming, "Spray Your Fat Away With This Doctor-Endorsed Miracle," or "You Can Quit Your Job Today and Still Make a Million $." Most, if not all, of these are spam, or the electronic equivalent of junk mail. How can you avoid falling into the clutches of these wicked people? One way is to make your e-mail address difficult to use "as is." You can add a totally extraneous word to your e-mail address and include a message to "real" people in your electronic signature or at the bottom of the message to remove the fake portion of the address. For example, add a message to your e-mail that says, "To send me mail, delete "nospam" from my address."

Follow these steps to change your newsgroup persona:

1. Click Tools → Accounts to open the Internet Accounts dialog box.

2. Click the News tab.

3. Click Properties to open the Newsgroups Properties dialog box.

4. On the General tab, edit the User Information to include an extraneous word in the e-mail address. For example, if your e-mail address is "Sally@isp.com," change it to "Sally@nospamisp.com."

5. When someone reads your message in a newsgroup, they'll see your tip at the bottom of your message. When they hit the Reply to Author button, your e-mail address will include "nospam." The reader simply deletes "nospam" from the address and sends the reply on its way.

Adding Your Two Cents to the Conversation

A conversation is always much more fun when you're actively participating in it, rather than simply listening or observing. This is as true in the virtual world of newsgroups as it is in actual interpersonal relationships. Take the time to get involved. Answer someone's question if you can. Send in your own question. Or, simply add your two cents to a conversation. It makes all the difference in how much you get out of a newsgroup.

You can send a message (also called a *post* or an *article*) with a new subject line and start your own conversation, or you can respond to a message already posted. When you respond to a message, you can respond to the entire newsgroup or to the sender who posted the message. Newsgroup mail is e-mail, so be sure to read through Chapters 11 and 12 if you're at all uncomfortable with the process. Pay special attention to the information about quoting from the original message in Chapter 12.

Starting a New Thread

Suppose the rec.food.cooking newsgroup doesn't have any messages about portobello mushrooms and they're your favorite thing in the world. You can start a new conversation or thread in the newsgroup about portobello mushrooms.

Follow these steps to send a new message to a newsgroup about a topic of your choice:

Compose Message

1. Click the Compose Message icon in the toolbar. It doesn't matter what message is selected when you do this. A New Message dialog box appears with the newsgroup name already entered, but with a blank subject line.

2. Enter a new subject line (e.g., "Wanted: Recipes for Portobello Mushrooms").

3. Complete the message as you normally would.

Sending a Reply to the Group

Lurking in the real world is not a very good thing to do. In the virtual world of newsgroups, it simply means that you read the messages without taking an active role in the newsgroup. Lurking can actually be a good thing when you first sign up for a newsgroup. It gives you a feel for the culture of the group (and each group does have its own culture) and a sense of how questions and replies are handled. There will come a time, however, when you want to unveil, as it were, and join the group.

Follow these steps to reply to a message and send your response to the newsgroup so that everyone can read it:

1. While the original message is selected, click the Reply to Group button in the toolbar. A compose message dialog box appears with the newsgroup name filled in and "Re: *original subject*" in the subject line.

2. Complete and send the message as you normally would.

 If you find that your response includes the entire original message, choose Tools→Options, and then go to the Send tab and confirm that the last item on the tab, "Include message in reply," does *not* have a checkmark. See Chapter 13, "Subscribing to Newsgroups," for more details on the Options dialog box.

Sending a Message to the Author

Sometimes you want to send a message to the author and not to the entire newsgroup. (e.g., Sheryl, I lost your recipe for Spanish chicken and rice. I loved it and would greatly appreciate it if you'd send it to me personally.) A private response is an especially good way to deal with a personal disagreement you may have with the author. Although it's totally appropriate to send a professionally worded disagreement about the content of a post to the entire group, sending negative comments about a particular author or post to the entire newsgroup can result in a *flame war,* with people weighing in on one side or the other. Flame wars can be nasty things and are always unnecessary. It's best to keep pointed disagreements private. Think about how you deal with a colleague in a meeting. If your disagreement affects the ongoing conversation, it should probably be said in public. However, if it's more personal in nature (e.g., "I can't believe you didn't support me on that one!"), it's best said in private.

When sending messages to newsgroups, it's best to keep disagreements private, rather than post them to the entire newsgroup, which could result in a flame war.

Follow these steps to send a reply only to the author of a message:

1. While the original message is selected, click the Reply to Author button in the toolbar. A Compose Message dialog box appears with the author's name and the subject line filled in.

2. Complete the message and send it the way you normally do.

Forwarding a Message to an Outsider

If you get a terrific portobello mushroom recipe as a response to your post, you can send it to your sister with a click of your mouse.

Follow these steps to forward a newsgroup message:

1. While the message is selected, click the Forward Message button in the toolbar. The Compose Message dialog box appears with the subject line filled in and the original message in the bottom part of the dialog box (see Figure 14-5).

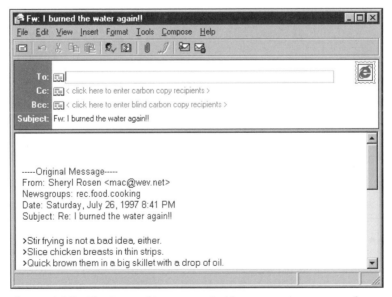

Figure 14-5 The Forward button sends this message to a person of your choice even if they're not in the newsgroup. Edit the original message as you see fit.

2. Enter the name of the person who'll get this message.

3. Change the subject line if you want.

4. Type an introductory sentence or two above the original message to let your sister know what this message is about.

5. Edit the header information from the original message as you see fit.

6. Send the letter as you normally do.

Sorting Messages

You can sort newsgroup messages in a variety of ways. For example, if you've been reading the newsgroup for a while and are familiar with the names of the people who participate, you can search for their posts by name. If you've been busy lately and haven't had a chance to check the newsgroup, you may want to sort by date to see the latest posts. Below, we describe the various ways to sort the messages in a newsgroup. Try out the different methods and see what happens on your screen. Notice that the standard, or default, way that newsgroup messages are sorted is by thread. Notice, too, that the sort method you choose will stay in effect until you change it.

TIP   **A brief note on the way Outlook Express sorts: When you choose to sort by sender, Outlook Express sorts on the name exactly as written, meaning "Jane Smith" will be sorted by J, not S.**

There are two ways to sort messages:

✳ Click View in the menu bar and then click Sort By. Select the appropriate method.

✳ Click the column heading for the method you want. For example, click the Sent heading. The ▼ sorts with most recent dates at the top of the column and the oldest dates at the bottom. The ▲ sorts with the oldest dates at the top of the list and the most recent at the bottom.

Faster Than a Speeding Highlighter Pen

There are several ways to mark a message. You can mark a message you've read as unread. You can even mark a message you haven't read as read. Why would you want to do this? See the following sections. You can also mark a message so that Outlook Express will get it for you later. See the section on reading newsgroup mail offline later in this chapter for details.

I Did, But Let's Say I Didn't

Even after you've read a message you can tell Outlook Express to consider it unread. That way it will stick around longer in the newsgroup. When you mark a message as unread, the bold type will return, but the full-page icon to the left of the message listing won't turn back into an unread half-page icon.

To mark a message as unread, right-click the message and click Mark as Unread on the shortcut menu.

I Didn't, But Let's Say I Did

Even though Outlook Express is set to mark a message as read after you've looked at it for only five seconds, you may not want to bother clicking on each message and waiting for a full five seconds for each one to be marked as read. You, after all, have places to go and things to do. Besides, you can probably tell from the subject line whether you want to bother with the message at all. Or, a message may have an old date, but is still being listed in the newsgroup even though you can't access it. With Outlook Express you can mark a message as read without even clicking on it. In fact, you can mark a whole bunch of messages at the same time. After you mark messages as read, you can tell Outlook Express to show you only unread messages.

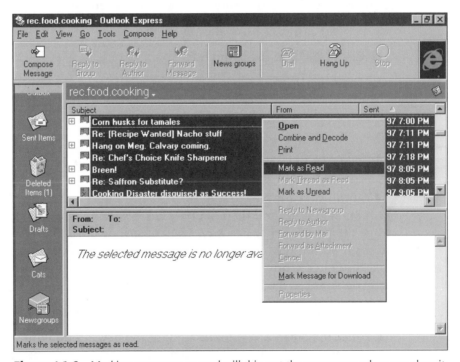

Figure 14-6 Marking messages as read will thin out the newsgroup when you close it.

Follow these steps to mark messages as read:

1. Click the message you want to mark. To mark multiple messages at once (see Figure 14-6), use the standard Windows selection procedures below:

   * Click the first item you want to select.

   * Hold the Shift key on your keyboard and click the last item you want to select. All items between clicks will be selected (highlighted).

   * If you want to select items that are not in a row but are scattered throughout the list, click the first item to highlight it. Hold the Ctrl key on your keyboard and click each item in turn. Each clicked item will be highlighted.

2. Right-click a highlighted message and then click | Mark as Read | on the shortcut menu. (If you selected multiple items and the highlighting disappears when you right-click, it's because you didn't place your mouse pointer on top of one of the highlighted items. You'll have to select the items once again and repeat the process.)

Viewing Only Unread Messages

Outlook Express is set up to show all messages, even those you've already read.

To see only unread messages, do the following:

1. Click | View | in the menu bar.

2. Then click | Current View | → | Unread Messages |. Your screen refreshes itself and shows only unread messages.

Going to Another Newsgroup

You can click the Newsgroups icon in the Outlook bar to go back to the list of newsgroups and then double-click a specific newsgroup to open it. But wait! There's an easier way. The Folder bar of the news reading window contains a button that lists all of the folders in Outlook Express, including the Inbox, the Outbox, any folders you've created, and the individual newsgroups to which you've subscribed.

Follow these steps to go to any other folder in Outlook Express:

1. Click the down arrow to the right of the newsgroup name. A list of folders within Outlook Express appears with the current newsgroup highlighted (see Figure 14-7).

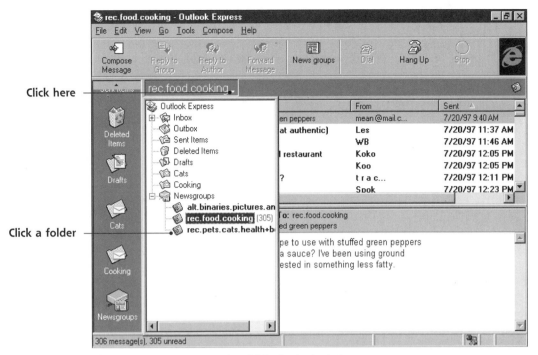

Click here —

Click a folder —

Figure 14-7 Go to any other folder in Outlook Express.

2. Switch to another newsgroup by clicking its name at the bottom of the list.

Printing a Message

To print a message, right-click it and then click Print on the shortcut menu. Unfortunately, Outlook Express prints only the body of the message and does not include any of the identifying header information, such as name, e-mail address, etc. This is very annoying if you want to keep a record of the sender's name. Refer back to the section "Who Is That Masked Man?" to get the person's e-mail address.

Saving a Message

You'll find that newsgroups are a never-ending source of information on all sorts of topics. You'll undoubtedly want to save some of the messages for future reference. There are two ways to save messages.

Saving a Message to a Folder

Saving a message within Outlook Express couldn't be easier. You simply drag and drop it into the appropriate folder. (Click File→Folder→New Folder to create a new folder.)

Follow these steps to save a message to a folder:

1. Click the message you want to save to highlight it.

2. Click the down arrow at the bottom of the Outlook bar until you can see the folder where you want to save the message. We named our folder Cats.

3. Drag the message icon in the top pane onto the folder in the Outlook bar. You'll see a + sign attached to your mouse pointer as you drag (see Figure 14-8).

4. Click your folder in the Outlook Express toolbar to open it and see the messages you've saved.

TIP If you don't like dragging files, click Edit→Copy to Folder, and then select the appropriate folder.

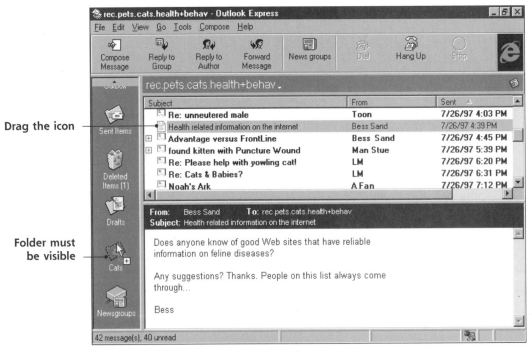

Figure 14-8 Drag a message onto a folder to save it.

Saving a Message as Text

Dragging a message to a folder is incredibly easy; however, it means that you must be in Outlook Express in order to get to the message. You can save the message to any other folder on your computer if you save it as a text file with a .txt extension. You can then open it in your word processing program and have your way with it.

Follow these steps to save a message as a text file:

1. Click the message listing to highlight it.

2. Click **File** → **Save As** to open the Save Message As dialog box you see in Figure 14-9. The default folder in which the message will be saved may be Outlook Express or Windows.

3. Click the down arrow to the right of the Save in box and navigate to the drive and folder where you want to save the message.

4. Rename the file if you want, by typing a new name in the File name box.

5. Click the down arrow to the right of the Save as type box and select Text Files (*.txt) as the file type.

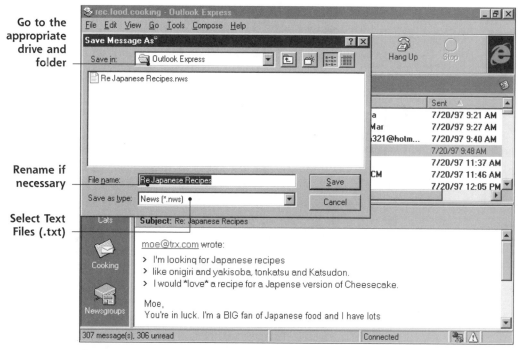

Go to the appropriate drive and folder

Rename if necessary

Select Text Files (.txt)

Figure 14-9   Save a newsgroup message as a text file that can be opened in your word processing program.

6. Click the Save button. You can now use your word processing program to open this file. Remember to change the file type in the Open dialog box to text file. Or, double-click the file in Windows Explorer or My Computer to open it automatically in Notepad.

Reading Messages Offline

Suppose you'll be flying out on a business trip tomorrow or, better still, going on vacation. You have a laptop, but you don't want to spend a long time online while using airport phones and you certainly can't connect while in flight. Never fear, help is here. You can identify selected messages (or the entire newsgroup) and then download them to be read offline. You can now spend your airport and/or flying time productively or entertainingly, as the case may be, without having to be "connected." Reading messages offline involves a two-step process. First, you mark the messages you want to download. Second, you actually download them.

Marking Selected Messages for Download

If you want to follow certain threads or read messages from specific authors, you can mark only those messages for downloading. If you want to download all of the messages, see the next section, "Downloading Messages."

Follow these steps to mark selected messages for downloading for offline reading:

1. Expand the top pane by dragging the divider down. This will let you see many more subject lines (see Figure 14-10).

2. Highlight the messages you want. See the previous steps to mark a message as read in "I Didn't, But Let's Say I Did."

3. Right-click a highlighted message and select Mark Message for Download. Messages will appear with a download arrow to the left of the message listing.

TIP If you change your mind and want to unmark the messages or newsgroups, highlight the appropriate messages first and then right-click a highlighted selection. On the shortcut menu, click Mark for Retrieval→Unmark.

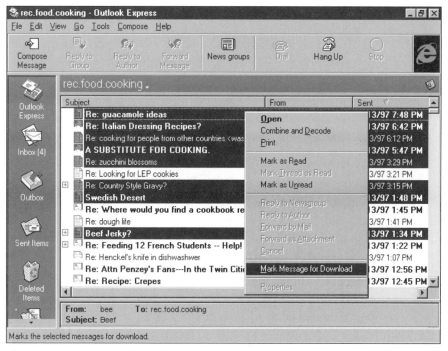

Figure 14-10 Mark only highlighted messages for downloading.

Downloading Messages

In order to read a message offline, you have to have the body of the message available to you. Outlook Express downloads only message headers when you connect. If talking about heads without bodies brings back memories of Ichabod Crane in the *Legend of Sleepy Hollow,* you might want to take a look at the Side Trip later in this chapter.

Follow these steps to download messages:

1. While you're in the newsgroup, click [**Tools**] → [**Download this Newsgroup**]. The Download Newsgroup dialog box shown in Figure 14-11 appears.

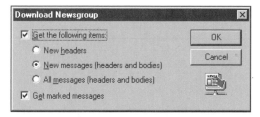

Figure 14-11 Customize your download of newsgroup messages.

2. If you've marked messages, there will be a check beside "Get marked messages" at the bottom of the dialog box.

3. Click "Get the following items" to enable the choices below it.

4. Click the appropriate choice. See the Side Trip "Heads Without Bodies" for a discussion of headers. If it's a large newsgroup and you select "All messages" (headers and bodies), be prepared to wait a very long time for the download to complete.

5. Click OK. An Outlook Express dialog box appears showing the progress of the download. Click the Stop button if you want to stop the download.

6. Click the ⊠ to close the dialog box.

Marking All Newsgroups At Once

In the sections above you learned how to select messages within a newsgroup for downloading. If you're into being super-efficient, you can mark all of your newsgroups in, as Inspector Clouseau would say, one swell foop.

Here's how to mark all newsgroups for downloading:

1. Go to the folder that lists all of your newsgroups. You can click the Newsgroups button in the Folder bar of the current newsgroup to see the list of all folders in Outlook Express (see Figure 14-7 for its location), or you can click the Newsgroups icon in the Outlook bar to the left of your screen.

2. Hold the Ctrl key as you click each newsgroup. All selected newsgroups are highlighted.

3. Right-click one of the highlighted newsgroups. Click Mark for Retrieval → New Messages (or any other choice you prefer). All selected newsgroups appear with the download icon to the left.

4. Click Tools → Download this Account . An Outlook Express dialog box appears and shows the progress of the download.

GETTING A HEAD WITHOUT A BODY

Outlook Express is preset to download only 300 message headers at a time. What exactly is a header? A header tells you the subject, author, size, and date of an article. It doesn't contain the actual message so it's much faster to download headers as opposed to complete messages. When you see the listing of articles in Outlook Express, you are in reality seeing the headers. When you click a header, notice that there is a slight pause as Outlook Express connects to your server and downloads the body of the article. Because most articles are text and are relatively short, this pause is barely perceptible. If you're in a newsgroup that contains pictures, however, the pause between clicking the listing (header) and getting the body can be mindnumbing. However, you don't necessarily want to get the bodies for all messages in the newsgroup for online reading. It's a waste of time and space because you undoubtedly won't read every message. The only time you must have the bodies is when you want to read offline.

If the newsgroup listing in the Newsgroup folder shows that there are over 1000 messages, you won't see them all unless you tell Outlook Express to get them. See the discussion of this feature in the section entitled, "Fine-Tuning Newsgroup Options," later in this chapter.

To get more message headers, click Tools in the menu bar, and then click Get Next 300 Headers.

Reading Messages in Mid-Air

Now that you've downloaded your messages, you're ready to read them offline (hopefully in an airplane headed to some exotic yet incredibly restful place).

Here's how it works:

1. Boot up Outlook Express. Click Cancel on the dial-up screen if necessary.

2. Click the Newsgroups icon in the Outlook bar, and then double-click the desired newsgroup.

3. You may have to cancel the dial-up box again. It is incredibly persistent.

4. Read the messages you previously downloaded.

Fine-Tuning Newsgroup Options

The Options dialog box contains settings that affect the way your newsgroups function. Now that you've had some experience with newsgroups, you may want to fine-tune the settings. Click Tools→Options and then click the Read tab, as shown in Figure 14-12.

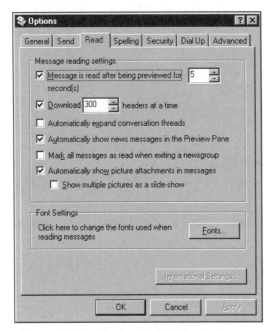

Figure 14-12 The Read tab of the Options dialog box affects newsgroups.

You can make changes in the following options on the Read tab (listed in order from first to last option):

✳ We suggest you keep the default time of five seconds for marking a message as read unless this timeframe annoys you.

✳ If you want more headers downloaded at a time, change this setting. If you do change this setting, the option on the Tools menu will change to reflect the new amount. (What clever people those programmers are!) If you click this option to *remove* the checkmark, Outlook Express will download *all* available headers each time you sign on.

✳ If you get tired of clicking on the + to open a thread, you can select this option to automatically expand threads.

* You can mark all messages as read when exiting a newsgroup. If you choose this option, you'll see only new messages the next time you open the newsgroup. However, you'll lose any messages you didn't get around to reading.

* It's fun to be able to automatically see a picture within a message instead of having to download it. Don't worry about the suboption of showing multiple pictures as a slide-show unless you know you'll be getting lots of these.

* You can change the font and the font size.

BONUS

Displaying and Saving Graphics from Newsgroups

Outlook Express displays graphics inside the message, which is very cool. You don't have to download the graphic in order to see it. You can save a graphic that you like, even use it as wallpaper.

Complete the following steps to save or display a graphic:

1. When you click a message that has a graphic, the graphic is shown in the preview pane at the bottom (see Figure 14-13).

2. Click the paper clip. A graphic label appears showing the name, type, and size of the file.

3. Click the label. An Open Attachment Warning dialog box, shown in Figure 14-14, appears.

4. Click Open it and then click OK. The browser opens and displays the picture. You may have to maximize the window to see it full-size.

14

Figure 14-13 Click the paper clip to show a label identifying the graphic file.

Photo taken by Jo A. Moore while in the Masai Mara, Kenya, during July 1997. Photo scanned and published on "A World Travels, Safaris, and Wildlife" site at http://www.inficad.com/~vmoore by Vern Moore.

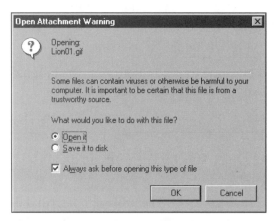

Figure 14-14 You may see a warning before opening a graphic in the browser.

Complete the following steps to save the picture to your hard drive. By the way, these steps work for any graphic that you see while cruising the Web.

1. Right-click the picture.

2. Click [Save Picture As] on the shortcut menu as shown in Figure 14-15. The Save As dialog box appears.

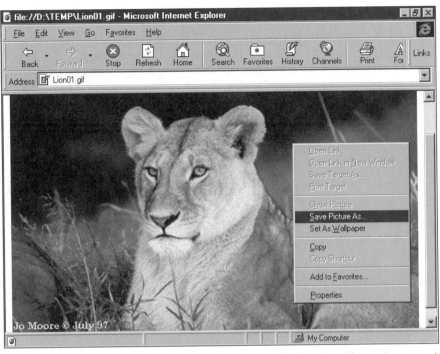

Figure 14-15 Right-click a picture in the browser and select Save Picture As to save it to your hard drive.
Photo taken by Jo A. Moore while in the Masai Mara, Kenya, during July 1997. Photo scanned and published on "A World Travels, Safaris, and Wildlife" site at http://www.inficad.com/~vmoore by Vern Moore.

3. Select the drive and folder where you want to save the picture and then click OK.

WEB PATH

Isn't the lion shown in the pictures above absolutely gorgeous? Vern and Jo Moore of Moore's Consulting & Services in Phoenix, Arizona, deserve the credit for the photo. They took the picture on their recent safari in the Masai Mara, Kenya. If you like animals or are interested in travel, safaris, and wildlife, visit their Web site. Vern says you'll find photos, articles, and much more.

Visit Vern Moore at http://www/inficad/com/~vmoore.

Summary

The world is so much easier to deal with when things are organized, and the messages in newsgroups can be organized to meet your needs. You can sort messages on four different variables. You can mark messages and even entire threads as read or unread. Even though you subscribe to a newsgroup you don't actually have to participate. You can simply read the messages that interest you and save those you want to keep. This isn't nearly as much fun as being an active participant, however. Once you start responding to newsgroup threads and contributing your own, you'll be hooked, and before you know it you'll be a full-fledged member of the Net news community.

HOLDING A NETMEETING

In these chapters, we introduce you to a new program included with IE 4 called NetMeeting. NetMeeting gives you the ability to interact with colleagues in "real time." No waiting for a response to the last e-mail, no mailing illustrations or diagrams back and forth through the postal service, just instant collaboration over the Internet.

NetMeeting automatically establishes an audio connection, and can also include video, if the computers involved in the meeting are equipped with video cameras. Other components of the program include "Chat," similar to the text-exchange chat feature available in The Microsoft Network, America Online, and other online services; and a "Whiteboard" that lets the people in the meeting share and edit images. A file exchanger and the ability to browse the Web together round out NetMeeting. After we show you how to install NetMeeting and get ready for your first conference, we'll give you the details about how the program works.

Studies of people who work at computer screens report that 91 percent complain of eyestrain, 70 percent experience blurred vision, 74 percent to 80 percent have irritated or burning eyes, and fully 40 percent have a change in color perception. In addition, computer users have many more headaches, are more irritable and tired, and are absent from work more often than those who don't work at a computer screen.

We could be founding members of the tired eyes club. We spend more time than we want to admit glued to our chairs and staring at our screens. However, during a brief outing to the grocery store, we met one of the most interesting people we've run into in a while—Dr. Arthur Seiderman, an internationally recognized authority on vision therapy, and founder of the Vision Development Center in Plymouth Meeting, Pennsylvania.

Arthur is also the author of two books, *20/20 Is Not Enough: The New World of Vision* (Alfred E. Knopf Publishers) and *The Athletic Eye: Improved Sports Performance Through Visual Training* (Hearst Books). During subsequent conversations, he talked about the reasons that computer work causes eye problems: "A computer image is comparatively blurred and is constantly moving and flickering. Computer screens magnify, multiply, and compound the usual visual problems associated with desk work." Boy, is he right!

If you feel you qualify for the tired eyes club, consider implementing some of Dr. Seiderman's suggestions:

✓ Frequently look out a window at the most distant object you can see. You can continue your train of thought while you gaze at the horizon.

✓ Relieve occasional blurring by shifting focus between your computer screen and, say, a painting on the wall.

✓ Work 30 to 45 minutes and take a three-minute break. Don't read. Get up. Walk around. Drink some water.

✓ Get the best screen with the best resolution you can afford.

✓ Set up your work station so that you are looking down on your screen at about a 30° angle.

✓ Use diffuse, indirect lighting with full-spectrum lightbulbs.

✓ If you wear glasses, run—don't walk—to an optometrist who can make you a special pair designed specifically for computer work.

✓ If you wear bifocals, have a special pair redesigned to put the bifocal portion much higher (so that you're not constantly tilting your head) and the distance portion only at the very tippity top.

CHAPTER FIFTEEN

SETTING UP A NETMEETING

IN THIS CHAPTER YOU LEARN THESE KEY SKILLS

Maybe you've seen those ads on TV with the woman who works from home, sending e-mail over breakfast and holding online conferences in her bunny slippers. With Microsoft NetMeeting, that can be you! The bunny slippers are optional.

Microsoft NetMeeting is the next best thing to being there. It gives you "real-time" exchange that includes text chat, a whiteboard that can display files or images, joint Web browsing, file exchange, and even sound and video, all over your Internet connection. Unlike a regular phone call, you "dial" using the other person's e-mail address, so you won't be running up a huge bill, even if you're conferring with a colleague in Tahiti. (In this situation, though, maybe you don't want the "next best thing" to being in Tahiti.)

NetMeeting works best if you have a sound card and microphone installed so that you and the others in your online conferences can speak with one another, but these options aren't necessary for using all of NetMeeting's features. Likewise, the video options depend on special equipment that your computer may not have, and are not essential to NetMeeting's operation.

Getting Your Act Together

There's an old New England expression: "You cahn't get theyahh from heahh." Well, you can't get to NetMeeting from Internet Explorer or Outlook Express until you install and set it up. This chapter assumes that you chose to install NetMeeting when you installed IE 4. If you didn't, see the Bonus for Chapter 3, "Updating Explorer," for directions on adding NetMeeting to your suite of IE 4 programs. After the program is installed, you're ready to set it up.

Follow these steps to set up NetMeeting:

1. You can go online now or let NetMeeting automatically connect you to the Internet later.

2. If you're in Internet Explorer or Outlook Express, click `Go` → `Internet Call` .

or

Click `Start` in the taskbar and then click `Programs` → `Mircosoft NetMeeting` . The first time you open NetMeeting with either of these methods the Microsoft NetMeeting Wizard starts up.

We're Off to See the Wizard

The NetMeeting Wizard opens with general information about what you can do with NetMeeting, and then presents you with dialog boxes of information and options for the various things you have to set up to use the program (see Figure 15-1). When there are options to choose between, we suggest that you accept the default settings that the Wizard makes for you, except for logging on to a directory server when NetMeeting starts. All of the setup options can all be changed later should you want to do so. The Wizard presents dialog boxes for the following options, in turn:

✳ Select a directory server that will list you and others who can be contacted using NetMeeting. This is where you set the DLS (Dynamic Look-Up Service) server that you will be registered on and use by default for connecting with others. There is no cost for being registered on a DLS server, it's just a part of using the Internet for NetMeeting. Accept the default setting or, if you're already listed in another server, select it from the drop-down list. The option, "Log on to a directory server when NetMeeting starts" is also in this dialog box. We suggest clicking this option to remove the ✓ from the box next to it. We'll tell you our reasons later; you can always change this option should you want to do so.

✳ Enter your name, e-mail address, and other pertinent information for your directory listing.

* Select a category for your directory information.
* Adjust audio settings for your modem, sound card and microphone. (If you don't have these installed in your computer, you'll see the final NetMeeting Wizard dialog box. You can still use the Chat, File Exchange, Collaboration, and Whiteboard features if you do not have a sound card.)
* Select your video camera (if you have a video camera installed).

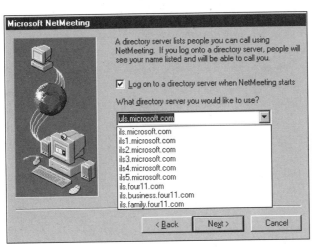

Figure 15-1 The Microsoft NetMeeting Wizard walks you through the setup process.

When the NetMeeting Wizard finishes, NetMeeting opens (see Figure 15-2).

Checking Out Your Options

The NetMeeting window (see Figure 15-2) has a few features we'd like to point out:

* Toolbar handles—You can drag these to rearrange the toolbar and volume control bar.
* Microphone and speaker volume controls—These let you adjust volume during a call by dragging the volume level indicators left or right.
* Tabs along the left side of the window—These let you display *History* information about previous calls, *Current Call* information, your *SpeedDial* list, or the list of people in the *Directory* you selected to use.

When NetMeeting first starts up, it begins to connect you to the Internet. If, in the setup Wizard, you selected "Log on to a directory server when NetMeeting starts," NetMeeting logs you on to the server. We suggested that you de-select this option during setup. The reasons are 1) you may not want to use the directory every time to make your connection, and 2) you may want to make changes to certain setup options for a particular NetMeeting connection before you make a call. For example, you may want to turn off audio or video before you make some calls. There are some other options discussed in the list below that you have to change if you want to keep NetMeeting from automatically connecting to the Internet each time you start it up.

Before you log on to a directory server and get your first meeting under way, there are a few options that the setup Wizard didn't give you and that you should be aware of.

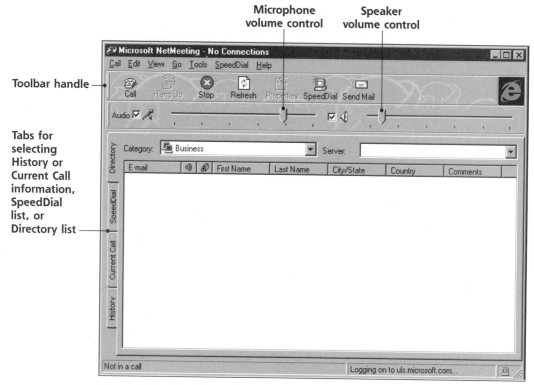

Figure 15-2 The Microsoft NetMeeting window.

Follow these steps to check out all of your NetMeeting options:

1. Click **Tools** → **Options** . The Options dialog box opens with the General tab at the front. Some of the options you may want to make use of or disable on this tab include:

   ✳ Run when Windows starts... (if you want to use NetMeeting every time you use your computer)

   ✳ Show the SpeedDial tab... (if you want to use SpeedDial for most or all of your connections)

   ✳ Automatically accept incoming calls... (if you don't want to screen them)

✳ Show Intel Connection Adviser... (highly recommended so that you can use the automatic connection monitoring and troubleshooting help that this option provides).

2. Click the My Information tab to bring it to the front. This tab is where you can change your directory information. You may want, for example, to leave your location off of the directory listing for some calls.

3. Click the Calling tab to bring it to the front. If you don't want to automatically log on to a directory, or don't want to be listed in it when you log on, this tab is where you select these options. This tab also has several options related to SpeedDial. If you do not want NetMeeting to automatically connect to the Internet when you open it, click "Log on to the directory when NetMeeting starts," "Refresh directory listing when NetMeeting starts," and "Refresh SpeedDial list when NetMeeting starts," to *remove* the ✓ next to each of these options.

4. Click the Audio tab to bring it to the front. This tab includes the option "Enable full duplex audio...," which lets you speak and listen to audio at the same time. This does not work for all connections; check the online help in the Intel Connection Advisor for more information on this option.

5. Click the Video tab to bring it to the front. If you have video, but don't want to use it for all of your calls, click the two options under "Sending and receiving video" to remove the ✓ next to them.

6. The Protocols settings generally should not need to be changed from what the Wizard set up for you. Click OK in the Options dialog box to save your choices and close the dialog box, or click Cancel to close it without making any changes.

What's on the Menu?

NetMeeting's menus contain a couple of choices that you may want to make use of depending on the choices you make in "Checking Out Your Options." These include:

✳ Call→Do Not Disturb if you selected "Automatically accept incoming calls" and you don't want to receive any for a while.

✳ Call→Log on to... if you de-selected "Log on to the directory server when NetMeeting starts," and you want to log on for making calls. If you are not connected to the Internet, NetMeeting starts making the connection when you select this option.

✳ Call→Change My Information to alter your directory information before making a call.

* View→Refresh when you have the SpeedDial tab at the front in your NetMeeting window if you de-selected "Refresh SpeedDial list when NetMeeting starts." If you are not connected to the Internet, NetMeeting starts making the connection when you select this option.

* View→Refresh when you have the Directory tab at the front in your NetMeeting window if you de-selected "Refresh directory listing when NetMeeting starts." If you are not connected to the Internet, NetMeeting starts making the connection when you select this option.

Instead of selecting View→Refresh, you can also click the Refresh button on the toolbar to refresh the directory or SpeedDial list. Now that we've gone over these basic elements and options available in NetMeeting, you're ready to make a call.

Making a Call

There are several ways to initiate a call in NetMeeting. But before you make a call, it's a good idea to arrange a date and time with your NetMeeting partner or partners. Everyone in the meeting should be online and have NetMeeting running at the same time. First we'll tell you about the ways to make a call from within NetMeeting, and then we'll outline the ways to start a NetMeeting call without the program running.

Calling with NetMeeting Open

Follow these steps to make a call using the Directory tab:

1. Click `Call` → `Log on to...` to connect to the Internet and log on to the directory if you have not already done so.

2. Click the Directory tab, if needed, to bring it to the front (see Figure 15-3).

3. Click the column in the directory that you want to sort the listings by. For example, to sort the listings alphabetically by last name, click the Last Name column.

4. Double-click the listing for the person you want to meet with. NetMeeting begins to make the connection.

Follow these steps to make a call using the SpeedDial or History tab:

1. Click the SpeedDial or History tab to bring it to the front.

2. Double-click the listing for the person you want to meet with. NetMeeting begins to make the connection.

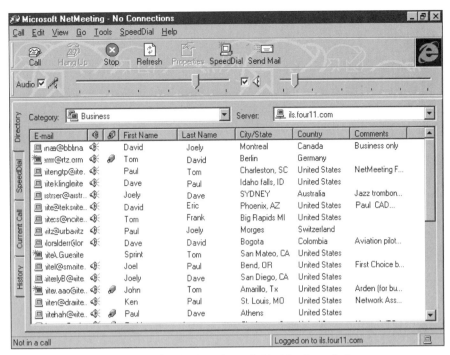

Figure 15-3 The Directory tab in the Microsoft NetMeeting window.

You can use the New Call dialog box to connect to another person using their e-mail address or their computer's IP (Internet Protocol) address.

> **NOTE** An IP address is a unique, permanent numerical Internet address assigned to a computer, and is most useful in this case for making a connection between two computers on company networks. An IP address would look something like 123.123.123.000, and is used to indicate one particular port on the network. Most ISPs (Internet Service Providers) do not assign an IP address to their dial-up customers. Instead, they assign a fixed number of IP addresses *dynamically*. That is, you are assigned the address only for as long as you're connected to the ISP. That way, when you disconnect, it's available for someone else. This saves equipment expenses and complications for the ISP.

Follow these steps to make an automatic call:

1. Click the Call button in the toolbar or click **Call** → **New Call**. The New Call dialog box appears (see Figure 15-4).

2. Type the e-mail address or IP address of the person you want to meet with into the Address box.

3. Click Call. NetMeeting begins to make the connection.

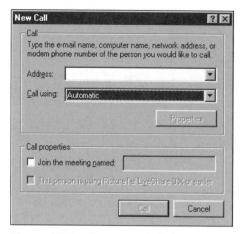

Figure 15-4 The New Call dialog box.

Calling with NetMeeting Closed

You can also use your Windows Address Book or the Run dialog box to start a NetMeeting.

Follow these steps to make a call using your Windows Address Book:

1. Open your Windows Address Book.

2. Click the listing for the person you want to call.

3. Click the Properties toolbar button. The Properties dialog box for the person's listing appears (see Figure 15-5).

4. Click the NetMeeting tab to bring it to the front.

5. Select the person's e-mail address from the drop-down list under Conferencing E-Mail.

6. Select the directory server, or type the server's name into the Add new box and click Add.

7. Click the Call Now button. NetMeeting opens and begins to make the connection.

Follow these steps to make a call using the Run dialog box:

1. Click Start on your taskbar to open the Start menu and select ⬚ **Run** .

2. Type **callto:** followed by the person's directory server and e-mail address, and then press the Enter key. For example, type **callto:uls. microsoft.com/Sunsethaus@blablablabla.com** and press Enter. NetMeeting opens and begins to make the connection.

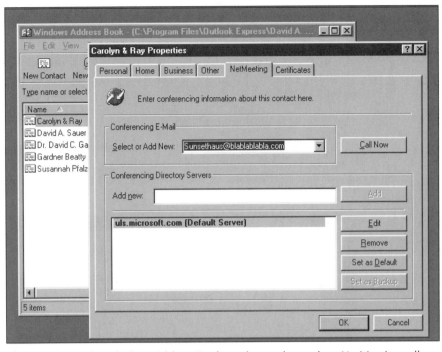

Figure 15-5 The Windows Address Book can be used to make a NetMeeting call.

Accepting or Declining a Call

If you did not set your options to "Automatically accept calls," a dialog box appears when you receive a call (see Figure 15-6). Click Accept to take the call and start a NetMeeting, or click Ignore to decline the call. The caller receives a message that you did not accept the call (see Figure 15-7). This same message is sent whether you actually decline a call or simply are not there to accept it.

Figure 15-6 The incoming call dialog box.

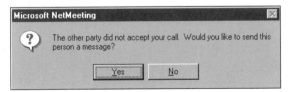

Figure 15-7 NetMeeting can automatically send e-mail if your call is not accepted.

Leaving a Message

I f your call is not accepted (for whatever reason), a dialog box appears that gives you the option of sending the person you called an e-mail message (see Figure 15-7). Click No if you don't want to leave a message, or Yes if you do.

Follow these steps to leave an e-mail message if your call is not accepted:

1. Click Yes in the dialog box that tells you the call was not accepted. A form with the recipient's name, the subject, and a generic message filled in appears (see Figure 15-8).

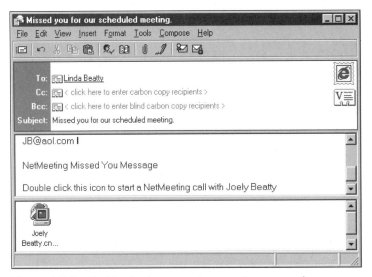

Figure 15-8 NetMeeting's automatic, generic message for unaccepted calls.

2. Click the Send icon in the toolbar or click File → Send . An Outlook Express dialog box appears and lets you know when the message has been sent.

BONUS

Holding Family Conferences

NetMeeting can be a very useful way for families to keep in touch without running up big phone bills, especially if your family members are in different countries. Letters that have been written in advance can be sent back and forth using the file exchange or copied and pasted in Chat, and family pictures that have been scanned into electronic format can be shared and saved using the Whiteboard. You may even be able to collaborate with family members on a shared application such as a genealogy program.

Families can keep in touch using NetMeeting instead of running up big phone bills.

However, you would have to plan your family get-together in advance, because NetMeeting has to be running on the computers involved at the time of the call. This could be arranged in either a quick, low-cost telephone call or by e-mail.

To set up your family conference, both parties or groups should remember to do these things in advance:

1. Arrange the time and date of the conference using e-mail or a quick phone call. Keep time differences in mind if you're in different time zones or in countries on different continents.

2. Write and save letters using Notepad, or use your word processing program. Just remember to save the letters as text files so that Chat or the file exchange can display them clearly. Save the letters in a folder by themselves so they're easy to locate during the conference.

3. If you have a scanner, scan any pictures that you want to share using the Whiteboard. Many copy services, office supply stores, and "mail box" stores offer scanning services if you don't have a scanner at home. Just remember to copy the scanned files to your computer's hard disk before the conference. You may want to save the files in the same folder as the letters (see Step 2) for convenience.

4. Review the information and steps in the next two chapters to help the conference go as smoothly as possible.

15

Summary

NetMeeting's setup options give you great flexibility in controlling how the program behaves in online meetings. The many methods you can use to initiate a NetMeeting, from within the program or with it closed, put its powerful features only a few mouse clicks away.

CHATTING AND USING THE WHITEBOARD

IN THIS CHAPTER YOU LEARN THESE KEY SKILLS

You can have a NetMeeting with one or more people. If you're "wired for sound" you can actually talk, but only to one person at a time. The same is true of video. No matter how many people there are in the meeting, you can see only one person at a time. Use the Switch button in the toolbar to switch the audio or video to another person in the group. Two people can sit at the same computer, of course, and share a microphone. If each person is using a separate computer, however, you have to "switch" to that person to hear or see them. Interestingly enough, you can receive video even if you don't have video on your end.

Even if you don't have sound or pictures, you'll find NetMeeting to be a fun way to meet with friends and an interesting way to conduct a business meeting. This chapter focuses on how to use Chat and the Whiteboard without sound or video. It assumes that you've done the setup required in Chapter 15 and that you've made the call. Now that you're connected, we'll show you how to chat and use the Whiteboard.

16

Chatting with Friends in NetMeeting

The Chat feature in NetMeeting works like the online chat sessions that are so common in services like America Online. Text is sent back and forth and shows up on both people's screens. With NetMeeting you can even save the text of a chat session if it contains information you want to keep. (Hint, hint...don't "say" anything in a chat session that you don't want the other person to have in writing.)

TIP This chapter is all about using the Chat feature in NetMeeting. However, there's another way to chat. When you installed Internet Explorer, a program called *Microsoft Chat* was put on the Start→Programs menu. You can join a chat room already in progress or start your own. Take a look.

Assuming that you're online and you've made the call (or received one) and both of your names are listed in the Current Call window, you're ready to start chatting. If the Current Call window is not on your screen, click the Current Call tab on the left of the window to bring it to the front.

Follow these steps to chat in a NetMeeting call:

1. While in the Current Call window, click the Chat button shown in Figure 16-1. The Untitled Chat window appears. (If you don't see a Chat button you're not in the Current Call window.) Notice that this is a chat session with three people.

2. You can manually size the Chat window to make it bigger or fully maximize it to fill your screen.

3. Type your message in the Message box at the bottom of the window. Let your text run across one line. Don't press the Enter key to make a new line because pressing the Enter key "sends" whatever you've written up to that point to the chat screen.

4. Press the Enter key on your keyboard or click the icon to the right of the Message box to send your text to the screen. Your message appears with your name and everyone in the chat session can see it.

NOTE If you want to save a record of the chat session, click File→Save As in the Chat menu bar. Chat files are saved as .txt files and can be opened in your word processing program.

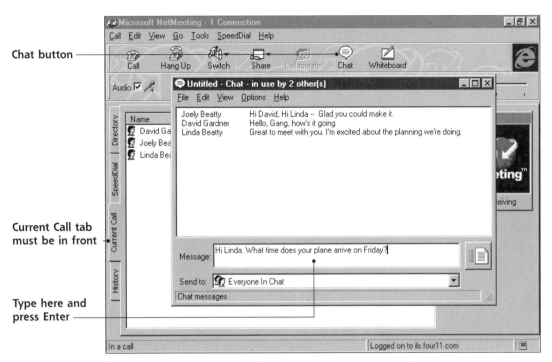

Chat button

Current Call tab
must be in front

Type here and
press Enter

Figure 16-1   You can chat with one or more people in NetMeeting.

Whispering

We know your mother taught you that it's not polite to whisper around other people but in NetMeeting no one else can see or hear you "whisper." So does that mean, at least when you're in NetMeeting, that because no one hears a tree fall in the forest it doesn't make a sound? In a chat session with more than one person, you can "whisper" to a particular person. Your comment will show up on that person's screen in italics with "(private)" preceding the text (see Figure 16-2).

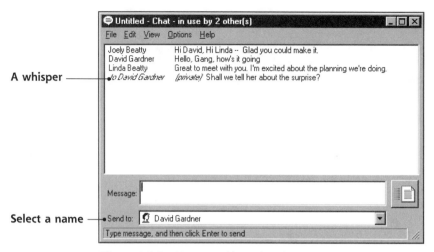

A whisper —

Select a name —

Figure 16-2 You can whisper in private to one person in a group chat session.

Follow these steps to whisper:

1. Click the down arrow to the right of the Send to box at the bottom of the Chat window. A list of people in the chat session appears.

2. Click the name of the person into whose ear you want to whisper.

3. Type your comment and send it as usual. Your comment appears on your screen and the screen of the person to whom you whispered. It's preceded by the word *private* in parentheses. This comment does not show up on anyone else's screen and the other people in the session don't know that you whispered anything to anyone. On the recipient's screen (the whisperee ?), the comment appears as "from *your name (private)* blah, blah blah."

Being the Host with the Most

You can set up a meeting and invite people to join you. With NetMeeting, you don't even get stuck providing the refreshments. It's strictly BYO. As the gracious host that you are, however, you can include the online equivalent of a response card with your e-mail invitation.

Sending the Invitation

When you're supposed to RSVP to an invitation, don't you appreciate getting that response card that you can mail back instead of having to dig out stationery and pen and writing your response?

Here's how to send the electronic equivalent:

1. While you're online and logged on to your directory server, click Call in the NetMeeting menu bar and then click Create SpeedDial . The Add SpeedDial dialog box shown in Figure 16-3 appears. Notice that it has your address already listed.

Figure 16-3 Send an electronic reply form to the people you invite to a NetMeeting.

2. Click Send to mail recipient to put a dot in the circle.

3. Click OK. After a brief pause, a New Message e-mail window appears with a direct link icon in the bottom pane. When your invited guest clicks on this icon she'll dial right into you. Complete and send the letter as you normally do. Just remember, when people try to come to your party, you must be online, waiting in NetMeeting, and logged onto your directory server.

TIP If you click Save on the desktop in Step 2 above, you'll save a SpeedDial icon on *your* desktop that has a SpeedDial to your computer. When you want to send your SpeedDial icon to someone, right-click the shortcut on your desktop and click Send To→Mail Recipient. An e-mail window appears with the SpeedDial icon already included.

Joining a Meeting

Joining a meeting is easy. Call the person hosting the meeting. You'll see a message that says: "The person you called is currently in a meeting. Do you want to try to join the meeting?" Click Yes and you're in.

Using the Whiteboard

The Whiteboard lets each person in a meeting draw on a shared board so that everyone can see the emerging picture. You can sketch ideas cooperatively, with each person adding or changing elements in the design.

If you've used Microsoft Paint or Paintbrush, you're already familiar with most of the tools in the Whiteboard. If you haven't used any kind of drawing program before, you'll find them a little awkward to use at first, but it's nothing you can't handle.

TIP If you're not familiar with how a Whiteboard works and haven't used the tools before, you can practice on your own. After you've connected to NetMeeting and clicked the Current Call tab, log off from your directory server (if necessary) and disconnect from your ISP (if necessary). Now you're free to play around with the Whiteboard in private.

Follow these steps to open the Whiteboard:

1. Click the Current Call tab.

2. Click the Whiteboard icon in the toolbar. (If you don't see a Whiteboard icon, you're not in Current Call.) You may see a message that says its searching for other Whiteboards. When NetMeeting locates them all, the Whiteboard appears.

3. Click the maximize button to enlarge the Whiteboard.

Becoming a Computer Picasso

The drawing tools in the Whiteboard are elementary. You won't be able to rival Monet, but a simplistic cubist approach to your subject could work well. Figure 16-4 shows a Whiteboard with shapes drawn on it. The color palette at the bottom of the Whiteboard and the line widths at the left don't appear until you click a tool that requires them.

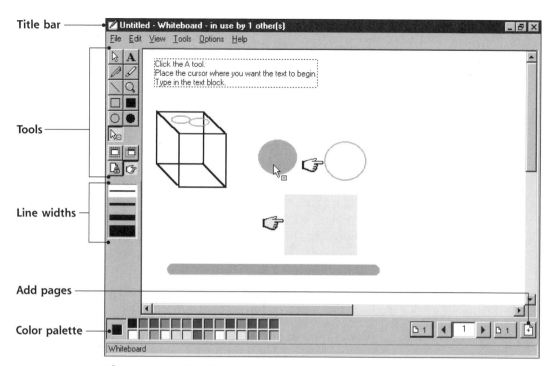

Figure 16-4 The Whiteboard gives NetMeeting participants the opportunity to collaboratively put their thoughts "on paper."

Notice the following items:

✳ The Title bar tells you how many are in the meeting. If you're practicing, the Title bar will say "Not in call."

✳ The 15 icons on the left side of the Whiteboard are the tools. They're also listed on the Tools menu, but it's much easier to display the toolbar so they're handy. We'll discuss using the tools in a little while.

✳ The four line widths under the tools appear only when you've selected a tool that can use a line width.

✳ The color palette at the bottom of the Whiteboard appears only when you've selected a tool that can be used with color.

✳ You can add pages to your Whiteboard using the icons in the lower right. We'll show you how later.

A Craftsman Is Only as Good as His Tools

There are 15 tools in the Whiteboard. There are three major things to remember about tools:

* The tools take a little getting used to. In the "real" world, you have to pick up a tool before you can use it. The same is true in the virtual world of the Whiteboard. You must click a tool before you can use it. The disconcerting part is that the tool doesn't go away after you've done what you want to do with it. It becomes yours for life until you click another tool.

* Many of the tools can use line width and color. For example, you can draw a square with a thin line or a thick line and you can draw it in any one of 28 colors. When you select a tool that can use line width or color, these elements appear as shown in Figure 16-4. You can select line width and color before *or* after selecting the tool, but these choices stay in effect until you change them.

* There is no Undo in the Whiteboard. You have to erase what you don't want. See the description of the Erase tool in Table 16-1.

Following is a summary of the tools and what they do. You can see the name of each tool by holding your mouse pointer on top of a tool. A label pops up with its name. Play around with the different tools. Be adventurous. If the Whiteboard gets crowded, click Edit→Clear Page.

TABLE 16-1 Whiteboard Tools

Tool	Name	How to use it
⌖	Selector	It doesn't do anything by itself. It "selects" shapes already drawn. After you've drawn a shape or typed text, click the Selector, then click the shape or text. A dotted line appears around the item. You can now move it by dragging it to another spot on the screen, or change its color by clicking a color on the palette.
A	Text	Click it and your cursor becomes an I-beam. Place the I-beam where you want the text to begin. When you click your mouse, a text block will appear. A Font Options button also appears to the right of the color palette. Click this button to customize the font. The border around the text will disappear when you click the Whiteboard or select another tool. To edit the text, click it again with the Text tool.
✎	Pen	You can write or draw with this tool. Select the line width by clicking the one you want. Choose the color you want by clicking one of the squares in the palette. The color will appear in the single square to the left of the palette. Remember, this color will stay in effect until you change it.

Tool	Name	How to use it
	Highlighter	Use like a highlighter pen. After you click it, choose the width and color as described above.
	Line	When you click it, your cursor turns into cross hairs. Place the cross hairs where you want the line to begin. Then click and hold your mouse and drag until you want the line to stop. You can make straight lines in any direction. (To make curved lines, use the Pen.) Choose the line width and color. If the line looks a little jagged, continue to hold the mouse button as you straighten it out. It will actually print straight no matter how jagged it looks.
	Zoom	This zooms in on the last part of the screen you worked in. Unfortunately, you can't direct the zoom to a specific part of the screen. Click the Zoom tool again to zoom out.
	Unfilled Rectangle	When you click this tool, your cursor turns into cross hairs. Place the cross hairs where you want the shape to begin, and then drag to form a square or rectangle. For some reason the shape appears with a thin black line until you release the mouse button, and then it changes color and line width.
	Filled Rectangle	Ditto the directions for using the Unfilled Rectangle.
	Unfilled Ellipse	Ditto the directions for the rectangle tools except that the ellipse (or circle) appears with a thin colored line until you release the mouse button.
	Filled Ellipse	Ditto the above.
	Eraser	When you click this tool, your mouse pointer appears with a little minus sign attached. Click the shape you want to erase. If a shape is made up of multiple lines, you have to erase each line.
	Select Window	You'll see a message that says "The next window you click will be pasted into the Whiteboard." You go to the Current Call window and, literally, the next window you click will be pasted into the Whiteboard. It's kind of weird. If you change your mind while you're in the Current Call window, press the Esc key to get rid of the tool. If a window gets pasted into the Whiteboard, click the Selector tool, click the picture of the window to get the dotted line around its border, and then press the Delete key on your keyboard.

Tool	Name	How to use it
	Selected Area	You'll see a message that says, "Select an area on the screen to paste into the Whiteboard." Click OK and you go to the Current Call window. You can drag the cross hairs around the part of the window you want to copy to the Whiteboard. Once in the Whiteboard, use the Selector tool to select it and then move it. Ditto the comments above.
	Lock/Unlock Contents	Click this icon to prevent others in the meeting from changing the contents of the Whiteboard. Click it again to remove the lock. The first person to click this tool locks the Whiteboard. Everyone else sees a lock attached to their mouse pointer and the only tool available is the Remote Pointer (see below).
	Remote Pointer On/Off	This is a cool tool. Click it to insert a hand onto the Whiteboard. Each person can insert a pointer hand and each hand will be a different color. While this tool is selected, your mouse pointer is an arrow. Use the arrow to drag the hand to different parts of the Whiteboard to point to different items.

 NOTE Printing the contents of the Whiteboard is just like printing any other page. Click File→Print and make the appropriate selections in the Print dialog box.

Adding a Page to the Whiteboard

To add pages to your Whiteboard, click the Insert New Page icon shown in Figure 16-5. This inserts a page after the current page. You can also use the Edit menu to insert a page before or after the current page. When you have more than one page in your Whiteboard, use the following icons:

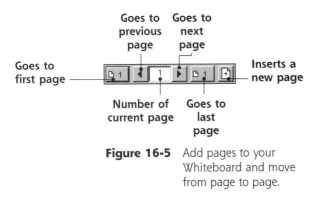

Goes to first page —

Goes to previous page

Goes to next page

Inserts a new page

Number of current page

Goes to last page

Figure 16-5 Add pages to your Whiteboard and move from page to page.

Ending A NetMeeting

When you're finished with your call, simply click the Hang Up button in the NetMeeting toolbar. When you're ready to leave NetMeeting, click the Close button in the Title bar. You'll still be online, so disconnect if you're through with Internet Explorer.

BONUS

The Whiteboard Is Cool But What Do I Use It For?

Unless you're into creating layout designs or flow charts, you may be wondering how you can actually use the Whiteboard other than for entertainment. Here are a couple of ideas:

Giving Directions

Pretend you need to give meeting participants directions to a company function. Figure 16-6 shows a map that you created in advance and saved with File→Save As. If you don't have audio, discuss the directions in Chat and tell people you'll show them a map in the Whiteboard. Go to the Whiteboard and open the map with the File→Open command. Meeting participants can print the map from the Whiteboard.

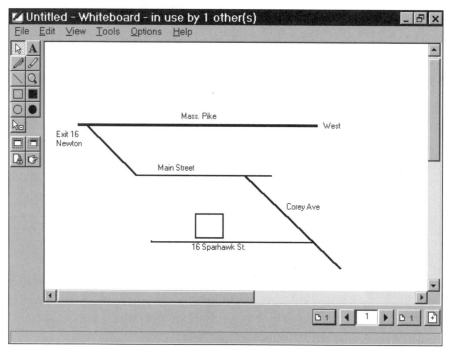

Figure 16-6 Create a map in the Whiteboard in advance of a meeting. Save it, and then open it during the meeting.

Sharing Pictures

You can share graphics with people using the Whiteboard.

Unfortunately, there's no direct way to open a graphic file in the Whiteboard, so here's a way around that:

1. Click the Browser icon in the Quick Launch toolbar.

2. Click **File** → **Open** , and then browse to the folder and graphic file you want to show. Be sure to select the appropriate file type in order to see the file. Open the file in the browser window.

3. Right-click the picture and click Copy.

4. In the browser toolbar, click **Go** → **Internet Call** to go back to NetMeeting.

5. Click the Whiteboard button in the taskbar.

6. In the Whiteboard toolbar, click **Edit** → **Paste** . The picture appears in the Whiteboard.

In truth, you can share pictures in the browser by doing collaborative browsing (see Chapter 17). The difference is that you don't have any of the tools from the Whiteboard available in the browser. The photo you see in Figure 16-7 was taken by Vern and Jo Moore. See Chapter 14, "Participating in Newsgroups," for more about them.

Figure 16-7 Copy pictures in the browser and paste them into the Whiteboard.
Photo taken by Jo A. Moore while in the Masai Mara, Kenya during July 1997. Photo scanned and published on a "World Travels, Safaris and Wildlife" Web site at `http://www.inficad.com/~vmoore` by Vern Moore.

Summary

NetMeeting has two very cool tools: Chat and the Whiteboard. Even if you don't have a sound card you can "talk" back and forth to one or more people in Chat. And even if you don't have a video card and camera, everyone in the meeting can "look at" the contents of the Whiteboard and contribute.

CHAPTER SEVENTEEN

EXCHANGING FILES AND WORKING TOGETHER

17

IN THIS CHAPTER YOU LEARN THESE KEY SKILLS

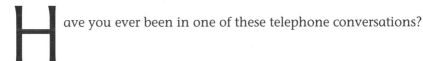

ave you ever been in one of these telephone conversations?

* *You* (sounding cool, calm, and professional): Take a look at page 17 of the contract.
* *The Other Person* (sounding frustrated): Page 17? I don't see it. Oh, wait, here it is. Where am I supposed to look?
* *You* (still sounding professional): Look half-way down the page at paragraph 14a.
* *The Other Person* (sounding totally confused): Paragraph 14?
* *You* (gritting your teeth): No. Paragraph 14*a*!

You can finally unclench your teeth and relax. Thanks to NetMeeting, you and the ninny in the above conversation can now view the same file on each of your computer screens, so there's no confusion about where you are in the document. And if the person isn't a ninny at all but a close colleague (or better yet, a paying customer), you can actually work on the file together.

If your partner in the NetMeeting is a friend and you want to point out a really terrific Web site, you can even browse the Web together. What will they think of next?

You Can Look But You Can't Touch

M icrosoft has a strange definition of "sharing." In NetMeeting, it means that the other person can look at your file but they can't actually use it or change it. That's not what Miss Brooks, my kindergarten teacher, taught me about sharing. However, I must admit that Microsoft's view of sharing is much closer to what *I* had in mind in kindergarten. Still, "sharing" files in NetMeeting is pretty cool, and there are times when you definitely don't want other people in the NetMeeting to be able to change the document or file on the screen.

In order to share a file, both (or all) of you must be in a call together. One person takes the lead and opens the file and the others in the meeting share it. For the purposes of this discussion, we'll call the first person the leader and the other person the follower.

The leader should complete these steps to begin sharing a file:

1. Go to the Current Call tab.

2. Open the file—a spreadsheet in Excel, for example—and then minimize it so you can see NetMeeting.

Meanwhile, back at the ranch, the follower should:

1. Go to the Current Call tab.

2. Sit and wait.

The leader, who has more work to do, completes these steps:

1. Click the Share button in the Current Call toolbar. A list of open applications/files appears, as shown in Figure 17-1.

2. Click the file you want to share. You'll see a Microsoft NetMeeting message that says, "You have chosen to share an application, etc." Click OK. Nothing else happens until you do Step 3.

3. Now go to the Windows taskbar. Click the file button in the taskbar to open the file on your screen. At this point, there's nothing else *you* have to do to "share" the file besides wait for the other person to open his or her copy of the shared file. You should know, however, that whatever you have on your screen is what the other person sees, so if you maximize the file window, the other person will see a maximized file

window. If you click a cell in the spreadsheet, the other person sees that cell selected on his or her screen. If you—well, you get the point.

Share an open file —

Click to open the file on your screen —

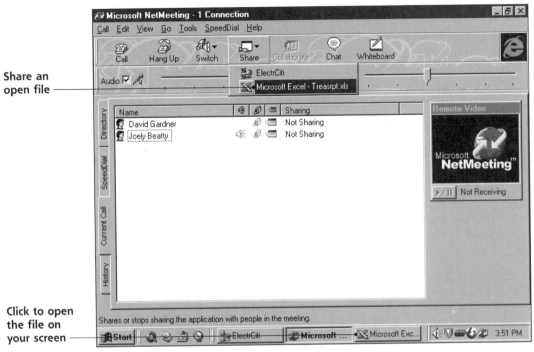

Figure 17-1   Open files are listed on the Share menu. Click the file you want to share, and then click the file in the taskbar to let others in the meeting see it.

Now it's the follower's turn to open the shared file:

1. As the follower, there is a button on your taskbar that has a picture of a hand holding a file, as shown in Figure 17-2. If you hold your mouse pointer on the button, a label appears with the filename and the leader's name.

Figure 17-2   After the leader selects a file to be shared, a button appears on the taskbar of others in the meeting. Click the button to open the shared file.

2. Click the button and the file appears on your screen. Whatever the leader sees on his or her screen is what you see on yours. You can't do anything with the file. If you click it, you'll see a message box that says, "You cannot work in this application because the person sharing is not collaborating." This message box goes away eventually, but I bet the person who wrote the message was a tattletale in kindergarten.

MORE TOOLBARS THAN YOU KNOW WHAT TO DO WITH

You know, of course, about the taskbar at the bottom of the Windows 95 screen. Internet Explorer puts a Quick Launch toolbar on the left side of the taskbar. When you start NetMeeting, another icon appears on the right side of the taskbar in an area called the *status area*. The status area in the following figure shows icons for a sound card, a virus protection program, an active modem, the Intel Connection Advisor and NetMeeting (both of which are put there by Microsoft), and, of course, the time.

NetMeeting icon

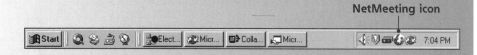

When you click the NetMeeting icon, you see the Quick Access toolbar shown in the following figure. The Quick Access toolbar is especially useful when you've maximized a shared application, the Whiteboard, or the Chat window, and you want to have the NetMeeting commands available without having to minimize what's on your screen.

Go to whiteboard

Go to chat

Collaborate/stop collaborating

Share/stop sharing

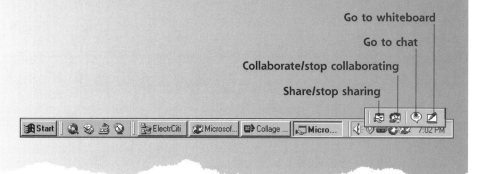

NOTE   The leader is the only person who can work in the shared file and who can close it. To close a shared file, click the Share button in the Current Call toolbar. The file appears with a checkmark on the Share menu. Click the filename again. The file is no longer shared and it disappears from the screens of other people in the meeting. That's all there is to sharing. If you're interested in a more cooperative type of sharing in which others can actually work on the file with you, see the next section on collaborating, "Many Hands Make Light Work."

Many Hands Make Light Work

Sharing as practiced in NetMeeting is very much a show-and-tell operation, with the leader doing all of the showing and telling and the follower simply observing. If you want others in the meeting to be able to interact with the file and make changes, you must "collaborate."

Collaborating

Collaborating is a two-part process. First you share a file and then you open the shared file for collaboration.

The leader completes the following steps to begin a collaboration:

1. Open a file for sharing as explained in the previous section.

2. After the file is open for sharing, click the Start Collaborating button in the Quick Access toolbar. See the Side Trip above for its location. A Microsoft NetMeeting message, shown in Figure 17-3, appears. Read the message and click OK.

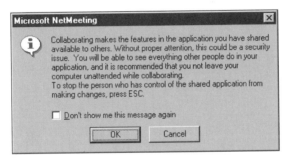

Figure 17-3 Open a shared file for collaboration by clicking the Collaborate button in the toolbar. Click OK in this message box.

3. For some reason the file is now minimized, so go to the taskbar and open the file on your screen.

4. If you make a change in the file, others in the meeting will see the change. You are now "in control" of the file. See the follower's process below. Then see the note about taking control.

The follower now completes these steps:

1. Click the Start Collaborating button in the Quick Access toolbar (see the Side Trip above for its location). You'll see a message about collaborating. Click OK.

2. The file is minimized, so go to the taskbar and open the file on your screen.

3. Notice the following: The initials of the person "in control" of the file appear on the screen (see figure 17-4).

4. When you try to use your mouse, you see a pop-up message that tells you to click the mouse to take control. Click your mouse. You're now in control and the other person sees *your* initials on *their* screen.

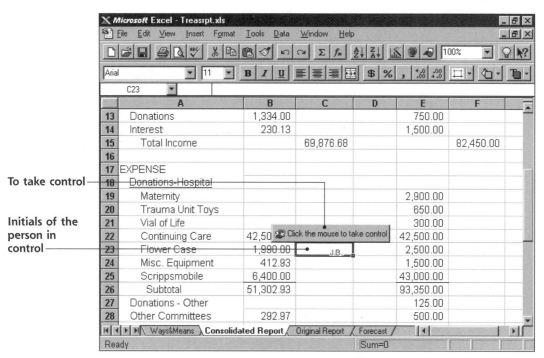

Figure 17-4 The initials of the person "in control" of the collaboration appear on the screen along with a message to click to take control.

NOTE Only one person can be "in control" at a time. Although the "follower" can see the file on his screen, he cannot make changes as a follower. He must click in the application window to take "control" and only then can he make changes. This control process prevents two people from trying to change the file at the same time. It makes mouse control and movement a little awkward, but if you have audio you can talk over the rough spots, which makes it workable.

Ending the Collaboration

Anyone in the meeting can end a collaboration on their particular machine by clicking the Collaborate button, but the person who originally opened the file is the only one who can actually close it.

✳ Anyone can stop collaborating by clicking the Stop Collaborating button in the Quick Access toolbar. A dialog box appears asking, "Do you want to stop collaborating?" Click OK.

✳ Although active collaboration on the file is stopped, it's still shared. In order to close the file, the original leader must click the Share button and click the filename on the menu to remove the checkmark. The file is now closed on everyone's computer but the leader's.

✳ If you, as the leader or host, want people in the meeting to have a copy of the changed file, you must send it to them. This is incredibly easy in NetMeeting. See the next section.

What's Mine Is Yours

While you're in NetMeeting, it's simple to send a file to the people in your meeting. Just think, all the "drudgery" of going to Outlook Express, opening a new letter dialog box, completing the letter, attaching the file, and sending it is gone <big grin>. Seriously, you'll love how easy it is to send a file, and it doesn't matter where you are in NetMeeting when you begin this process.

You can use NetMeeting to easily send a file to people in your meeting.

Complete these steps to send a file to the people in your meeting:

1. Click [Tools] in the menu bar, and then click [File Transfer] → [Send File]. The Select a File to Send dialog box appears.

2. Go to the folder where the file is located, click the file, and then click [Send]. The status of the transfer is shown in the status bar at the bottom of the NetMeeting window. When the transfer is complete, you see a message to that effect. Your part is done. Now the meeting participants have the file.

As a meeting participant, complete these steps to receive a file:

1. When the transfer is complete, you see the dialog box shown in Figure 17-5. You have the following choices:

✳ Click **Open** to open the file right now on your screen. If you open the file now, you can use the Save As command to save it to a folder on your hard drive.

✳ Click **Close** to close this dialog box. You can see the file in Step 2 below.

✳ Click **Delete** to delete the file from your computer.

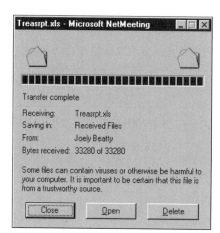

Figure 17-5 When you are sent a file from someone in a meeting, this dialog box appears on your screen.

2. If you chose to close the transfer dialog box, you can see the file at any time by clicking **Tools** → **File Transfer** → **Open Received Files Folder** . The Received Files folder you see in Figure 17-6 appears.

Figure 17-6 The Received Files folder has a copy of all files sent to your computer.

3. Double-click the appropriate file icon to open that file.

TIP The Received Files folder is on the C:\ drive under Program Files→NetMeeting. You can change the location of files sent to you through NetMeeting. Click Tools→Options, and then click the General tab and Change Folder. Then go to the folder where you want files sent.

Come Tiptoe Through the Tulips with Me

Let's say you want to plan a weekend of fun with a friend, and while browsing the Web you come across the Tulip Festival in Skagit Valley in the state of Washington. A weekend in the Northwest sounds like just the ticket, but you want your friend to be able to see the Web site too. You can, of course, e-mail the link to your friend, but there's a much more exciting way to do this. You can browse collaboratively! It's just like collaborating on a file, only it's the browser that's on your screen.

The Skagit Valley Tulip Festival is a real event in a real place, by the way. I discovered it by typing ? tulips in the Search bar. When the Autosearch result screen appeared, I linked to:

`http://www.tulipfestival.org/`.

Follow these steps to browse collaboratively:

1. Go to NetMeeting and call your friend.

2. Click Launch Internet Explorer on the Quick Launch toolbar. Or, click `Go` → `Home Page`.

3. When the browser is on your screen, click the NetMeeting icon in the taskbar and then click the Share button. On the Share menu, click Internet Start - Microsoft Internet Explorer (see Figure 17-7). (The browser page may become minimized during this process. It didn't seem to happen consistently for us. If it's minimized, click its button in the taskbar to open it again on your screen.)

4. When the browser page is open for sharing, click the Start Collaborating icon in the Quick Access toolbar.

5. Your friend can now click the Start Collaborating icon on his or her Quick Access toolbar. Your friend may have to click the button in the taskbar to open the browser, or the browser page may appear automatically.

You're now in business. Follow the steps above for sharing control and have fun!

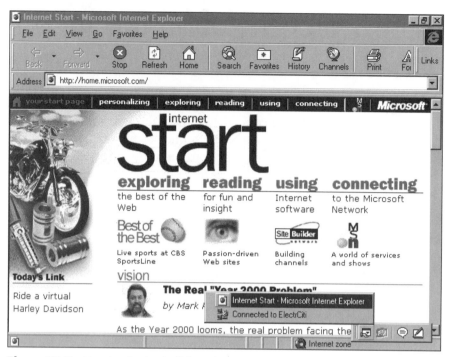

Figure 17-7 Use the sharing/collaborating process to browse the Web with a friend.
Screen shot reprinted by permission from Microsoft Corporation.

BONUS

Is It True That There's No Place Like Home?

As full-time authors and consultants, all three of us work at home and have done so for many years. Like everything else in life it has its good points and bad points, but it's definitely worth considering. There are a couple of myths about working at home that we'd like to discuss.

Myth #1: I'll work at home so I can be there for the kids.

Stop right now. You're setting yourself up for failure. If your children are very young you *must* hire help and then train the kids and your helper that you are not to be disturbed except in emergencies. You cannot expect to dish out cookies and monitor sibling squabbles and at the same time do a professional job at whatever it is you do. Working at home is just that—working. That said, working at home *does* give you more flexibility to schedule that teacher's conference or see the absolutely most important game of the season. But you still have to make up the time that was lost. So be prepared to work at night. And weekends.

Myth #2: Working at home is more relaxing.

It's true that you can forget the suit, briefcase, and heels (pick any two) on those days when you don't have to go to your client's office. And, thank heaven, the commute takes all of 15 seconds. These two issues alone start the day out right! However (and you just knew there had to be a "however"), when something goes wrong with your equipment or you run out of supplies in the office, you can, with a good conscience, say, "Not my problem," and expect someone else to fix it. When you work at home you must have a good support system of computer technicians, repair people, and office supply resources because, unfortunately, it *is* your problem. You can't pass the buck because there's no one to pass it to. If you're used to a support staff at work, being your own boss at home and the sole member of a staff of one is a culture shock.

On the other hand, if you're a disciplined person and have planned your transition well, working at home is wonderful.

WEB PATH Here are some resources to check out:

Home Office Association of America is a national club for full-time, home-based professionals. Get advice and benefits, such as airline discounts. Their Web address is:

```
http://www.hoaa.com/
```

American Home-Workers Association features more than 3,000 national companies looking for work-at-home employees. Get the benefits of working for a company with the freedom of working for yourself, without the risk of starting your own business. Their Web address is:

```
http://www.ahwa.com/
```

Summary

Using your computer and NetMeeting, you can work with people all over the world. You can *share* a file so that others in the meeting can see it, but can't change it. If you want others in the meeting to be more involved, you can *collaborate* on a file. This gives everyone in the meeting the opportunity to make changes to the file. It is then your responsibility as the host of the meeting to send all participants a copy of the final version. You can do this directly from NetMeeting, however, so there's no reason to forget to do it. You can even use the sharing/collaborating feature to browse the Web with other people.

PART FIVE

CREATING HTML DOCUMENTS WITH FRONTPAGE EXPRESS

THIS PART CONTAINS THE FOLLOWING CHAPTERS

Although the chapters in this part were written with Web pages in mind, you can also use the pointers you find here to create HTML documents to send via e-mail in Outlook Express. We'll take you through all the steps to plan, create, and post your Web page on the World Wide Web. Gone are the days of writing line after line of tedious HTML code. With FrontPage Express, you'll be creating Web pages in just a few minutes!

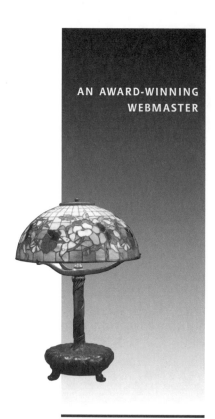

The term "Webmaster" came from the word "postmaster," the head of a post office. When the Web was still in its infancy, the "Webmaster" of a site was merely the person who designed and maintained it. In those days, if you were running your own Web site, you could call yourself a Webmaster.

Today, a self-anointed title is meaningless when a business tries to find itself a "qualified" Webmaster. There are no universities that offer "Webmaster" degrees and there is no list of requirements published in the Dictionary of Occupational Titles. Yet, designing, building, and maintaining a Web site with today's increasingly sophisticated technology requires an equally sophisticated background and experience. Today, a company Webmaster is not only responsible for coding HTML (the language of the World Wide Web), but also for coordinating with a company's system administrator, computer programmers, and graphic designers in order to keep the site operating at peak efficiency. In fact, in many companies, the person carrying the title of Webmaster is considered to be a top-level manager of an important business unit.

Just how does one become a real Webmaster when there is no clear career path? While every Webmaster's story about his or her career path is no doubt different from our award-winning Webmaster Bryan Maleszyk's tale, his is probably representative. Without realizing it, Bryan started his Webmaster career in a seventh-grade classroom when he wrote his first computer program in BASIC. The program made the words "This class is boring" appear on the screen in randomly different colors, and repeated itself 10,000 times.

As a freshman philosophy major at Boston University, Bryan discovered the Internet. Boston University did not have a Web page at that point, so he helped design a student-run site. He became more and more involved as a Webmaster for other sites. In fact, he took a year off from school and, with a partner, started a business designing and maintaining commercial Web sites.

Bryan won a national award for one of Boston's most popular web sites, WHDH-TV Channel 7, an NBC affiliate TV station. With a staff of only two (it's much larger now), Bryan doubled the "hits" of the site by making it a state-of-the-art place to visit.

Now back in school and a senior at Boston University, he has, as you may have guessed, changed his major from philosophy to business and computer science. According to Bryan, "One of the basics of being a good Webmaster is keeping up because what you're doing now will be obsolete in one year."

CHAPTER EIGHTEEN

PLANNING YOUR WEB PAGE

IN THIS CHAPTER YOU LEARN THESE KEY SKILLS

Although lots of companies now have Web sites, you don't have to be a business to have one. You can create a Web page for a fund-raising activity, to promote your local school, or as a fun site where you can share pictures and activities with family and friends. If you're looking for a job, you can create a Web page with your resume.

You have probably heard some of the buzz words associated with Web pages: hypertext, links, HTML (HyperText Markup Language), SGML (Standard Generalized Markup Language), markup tags, and on and on. The language of the Internet, like the Internet itself, is evolving. Much of it is incredibly technical and very intimidating to those of us newbies (newcomers) who don't have a technical background. However, you don't have to be intimidated anymore! Explorer's FrontPage Express makes it possible for you to create a Web page from scratch without knowing all the technical stuff that goes on in the background. You'll be able to insert pictures, create links to other sites, add colors, textures, tables, and section dividers, and reply e-mail. In short, you can create a professional-looking Web page almost as easily as typing a document. And if you don't want to start a page from scratch, you can use a template provided in FrontPage Express.

However, the point of this chapter is that no matter how easy the actual process of creating a Web site may be, a good Web page takes planning. You have to think about the visual impact you want to create, the message itself, and the flow from one section of your site to another. We'll help you through the process and point you in the direction of some terrific help that's available on the Web.

Don't Reinvent the Wheel

Because a Web page is a visual statement as much as a textual statement, you have to put as much thought into what your Web page will look like as into the words you want to use. We recommend looking for models that you can print and then review. The models in FrontPage Express are actually templates, meaning you can use them to create your own Web page. Once you're in FrontPage Express, you can find them by clicking **File** → **New** . To be honest however, we thought they created some pretty pedestrian results. The good news is that we know where you can find some great-looking models. They happen to be in Netscape, but one of the wonderful things about the Internet is that you can avail yourself of resources from any number of sites. You're not limited to what's provided (or not provided) with a given product.

Follow these steps to locate and print Web page models:

1. Type the following URL. It's a long one, so be careful to type it exactly.

   ```
   http://www.netscape.com/home/gold3.0_templates.html
   ```

2. Scroll about halfway down the Netscape Web Page Templates page until you see the following categories of templates:

   * Personal/Family
   * Company/Small Business
   * Department
   * Product/Service
   * Special Interest Group
   * Interesting and Fun

3. Click any link that interests you to open the associated template. If you like the looks of a particular layout, or some facet of the layout interests you, print the page. You're perfectly free to use these models for ideas. (You can't use the actual template unless you're using Netscape software, but, hey, how generous do you expect them to be?)

Mapping Your Web Site

Think about how you look at a map. First, you get a general impression and an overall view. (What is this map about? What are the main features?) Next, you zero in on a specific area. (Where is North Paradise Lost?) Then you look for the connection between one area and a second area. (How do I get from North Paradise Lost to South Nirvana?) On a visual level, people look at your Web site much as they do a map. What is this Web site about? What are the main features? How do I get to an area that interests me and once there how do I get back home again?

People look at your Web site much as they look at a map.

Get some paper and map out your Web site. Don't worry about details like what the text will say or what the graphic elements will be. That will come later. Right now, you're concerned only with the visual overview and the connections, or links. Be sure to plan for links in your page. They're what make a Web page fun. Think how boring it would be to scroll through one long page. In addition, a long page can take a very long time to appear on someone's screen. Web surfers aren't known for their patience, so downloading problems don't help your "hit" rate. Links, on the other hand, fit right into today's cultural consciousness: I see it, I want it, I gotta have it NOW. (And you thought you were just building a simple Web site!)

Figure 18-1 shows a map of a Web site that has four pages, or sections. Page 1 is the home page of your Web site. An effective home page contains the following features:

* A title to let the reader know what the Web page is about.

* A graphic element for visual interest. This can be a picture, an interesting font in the title, or a creative use of color, for example.

* Text bytes, catchy snippets of text that grab a reader's interest and contain links to more information. (Think sound bytes but with written words.)

* An e-mail link that brings up a self-addressed e-mail letter so the reader can get in touch with you.

How many pages should you have in your Web site? As many as you need. There's no rule about the appropriate number of pages, but your ISP will have some rules about how much space you can take up on their server without being charged extra money. Most package deals that we see from ISPs include one to two megabytes of storage space for your Web site. This is more than adequate for personal or small business use. Although the map we show in Figure 18-1 shows four pages in the Web site, two pages may be all you need.

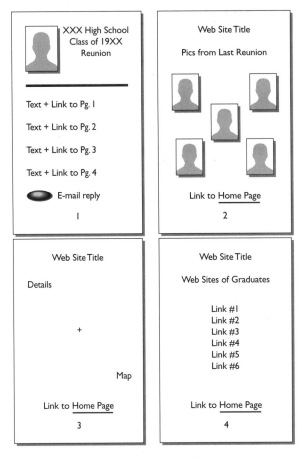

Figure 18-1 Draw a map of your Web site as part of the planning process.

The second page of a Web site (as well as the third, fourth, etc.) should have the following features:

* The Web site title so people don't forget where they are. It doesn't have to be as big or as graphic as on the first page, but it should be there.
* More information about the text byte on the first page.
* A link back to the home page.
* If you're feeling ambitious, you can put an e-mail link on every page.

Being More Than a Pretty Face

It's important to make your Web site attractive so that it invites people in. But once they're in the door, what are you offering? You need content, and content involves writing. Are you one of those people who finds writing difficult, if not downright painful? Join the club—most people do. If you freeze at the sight of a blank page or screen, try this technique: Shut your eyes and imagine that you're talking to a friend about whatever it is you're writing about (your personal Web page, your business, a special charity event). You want your friend to be as excited about this topic as you are. What would you say? Carry on a conversation with your friend in your mind. Get excited in your mind. See your friend getting excited and asking questions. Now, start making notes about what you said and the questions your friend asked. Don't worry about making sentences or even making logical sense. Go for the feelings and the excitement. That's what you write about!

Once you get some notes made, it will be easier to go back over them and organize them into text bytes and then into more detailed paragraphs. If you're still confused about what the heck a text byte is, think sound byte (like on TV) but in words. Quite honestly, we made the term up, but it's supposed to mean a short, eye-catching bit of text that invites the reader to look for more details. Type your text in a word processor. Words somehow look different when they're printed. And be sure to use the spell check and grammar check functions. There are few things more embarrassing than displaying errors for all the world (quite literally) to see. After you type your text, let it sit for a while. Time adds perspective, and what made total sense in the heat of excitement can be less than wonderful in the cold light of another day. Have other people review your text and really listen to their comments and suggestions.

When your text is written, you're ready for the really fun part—the graphics.

Getting Great Graphics for Free

The ability to show graphics is what makes the Web so cool. You'll certainly want to take advantage of this feature and include some graphic elements in your Web page. As mentioned previously, the graphic element doesn't have to be a picture. It can be an interesting font, background texture, color, separator, button, or icon. But let's be honest, pictures and clipart are really fun! You can find lots of free clipart and graphic elements on the Web. The real problems will be finding the time to cruise all the sites and making a final selection.

We know of two sites that are especially generous with clipart and advice, and we'll give you their Web addresses so you can go there directly.

Figure 18-2 shows the Web site for Page Works, a Web site developed *and* maintained (which is the much less glamorous but more demanding part) by Kitty Roach. If you have speakers, she plays great music. However, if you want to turn the music off, she considerately includes a stop button at the bottom of the page. The stop button is the square one.

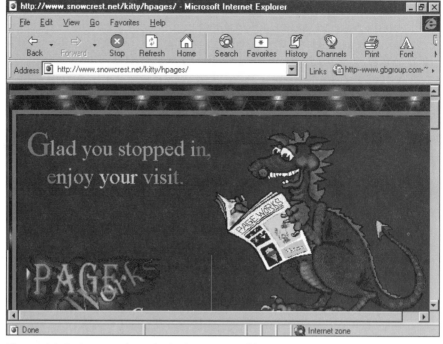

Figure 18-2 Page Works Web site is a source of free graphics and terrific advice.

 WEB PATH In addition to providing great clipart and animations, Kitty, the Webmaster, provides terrific advice and links to other knowledge-packed sites. Some of Kitty's excellent suggestions are included in the Side Trip below. The Page Works Web address is `http://www.snowcrest.net/kitty/hpages/`. It's well worth your time.

Figure 18-3 shows the Web site for TuDogs. They've spent a lot of time and effort to review and evaluate other sites. Scroll down the page a little until you see the links for "mirror" sites. Each of these represents a different server hosting the exact same site. Depending on traffic on a given server, one site may be faster than another, but the information you get will be the same.

The Web address for TuDogs is `http://www.tudogs.com/`.

Getting More Cool Clipart

Conduct a search for free clipart and we guarantee you won't have enough time to go through all the matches.

To search for free clipart, follow these steps:

1. Go to the Web browser.

2. Click the Search button on the toolbar.

DESIGN ADVICE FROM AN EXPERT

Kitty Roach, the Webmaster of Page Works (www.snowcrest.net/kitty/hpages/), was very generous with her time one Saturday morning and shared the following design advice for beginners:

* Get your personality into your Web page. You do this by incorporating design features you've seen that you especially like. For example, did a certain color really attract you? Did you like the look of a certain type style? Do you like light backgrounds, dark backgrounds, or textured backgrounds? If this is a personal page, include something specific about yourself, such as a hobby, an interesting aspect of your job, or a funny story about yourself. These are the things that make people react to your Web page and encourage them to send you mail.

* Keep your first page relatively lean. Don't load it up with tons of graphics because they will make your page veeeeeeery slooooooooow to load. Speed is important when loading a page. Keep the descriptions on the first page brief and include links to additional information. Once you catch the readers' interest, they're more willing to browse, but having to sit and twiddle thumbs while your page loads is an interest killer.

* Don't include too many animations. They take up lots of space and take a long time to load. When pressed, Kitty said four animations per page is too many. They start to interfere with one another.

* Put light lettering on a dark background and dark lettering on a light background if you want your text to be easy to read.

* Put a Home button or link on every page.

* Put an e-mail link on every page. People don't want to search for your mail link in order to send you a response.

* Make the color of your followed links much more faded than untried links. If your reader can't tell the difference between a link they've followed and one they haven't yet tried, they'll get frustrated and leave.

* And, most important, keep it simple and have fun!

3. Choose any one of the search engines listed in the Select Provider list box.

4. When the search page presents itself, go to the Computer or Internet or WWW section. Each search engine categorizes things a little differently. Pick the category that makes the most sense as presented by that particular search engine.

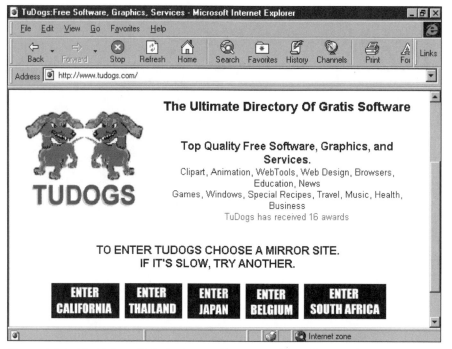

Figure 18-3 The TuDogs Web site is a terrific source of free clipart and other Web tools.

5. Type **free clipart** in the search box.

6. Be prepared to lose all track of time as you browse from site to site looking at what you can get for free on the Web.

7. If you're a glutton for clipart, repeat the search in all of the search engines.

Saving That Picture

When you find clipart or a graphic element that you want, it's easy to save it to your hard drive. Remember to look for a copyright symbol (©). If you see one, and even if you don't, ask permission to copy the graphic unless it is specifically identified as free clipart. Kitty Roach (`http://www.snowcrest.net/kitty/hpages/`) has taken the time to compile links to terrific information about copyright issues. Don't put yourself in a potentially compromising position by stealing and taking credit for someone else's work. Most artists who post their work on the Web are reasonable people and are happy to talk with you about using their image. Figure 18-4 shows how to save an image. The image you see in this example is "Today's Link" on the Microsoft Start Page.

Follow these steps to save a free graphic that you find on the Web:

1. Create a folder for your Web site by clicking File → New → Folder in Windows Explorer.

2. Right-click the graphic. A shortcut menu appears.

3. Click Save Picture As . The Save As dialog box appears.

4. Go to the folder you created for your Web site and save the graphic there.

Figure 18-4 Right-click a graphic to save it to your hard drive.
Screen shot reprinted by permission from Microsoft Corporation.

Getting Ready to Use FrontPage Express

Surprisingly, there's no icon for FrontPage Express on the Quick Launch toolbar that Internet Explorer installed in your taskbar. If you are going to build a Web site, you'll be using FrontPage Express a lot. Installing a shortcut icon on your desktop or on the Quick Launch Toolbar is a whole lot easier than using the Start menu every time you want to use FrontPage Express.

NOTE FrontPage Express was originally called FrontPad, so Figure 18-5 and the following directions show "FrontPad." By the time you read this book, however, Microsoft may have changed all the references to "FrontPage Express," so you'll have to do some quick translating in your mind as you go through these references. Oh well, a rose by any other name...

Follow these steps to install a shortcut icon for FrontPage Express on the Quick Launch toolbar:

1. Open Windows Explorer.

2. Go to the C:\Program Files folder (see Figure 18-5).

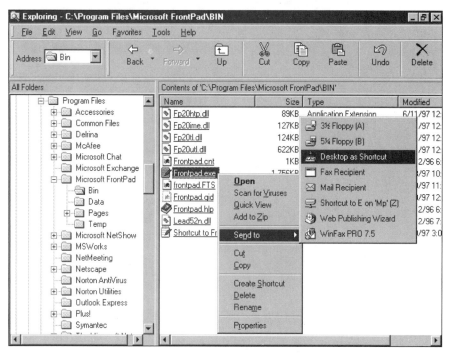

Figure 18-5 Create a shortcut icon for FrontPage Express and add it to the Quick Launch toolbar or send it to your desktop as a shortcut icon.

3. Go to the Microsoft FrontPad (or FrontPage Express) folder and then open the Bin folder.

4. In the Bin folder, right-click Frontpad.exe (or the equivalent .exe file for FrontPage Express). A shortcut menu appears.

5. Click [**Send To**] → [**Desktop as Shortcut**].

6. Close Explorer. Somewhere on your desktop is an icon that says FRONTPAD.

7. Drag the shortcut onto the Quick Launch Toolbar (or leave it on your desktop).

BONUS

Learning from the Masters

Y ou don't need to know HTML to create a Web page in Internet Explorer, but if you'd like to know more about it there are volumes of information available to you on the Internet just for the asking. Use the Autosearch feature in Internet Explorer to search for specific text. In Autosearch, you type the text you're looking for in the Address bar along with a question mark. The ? tells Internet Explorer to start an Autosearch for the text you entered.

To learn more about HTML, type **? beginner's html** in the Address bar (see Figure 18-6). Press Enter. A Yahoo! page appears with tons of links to terrific sources of information on HTML.

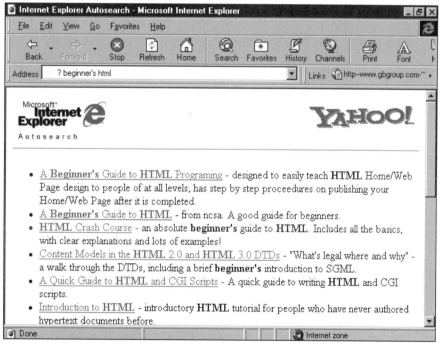

Figure 18-6 Use Autosearch to look for help on beginner's HTML.

Another way to learn from the masters is to use the View Source command on the shortcut menu.

Follow these steps to see the HTML coding for a Web site that you like:

1. Right-click a clear spot on a Web page that you like. A shortcut menu appears.

2. Click **View Source**. (If the View Source command isn't on the menu, move your mouse pointer to another spot and try again.) A Notepad window appears with the document that contains the HTML code for this page.

3. Scroll through the page. If looking at it makes your eyeballs spin, remember that you don't have to "speak HTML" to create a Web page in FrontPage Express.

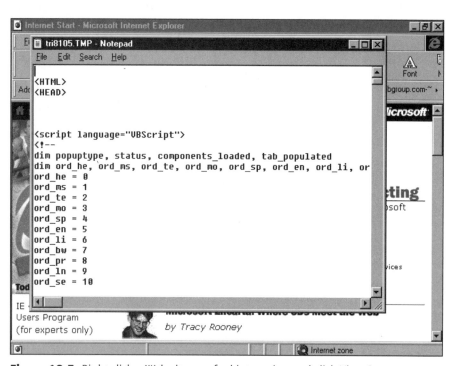

Figure 18-7 Right-click a Web site you find interesting and click View Source to see a copy of the HTML source document that created this particular page.
Screen shot reprinted by permission from Microsoft Corporation.

If you are especially impressed with a certain technique shown in the source code, you can copy the code and use it as a model for your own page. Remember, no wholesale duplication of code. It's not nice and it may be illegal.

Follow these steps to save a copy of the source code:

1. Click **File** → **Save As**. The Save As dialog box appears.

2. Notice that the file is set to be saved in the Tmp directory. Navigate to the directory you set up for your Web page.

3. Note that the current filename has a .tmp extension. Change the filename to one without an extension.

4. Save the file as a text document in the Save as type box.

5. Click OK. You can now open this file in Notepad or your word processing program.

Summary

The amount of work you invest in planning your Web page or HTML document will pay dividends in terms of your final product. Don't be shy about using models as a starting point. Use the Help menu and go to the Explorer home page to plug into all sorts of help from Microsoft. Make a map of your Web site that shows what you want to include page by page. Use the free clipart and graphics in Explorer or search the Web for some really terrific-looking stuff. If you're new to all of this, plan a simple site. You can always go back to revise and rebuild it later. In fact, a Web site is like a house. You can keep improving it forever.

CREATING AND PUBLISHING YOUR WEB PAGE

19

FrontPage Express, the HyperText Markup Language (HTML) editor that comes with Internet Explorer, gives you a full-featured, What You See Is What You Get (WYSIWYG) interface for creating Web pages, e-mail, or any other document that uses HTML. You can use it to create Web pages from scratch, edit pages you've made, or customize templates and sample pages that you download from sites that offer them on the Web.

FrontPage Express's toolbar and menus make creating professional-looking HTML documents as easy as using a word processor. After following along with our Web page example in this chapter, you'll feel like a pro.

This chapter assumes that you have some graphic files that you can insert into a test page and have located them in your My Documents folder.

Starting Your HTML Document

While FrontPage Express comes with Internet Explorer, it is not an integral part of Explorer. In fact, it is a neat little program on its own and is fully functional with or without Internet Explorer installed on your computer. What this means is that you do not have to go online or boot up Internet Explorer to work in FrontPage Express.

NOTE By the way, FrontPage Express is a "lite" version of FrontPage, Microsoft's full-fledged Web page composer program. Microsoft has also made it easy for you to upgrade if you need a more sophisticated Web page editor.

To start FrontPage Express from the Start menu, click Programs→Internet Explorer→FrontPage Express, or, if you are following along from the previous chapter, double-click your FrontPage Express icon, as shown in Figure 19-1.

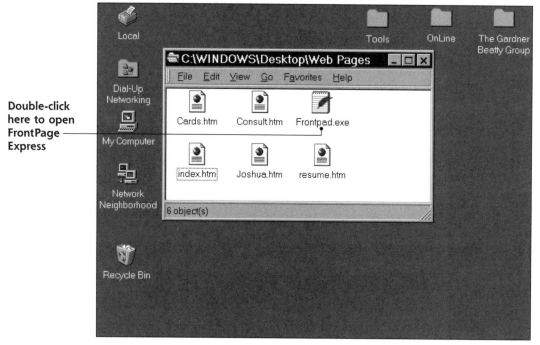

Double-click here to open FrontPage Express

Figure 19-1 Opening FrontPage Express from a Desktop icon.

CREATE A DESKTOP FOLDER FOR FRONTPAGE EXPRESS AND HTML DOCUMENTS

Notice that we have created a Desktop folder, called Web Pages, in which we store the FrontPage Express shortcut icon you created in Chapter 18, along with shortcuts to our HTML files. This way you don't have to flip around all the program lists on the Start Menu or browse with Explorer hunting for HTML documents. Follow these steps to create a folder for shortcut icons:

1. Anywhere on the Desktop, right-click the mouse button. A menu appears.

2. Click New → Folder . A Folder appears with the name text box highlighted.

3. Type a name for the folder in the text box and click anywhere on the Desktop to finish.

4. Move the folder to a nice, comfy spot on your Desktop.

5. Open the folder and drag the FrontPage Express icon into it.

6. In the open folder, click File → New to create shortcut icons for your HTML files. You can only create one shortcut at a time, which means you will have to use the Browse option to go to each file in succession. It's a bit of a pain but once you have them all in the folder, you'll find it a very convenient way to read and revise HTML files. Neat.

What Color Is My Room?

Just for the fun of it, let's add color to your Web page background before you do anything else.

Complete the following steps to add background color to the page:

1. Click Format → Background . A Page Properties dialog box appears with the Background tab in front, as shown in Figure 19-2.

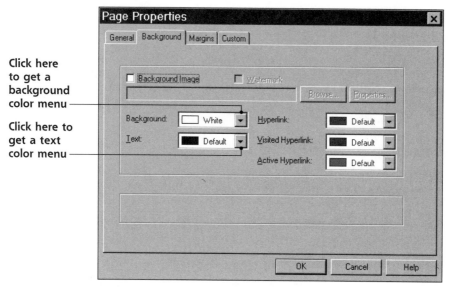

Click here to get a background color menu

Click here to get a text color menu

Figure 19-2 Changing a background color.

2. Click the ▼ to the right of the Background text box to open the background color selection menu.

3. Click the color of your choice. The color menu closes.

4. Click the OK button to complete the process.

NOTE You can follow the same process to change the text color.

Now that you have fiddled around with background colors, let's save the file. You know how cantankerous computers can be. Especially on a hot day!

Complete the following steps to save the file early in the game:

1. Click 🖫 to save the file. The Save As dialog box appears, as shown in Figure 19-3.

2. Type a name for the file in the Page Title text box. Choose the name carefully. The name you choose will appear in the Title bar of your Web page for everyone in the world to see. So, be warned!

3. Click the As File button. Another Save As dialog box appears. Browse to the folder in which you want to save this file.

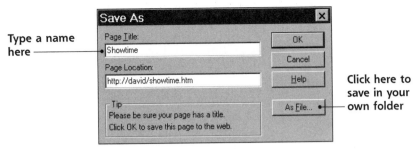

Type a name here ──────

Click here to save in your own folder

Figure 19-3 Saving and naming an HTML file.

Inserting and Formatting Text

N ow that you have selected your background color, left the text black (unless you changed its color), and saved your file, it's time to give the page a main heading and add some text. The main heading, or heading 1, acts as a title that appears on the page. In our example we typed **Auxiliary of Scripps Memorial Hospital - Encinitas**, pressed the Enter key, and then typed **Classic Car Show**. Once you have some text to work with, it can be customized by using the pull-down lists and buttons on the menu bar and the toolbar.

Follow these steps to insert and format text:

1. Type some text on the blank page.

2. Drag the cursor over the text to highlight it.

3. Click the arrow in the first list box on the left (with the word Normal in it) to open it, and then click Heading 1. The list will close and the text will become larger. Try out the font list box to the immediate right to change to various fonts. You can also fiddle around with the buttons in the same row to the right while the text is still highlighted to see what happens. If you make a mess, click the ↶ button to return to the previous state.

Text can also be altered using the commands in the Format menu and the submenus that open off of it.

✳ You can change fonts, font size, font style, and color when you click Format→Font to open the Font tab and avail yourself of the many options contained therein.

✳ You can also change styles and alignment when you click Format→Paragraph to open the Paragraph Properties tab.

Using a horizontal line to mark off parts of a page can improve the looks of your page. To do this, simply position the cursor where you want the line inserted and click Insert→Horizontal Line. Bingo, a line appears on your page. Once it's in place, right-click the line and select Horizontal Line Properties. The Horizontal Line Properties dialog box appears. Here you can select from a list of colors, widths, types of alignment, etc. Play with the line options for a while.

TIP If you choose to color a line (or anything on the Web page), keep in mind that 25 percent of all males are 25 percent color blind in the red-green spectrum. Primary colors are usually OK.

Inserting a Graphic

Graphic images are the raison d'être of the Web. Before the World Wide Web emerged, the Internet consisted of one text file after another and was completely colorless. In other words, boring. Inserting a graphic file to liven up your Web page couldn't be easier in FrontPage Express. If you are familiar with word processing programs, you will notice that FrontPage Express inserts graphic files the same way. You can either select Image from the Insert menu on the menu bar, or use the toolbar button for this command. The Insert Image button is on the toolbar below the editing bar, just under the small A.

Complete the following steps to insert a graphic:

1. Place the cursor where you want to insert the graphic and then click Insert → Image or click the Insert Image toolbar button. In either case, the Image dialog box appears with the Other Location tab at the front (see Figure 19-4).

2. Click From File to put a dot in the circle if it is not already there.

3. Click the Browse button and browse to the folder where the image is located.

4. Open the image into FrontPage Express. The image appears on the page where you place the cursor.

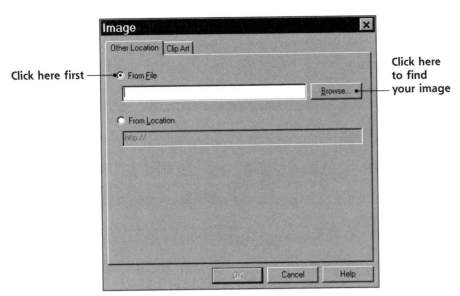

Click here first ——

Click here
to find
your image

Figure 19-4 Inserting an image.

Depending on which image you pick, it may be too large for your page design. You can resize the image in your drawing program and re-insert or you can resize it after you have inserted it into FrontPage Express.

Complete the following steps to resize your image:

1. Click the image with your mouse pointer. Little, black handles will appear on the outside edges as shown in Figure 19-5.

2. Place your mouse pointer on the handle at the lower right corner of the image. When the pointer turns into a two-headed arrow, move it up toward the upper-left corner of the image. The image will get smaller and smaller as you move the mouse. You may have to fiddle with it a little, but eventually you can get the size the way you want it.

If you want to play around with alignment (besides left, center, right), there are other options in the Appearance tab of the Image Properties dialog box. Simply right-click the graphic. A menu appears. Click Image Properties. When the Image Properties dialog box shows up, click the Appearance tab to bring it to the front. Experiment. Have fun!

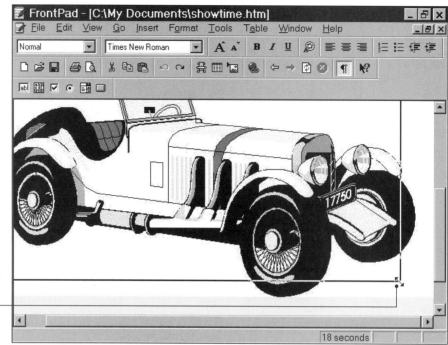

Move the two-headed arrow to resize

Figure 19-5 Resizing a graphic file.

Inserting Links

Y ou can create several types of links between text on your page and other Web pages you have made, other Web sites and graphics, and to e-mail.

A Link By Any Other Name

You can link any page you have created to any other page. To make another page, click File→New. The New Page dialog box appears, as shown in Figure 19-6. Choose Normal Page and click OK. You now have a blank canvas upon which to work your creative magic! Once you have created a second page, *make certain you save it in the same folder as the one to which you are going to link it.* It doesn't matter what name you give the new Web page. You can give the link one name and the HTML file another name and still make the connection.

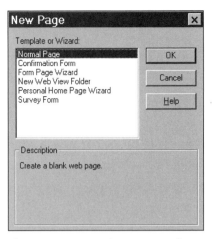

Figure 19-6 Opening a new Web page.

CREATING A PERSONAL WEB PAGE

One of your options in this dialog box is to create a Personal Home Page. When you select this option, a Microsoft Wizard will walk you through the basic steps. After you have created this very basic page, you can customize the page, add graphics, develop other pages to link to it, etc.

To link your new page to the master page, you must go to it before following the steps below. If the page is already open, just click Window→*Your master file name*. Once you are in your master page, simply type a name or phrase for the link. Any name or phrase will do. It doesn't have to be the name of the file to-be-linked. Follow these steps to create the link:

1. Highlight the name or phrase that you have given the link.

2. Click Insert → Insert Hyperlink . The Create Hyperlink dialog box appears.

3. Click the Open Pages tab to bring it to the front.

4. Click the page you want to link to highlight it.

The page you want to link (the "linkee") should be saved in the same folder and be open in FrontPage Express along with the master page (the "linker").

5. Click OK. The page is linked.

You can open your master page in Internet Explorer and click the link to see how it works.

To open the page for viewing in Internet Explorer, complete the following steps:

1. Open Internet Explorer.

2. Click **File** → **Open** . The Open dialog box appears.

3. Click the Browse button to browse to the folder where your new HTML files are stored.

4. Double-click the master page and away you go! Congratulations!

Linking Pretty Pictures

You can link a picture, art work, and other graphics to a page in much the same way as you linked the page above.

Here's how:

1. Create a new page and insert the graphic into it as you did earlier in this chapter.

2. Size the graphic so that it will be displayed the way you want it to look when the page is opened.

3. Repeat the steps in the Side Trip to link the page containing the graphic file.

Linking to Another Web Site

If you have been on the Web recently you've seen how people link their own sites to other sites. You might want, for example, to link your personal Web site to your favorite uncle's Web site or to your business Web site. Using FrontPage Express, the process of linking a site to yours is pretty simple. However, it's a good idea to get permission from the owner of the other Web site beforehand. Some site managers will object. (We assume your favorite uncle will not).

Complete the following steps to link your home page to another home page:

1. Type a name for the Web link. In this example, we typed **Visit Scripps Hospital's Web Page**. Highlight the phrase as shown in Figure 19-7.

2. Click **Insert** → **Hyperlink** . The Create Hyperlink dialog box appears.

3. Click the World Wide Web tab to bring it to the front if it is not already there.

4. Type in the Web site address as shown in Figure 19-8. Make sure you type the address exactly or the link won't work.

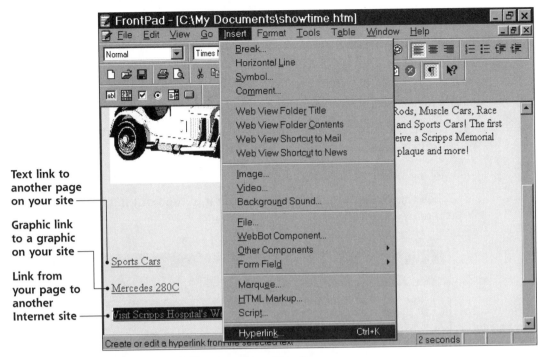

Text link to
another page
on your site

Graphic link
to a graphic
on your site

Link from
your page to
another
Internet site

Figure 19-7 Linking to another Web site.

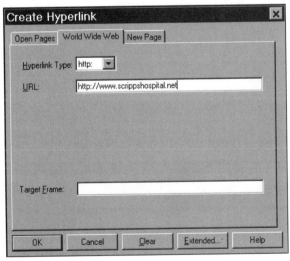

Figure 19-8 Type the Web link address correctly.

5. Click the OK button. All linked!

Linking to Your E-Mail Address

Want people to give you instant feedback when they visit your site? Linking your e-mail address to your home page (and, if your are compulsive, to all the pages on your site) is a good way to ensure that you do indeed get feedback.

Complete the following steps to link your e-mail address to your home page:

1. Type a word or phrase to tell people how to contact you. We typed **E-mail Us**. Next, highlight the word or phrase.

2. Click **Insert** → **Hyperlink**. The Edit Hyperlink dialog box appears.

3. Click the World Wide Web tab to bring it to the front if it is not already there (see Figure 19-9).

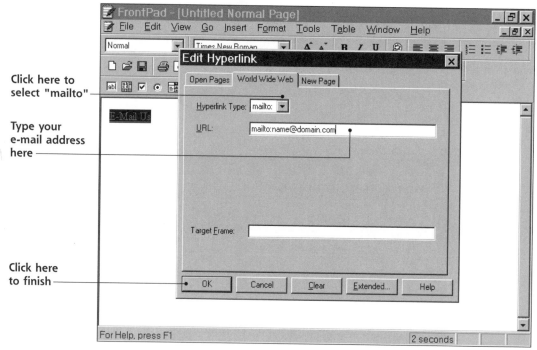

Click here to select "mailto"

Type your e-mail address here

Click here to finish

Figure 19-9 Creating an e-mail response page.

4. Click the ▼ of the Hyperlink Type box. A drop-down list of options appears.

5. Click "mailto" in the list. The list closes and mailto: appears in both the Hyperlink Type text box and the URL text box, as shown in Figure 19-9.

6. Type your e-mail address to the right of the colon with no spaces. It should look like this: **mailto:yourname@yourdomain**.

7. Click OK. You have created a link to your e-mail address!

Organizing the Facts

I f you want to show a bunch of data on a Web page to clients or coworkers, you can create a table with FrontPage Express in the same way you would create one in a word processing program. You can use tables to organize information, display a set of links, or present text in columns.

Making a Basic Table

Before you begin designing your table, create a new page and give it a name.

Complete the following steps to create a basic table:

1. Click `Table` → `Insert Table`. The Insert Table dialog box appears, as shown in Figure 19-10.

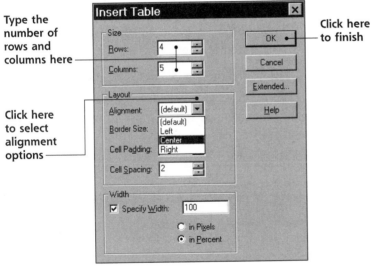

Type the number of rows and columns here

Click here to select alignment options

Click here to finish

Figure 19-10 Creating a basic table.

> **NOTE** You can insert a table using the Table button ⊞ on the toolbar. The problem with this is that you do not have all the options contained in Figure 19-10 at your fingertips. Moreover, you get a weird-looking little table that you then have to size and align.

2. Type in the number of rows and columns for your table.

3. Click the ▼ to the right of the Alignment box and select Center.

4. Click OK. A 4 × 5 table appears. Now let's fill it in.

5. Type in your information. Use the tab key to move from one cell to another.

6. Highlight the top row by clicking `Table` → `Select Row` and then clicking the Bold button on the tool bar to bold the column headings. You have just created a basic 4 × 5 table that quickly!

Jazzing Up the Table

There are many things you can do to jazz up a table. All you have to do is open the Properties dialog box for the basic table you just created and play with the options to your heart's content.

To jazz up your table, complete the following steps:

1. Click any cell on the table.

2. Right-click. A menu appears.

3. Click `Table Properties`. The Table Properties dialog box appears, as shown in Figure 19-11.

4. Add a border and size it by clicking repeatedly the ▲. Try 3.

5. Add some background color by clicking the ▼ to the right of Background color and select a color from the list that pops up.

6. Add color to the border by clicking the ▼ to the right of Border color and select a color from the list that pops up.

7. Click the Apply button. You can see part of the table and its changes without closing the dialog box. Looks pretty good, eh? No? Repeat the steps above and make your changes.

8. When you are finished fiddling around with the options, click the OK button to complete your jazzing up process.

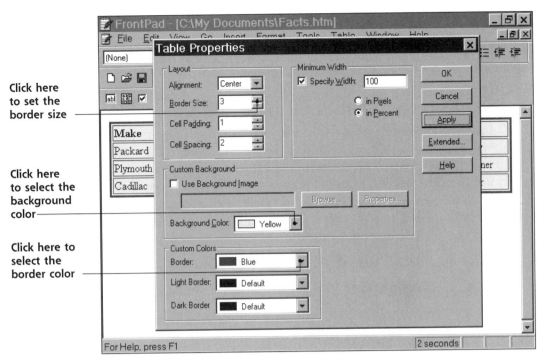

Click here
to set the
border size

Click here
to select the
background
color

Click here to
select the
border color

Figure 19-11 Jazzing up a table.

Publishing Your Web Page

"P ublishing" your page means making it available on the World Wide Web. Internet Explorer makes it quick and easy to publish the pages you create with FrontPage Express or any other HTML editor. To do this, you first have to have an account with an ISP or an online service, such as America Online or CompuServe, that gives you free space on their server to store your Web pages and graphic files. Check with your ISP or online service before proceeding with the steps in this section.

You will need to know the following:

* Whether their server and/or procedures are compatible with Explorer's publishing feature
* How much space is available for your pages and graphics
* The URL for their server
* What the procedures are for signing on to their server
* Your user name and password for access to their server, if it is different from your user name and password for other Internet access

* The path to the folder (or directory) on the server where you can store your files
* The URL you should use to view your page(s) using Internet Explorer

Starting the Web Publishing Wizard

Internet Explorer comes with an automated program, the Web Publishing Wizard, that simplifies the process of sending your HTML pages to a folder on your ISP's server so everyone can view it. Once you have started the Wizard, it is just a matter of filling in the information on a dialog box and clicking on Next to go to the next dialog box and so forth until you get to the Finish button. In the middle of all this, Explorer will connect you to your ISP's server and, after you click Finish, upload the files.

Follow these steps to open the Web Publishing Wizard:

1. Click `Start` on the taskbar. The `Start` menu appears.

2. Click `Programs` → `Internet Explorer` → `Web Publishing Wizard`. The first of a number of Wizard dialog boxes appears.

Filling In the Blanks

This is a rather tedious process, but if you have talked to your ISP technical folks, you should be able to get through it. One surefire way to handle this task is to get the technical person on the telephone and have him or her walk you through the process the first time. Keep notes so that the next time you want to update and/or send new files you'll remember how.

Complete the following steps to publish your Web pages:

1. Type the information requested in each dialog box as it comes up.

2. Once you are satisfied that you have filled in the correct information, click Next to move to the next dialog box. Figure 19-12 shows a dialog box requiring absolutely critical information needed to be a successful publisher!

3. Fill in your password and user name when asked. If you don't have this handy you might as well cancel out of the process (see Figure 19-13).

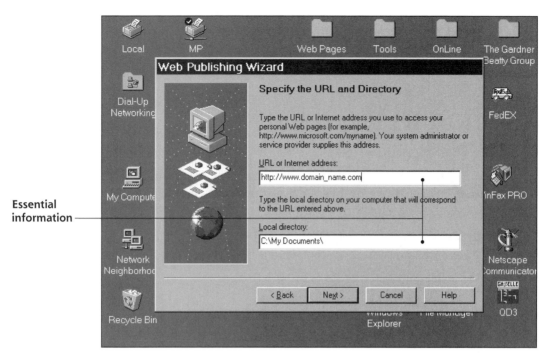

Essential information

Figure 19-12 Adding critical information to the Publishing Wizard dialog box.

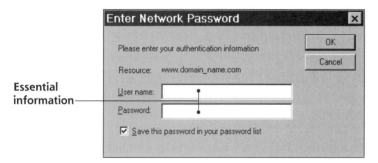

Essential information

Figure 19-13 Cancel now if you don't have this important information.

4. When you get to the Publish Your Files dialog box, click the Finish button, cross your fingers, and watch it happen. If you filled in the information in each dialog box correctly, you are in business as a publisher. Crack open a bottle of champagne and celebrate. If it didn't work, have another cup of coffee and call your ISP's technical service. Good luck!

BONUS

Getting the Word Out

Once you've created your Web page, you'll want people to know it's there. Whether you created the page for your business or your own pleasure, many free services are available that let search engines and World Wide Web directories know that you're there.

To locate lists of these services and more information about such "free advertising," check out this page of links by completing the following steps:

1. Browse to `http://www.yahoo.com/`.

2. Scroll down the page that appears.

3. Under the link "Computers and Internet" is a link in smaller print, "WWW."

4. Click the WWW link. Another link page appears.

5. Scroll down the page to find the "Information and Documentation" link.

6. Click the Information and Documentation link. Another linked page appears.

7. Scroll down the page to find the "Site Announcement and Promotion" link.

8. Click the Site Announcement and Promotion link.

Some of the page titles (links) that you'll find listed there include: "How Do I Publicize My Work?" "How To Announce Your New Web Site," "Promoting Your Page," and "300+ Free Link Sites." Have fun promoting your site!

Summary

In this chapter you learned how to create your own Web pages, including how to link them to other Web pages, to your e-mail address, and to a graphic file. You then learned how to publish the whole package on the Web. Just think, you did all that with Internet Explorer's FrontPage Express, in combination with Explorer's Web Publishing Program. This powerful combination gives you all the tools you need to continue to create professional-looking Web pages and publish them for all to see on the World Wide Web.

DISCOVERY CENTER

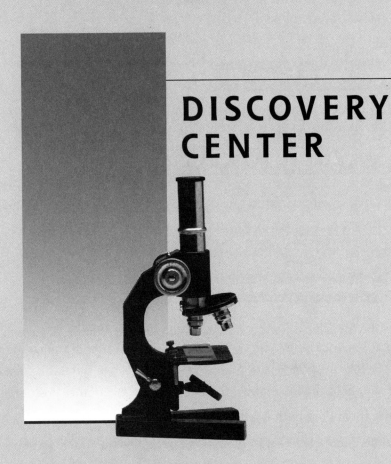

I n this section, you'll discover many of the important steps for accomplishing tasks in Internet Explorer 4. The Discovery Center is a handy reference to the most important tasks in the chapters. The quick summaries include page references referring you back to the chapters if you need more information.

CHAPTER 1

How to Open Explorer (page 14)

Click the icon named "The Internet" one time (or twice, if you turned off the Web Integrated Desktop) to open Internet Explorer.

How to Turn the Active Desktop Off and On (page 26)

1. Right-click an empty part of the desktop to open the shortcut menu.

2. Select `Active Desktop` → `View as Web Page` to turn the Active Desktop off or on.

How to Customize Toolbar Size or Arrangement (page 23)

1. Move the mouse pointer over the toolbar section's "handle" (the two vertical lines at the left end of the toolbar section) so that the pointer turns into a two-headed arrow.

2. Click and hold the mouse button as you drag it to another position.

3. Release the mouse button when the section is where you want it.

4. Drag the handle left or right to expand or reduce the toolbar section's size.

5. Drag the bottom edge of the toolbars up or down to add or remove toolbar rows.

How to Sort or Change Display Format for Folder Icons (page 23)

1. In any folder, including My Computer, Windows Explorer, or IE 4, click the `View` menu to open it.

2. Select `Toolbar` to choose which toolbars show, and to show or hide toolbar text labels.

3. Select `Large Icons`, `Small Icons`, `List`, or `Details` to display the icons the way you prefer.

4. Select `Arrange Icons` to sort the icons in the way you prefer.

How to Customize IE 4's "Look and Feel" (page 28)

Open My Computer and select Options from the View menu to open the Options dialog box, then:

* Select "Web style" for the new IE 4 look and feel.
* Select "Classic style" for the way Windows 95 used to work.
* Select "Custom" to choose a combination of features from both the Web and Classic styles.

CHAPTER 2

How to Customize a Folder (page 36)

1. Right-click a blank space in the folder background to open the shortcut menu, or click `View` in the menu bar.

2. Select `Customize this Folder` to start the Customize This Folder Wizard.

   The Wizard walks you through two different ways of customizing your folder: adding an image or pattern for the background, or creating an HTML document for the background. Except for "system" folders (My Computer, Control Panel and similar folders) every folder can be customized individually.

How to Use the New Start Menu Options (page 47)

* Click Start→Favorites to open the new Favorites menu. The Channels, links, and favorites that you set up in Internet Explorer are available from this menu.

* Click Start→Find to open the new Find menu. The Find menu also contains new options that you should try out. These include an option to search the Internet, and options for searching for people in your Windows Address Book or in Internet directories.

How to Edit Your Start Menu (page 49)

Drag icons or folders (that contain icons) from one part of your Start menu to another to set it up the way you want it.

CHAPTER 3

How to Customize the Taskbar (page 55)

1. Drag a shortcut to the Quick Launch toolbar to add a copy of it to the toolbar.

2. Right-click a shortcut on a toolbar and select `Delete` to remove it from the toolbar.

How to Create New Toolbars (page 58)

1. Right-click a blank space on the taskbar and select `Toolbars` to open the menu of possible toolbars.

2. Click the one you want to add or click `New Toolbar` to create a custom toolbar.

3. Drag the new toolbar to the desktop or to an edge of the screen to relocate it.

How to Modify Toolbars You Have Added (page 60)

1. Right-click the toolbar to open its shortcut menu.

2. Select the option you want to show or hide text, use large or small icons, Auto Hide, etc.

How to Use the Task Scheduler (page 64)

1. Select `Start` → `Programs` → `Accessories` → `System Tools` → `Scheduled Tasks` to open the Scheduled Tasks folder.

2. Click Add Scheduled Task to start the Add Scheduled Task Wizard.

How to Shut Down the Task Scheduler (page 70)

1. Open the Scheduled Tasks folder.

2. Select `Advanced` → `Stop Using Task Scheduler` to close down the Task Scheduler.

How to Upgrade Internet Explorer (page 70)

1. Go to the IE 4 home page (`www.microsoft.com/ie/IE40/`).

2. Select `Download` → `Internet Explorer 4.0 Components` to add or update IE 4 components.

CHAPTER 4

How to Customize the Active Desktop Background (page 75)

1. Create your own HTML background using FrontPage Express.

2. Right-click the desktop and select `Active Desktop` → `View as Web Page` to turn on the Active Desktop.

3. Right-click the desktop and select `Active Desktop` → `Properties` to open the Display Properties dialog box.

4. Click the Browse button on the Background tab of the Display Properties dialog box, browse to the HTML document you made for your background, and select it.

5. Click OK to save your settings and close the Display Properties dialog box.

How to Select and Subscribe to Channels (page 92)

1. Click a Channel category folder or sample Channel button on the Channel Bar to open the Active Channel Viewer.

2. Click the Channel Guide button to preview the available Channels.

3. Click the "Subscribe" button on the Channel's preview page to subscribe to it.

How to Download and Install Active Desktop Items (page 82)

1. Go to the IE 4 Active Desktop Gallery at `http://www.microsoft.com/ie/IE40/gallery/`.

2. Click a link to an Active Desktop Item to find out what it does.

3. Click the "Add to My Desktop" button on an item's information page to download and automatically install it.

How to Manage Channels (page 94)

1. Open My Computer or Windows Explorer.

2. Select `Favorites` → `Subscriptions` → `Manage Subscriptions` to open the Subscriptions folder.

3. Right-click a subscription in the Subscriptions folder to open its shortcut menu. Select the appropriate menu choice to copy or delete it, reschedule its updates, or manually update it.

CHAPTER 5

How to Use a Link (page 104)

Move the mouse pointer over an icon, graphic, or text. When the pointer turns into a 🖑, it is over a link. Click the link to go to the page it represents.

How to Use a URL to Go to a Web Site (page 107)

To go to a Web site other than the one appearing in the Address bar, follow these steps:

1. Click in the Address bar to highlight the current URL.

2. Type the URL of the site you want to visit.

3. Press the Enter key.

How to Go Backward (page 109)

Do any of the following:

* Click ⬅ Back in the toolbar to go back to the previous page.
* Click the down arrow to the right of the Back button to open a list of previously visited sites and then click the one to which you want to return.
* Right-click the page and click Back on the shortcut menu.
* Click File in the menu bar. A list of previously visited sites is at the bottom of the menu. Click the one you want.

How to Go Forward (page 109)

Do any of the following:

* Click $\boxed{\Rightarrow \text{ Forward}}$ in the toolbar to revisit in sequence pages you have already seen.

* Click the down arrow to the right of the Forward button to open a list of previously visited sites and then click the one to which you want to return.

* Right-click the page and click Forward on the shortcut menu.

How to Use the History List (page 110)

1. Click the History button.

2. Click the appropriate folder, and then click the Web icon to the left of the site name.

How to Add a Page to Your Links Bar (page 112)

Drag and drop a Web site icon onto the Links bar.

How to Add a Link to the Favorites Folder (page 114)

1. The Web site you want should be open on your screen.

2. Click ⬚Favorites⬚ on the menu bar, and then click ⬚ **Add to Favorites** ⬚. The Add to Favorites dialog box appears.

3. Click the Create in button. The dialog box expands.

4. Click the Links folder to highlight it.

5. Click OK. The link shown in the Name box is added to your Links bar and to your Favorites folder.

How to Delete a Link (page 115)

1. Double-click the Links bar handle to open the bar completely.

2. Right-click the link you want to delete.

3. Click ⬚ **Delete** ⬚ on the shortcut menu.

How to Print (page 117)

1. Right-click inside the frame (or page) you want to print. (Make sure your pointer is not over a link when you do this.) A shortcut menu opens.

2. Click `Print` to open the Print dialog box.

3. Within the Print frames section at the bottom of the dialog box, select the appropriate option.

How to Control What Your Kids See (page 119)

1. Click `View` in the menu bar and then click `Options` to open the Internet Properties dialog box shown below.

2. Click the Content tab to bring it to the front.

3. Click the Enable button. The Create Supervisor Password dialog box appears.

4. Type a password in the Password box, press the Tab key, and type the *same* password again in the Confirm password box.

5. Click the OK button. The Content Advisor dialog box appears.

6. Click the Ratings tab to bring it to the front of the Content Advisor dialog box if necessary

7. Click Language. A Rating scale appears below the Category list.

8. Slide the bar on the Rating scale to a spot that reflects your preference. Notice that the rating level is defined just below the scale.

9. Repeat Steps 2 and 3 for Nudity, Sex, and Violence.

10. On the General tab, select the appropriate option.

11. On the Advanced tab accept the default settings unless you have added specific software to your computer and want to use its rating system.

12. Click OK to apply the changes and close the Content Advisor dialog box.

13. Click OK in the Internet Properties dialog box to close it.

How to Override a Content Block with a Password (page 122)

When the Content Block message appears, type in your supervisor password. Click OK and you'll be able to open the Web site.

How to Set Up an Adult Browsing Session (page 123)

1. In the Internet Properties dialog box, click the Content tab.

2. Click the Disable button. The Content Advisor message box appears.

3. Click the OK button.

CHAPTER 6

How to Save a Favorite Web Site (page 128)

1. Go online with Internet Explorer and surf to a Web site you want to add to your favorites list.

2. Click ` Favorites ` → ` Add to Favorites `. An Add to Favorites dialog box appears.

3. Click the Create In button. Another Add to Favorites dialog box appears showing a list of folders where you can store the Web address.

4. The Favorites folder is highlighted. Click the OK button, and the Web address will be stored at the bottom of the Favorites list.

How to Create Your Own Favorites Folder (page 131)

1. Click ` Favorites ` → ` Organize Favorites `. The Organize Favorites dialog box appears.

2. Click the Create New Folder button to open a new folder.

3. Type a name for the new folder.

4. Click anywhere in the dialog box to complete the task.

How to Subscribe to a Web Page Online (page 137)

1. Go online to an awesome Web site that you want to add to your Favorites list.

2. Click ` File ` → ` Add to Favorites `. The Add to Favorites dialog box appears.

3. Click Subscribe to put a ✓ in the box.

4. Click OK. The Subscribe dialog box appears.

5. Click OK.

1. Open My Computer and click to highlight your C: drive.

2. Click **Favorites** in the menu bar.

3. Click the folder containing the Web site you want to add to your subscription list.

4. Right-click the Web site in question. A menu appears.

5. Click **Subscribe**. The Subscribe dialog box appears.

6. Click the OK button on the Subscribe dialog box.

CHAPTER 7

How to Use the Search Pane (page 148)

1. Go online and launch the browser.

2. Click the Search button in the toolbar.

3. Click the down arrow to the right of the Pick of the day to select the search engine of your choice.

4. Type a word or phrase and click the Search button.

5. Click a link to bring up the results in the right pane.

6. Click the Search button to close the Search pane.

How to Find It Fast (page 156)

1. Go to the Internet Explorer home page and click the link to Best of the Web.

2. Click any of the icons listed under Find It Fast.

How to Use Autosearch (page 157)

Type **Go** followed by a word or phrase in the Address bar. Press the Enter key.

CHAPTER 8

How to Set Up Microsoft Wallet to Buy Things Online (page 160)

1. Open Internet Explorer and click `View` → `Options` to open the Options dialog box, or right-click the icon on your desktop named The Internet to open the Internet Properties dialog box (they're actually the same thing).

2. Click the Content tab to bring it to the front.

3. Click Payments to open the Microsoft Wallet program and set it up for online purchasing.

How to Find Software Archives (page 168)

1. Open Internet Explorer and go to the Yahoo! directory (`http://www.yahoo.com`).

2. Click the link for Computers and Internet to go to the Computers and Internet page.

3. Click the link for Software to go to the Software page.

4. Scroll through the software links and try a few that look interesting to you.

How to Find Gophers (page 171)

1. Open IE 4, type **www.yahoo.com/Computers_and_Internet/Internet/Gopher/** in the Address box, and press the Enter key. The Gophers page at Yahoo! appears.

2. Click the link to Gopher Jewels for a list of the best gophers on the Net.

CHAPTER 9

How to Set Up an E-Mail Account (page 180)

1. Click `Tools` in the menu bar.

2. Click `Accounts` in the `Tools` menu to open the Internet Accounts dialog box.

3. Click the Mail tab to bring it to the front, and then click the Add button. A small menu appears.

4. Click Mail on the small menu. A series of Internet Wizard setup screens appear. Fill in the appropriate information as each Internet Connection Wizard dialog box appears, and click Next to go to the next screen.

5. Click Finish when done.

How to Set Up an Automatic Signature for Messages (page 185)

Method 1:

1. Click `Tools` in the menu bar. A menu appears.

2. Click `Stationery`. The Stationery dialog box appears. You can click the Text option and type any text message in the text box.

3. Click OK.

Method 2:

1. Click `Tools` in the menu bar. A menu appears.

2. Click `Stationery`. The Stationery dialog box appears.

3. Select the File option and click the Browse button to select a customized text file of your creation. Whatever text is in your customized signature file will be added to the bottom of your outgoing messages. Use Windows Notepad to set up a personal signature file in advance.

CHAPTER 10

How to Set Up the Address Book (page 194)

Click `Address Book` in the toolbar and do any of the following:

Add a name	Click the New Contact button on the Address Book toolbar to open a blank Properties dialog box.
	Enter the appropriate information in each tab of the Properties dialog box. Click OK.
Edit	Click the name of the addressee that needs editing to highlight it. Next, click the Properties button on the toolbar. The Properties dialog box for that person appears. Edit fields on appropriate tabs as needed. Click OK.
Add Personal and Business Information	Double-click the addressee's name in the Address Book list. The Properties dialog box appears. Click the Home tab and add appropriate information. Click the Business tab and add appropriate information. Click OK.

How to Create a Mail List (page 202)

1. Click [New Group] on the Address Book toolbar.

2. Type a name for the group.

3. Click the Select Members button on the dialog box to open a second dialog box.

4. Click the person's name you want to add to highlight it and then click the Select button.

5. Repeat process to add additional names.

6. Click OK. Click OK again.

CHAPTER 11

How to Compose an E-Mail Message (page 208)

Complete the following steps to compose a new message:

1. Click the Outlook Express icon on the Quick Launch Toolbar to the right of the Start button on the Taskbar to open Outlook Express.

2. Click the Compose Message button on the toolbar. A New Message dialog box appears.

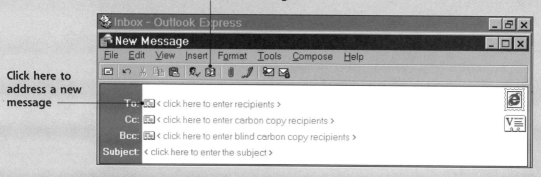

Click here to address a new message, too

Click here to address a new message

3. Click the little Rolodex card 📇 to the immediate right of "To" to open the Select Recipients dialog box (another view of the Address Book) or click the Address Book button on the toolbar. Either way, the Select Recipients dialog box appears.

4. Click the name of the person to whom you want to send a message to highlight it.

5. Click the To: button. The addressee's name moves to the Message Recipients To: section.

6. Click the name of the person you to whom you want to send a carbon copy to highlight it.

7. Click the Cc: button. The addressee's name moves to the Message Recipients Cc: section.

8. Click the name of the person you to whom you want to send a blind carbon copy to highlight it.

9. Click the Bcc: button. The addressee's name moves to the Message Recipients Bcc.

10. Click the OK button. All Done!

How to Attach a File to a Message (page 213)

Complete the following steps to attach a file to your message:

1. Click Insert → File Attachment . The Insert Attachment dialog box will appear.

2. Type the filename and click the Attach button.

How to Send a Message (page 215)

Click the Send button 🖃 in the far left corner of the toolbar.

CHAPTER 12

How to Get Your Mail (page 220)

1. Open Outlook Express and go to the Inbox.

2. Click the Send and Receive button. If you're not already online, Outlook Express connects you. After Outlook Express has downloaded your mail, the Outlook Express dialog box closes.

How to Read Your Mail (page 222)

Click a heading in the top pane. The letter will show in the preview pane. Each letter will have one or more of the following icons:

!	The message has been marked high priority by the sender.
↓	The message has been marked low priority by the sender.
📎	The message has an attachment.
✉	This message has not been read. The message listing appears in bold type.
✉	This message has been read. The message listing appears in light type.

How to Reply to E-Mail (page 223)

Click	To do the following
Reply to Author	Open a Compose Message box with the recipient's name and the subject already filled in.
Reply to All	Open a Compose Message box with all previous recipients' names in the To box and all Cc recipients' names in the Cc: box. The subject line will be filled in.
Forward Message	Open a Compose Message box with the original message included in the body of the letter. The subject is filled in.

How to Quote a Portion of a Letter (page 225)

1. Highlight the text you want to quote.

2. Right-click the highlighted text and click `Copy`.

3. Click the appropriate reply button.

4. Right-click in the message section of the new window and click `Paste`.

5. Insert a > to the left of the line of quoted text. If you're quoting many lines of text, consider putting a line of asterisks above and below the text instead of inserting the >.

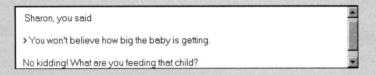

How to Save a Letter (page 227)

1. Right-click the message listing in the top pane, and then click `Move to`.

2. Click the folder where you want to send the letter.

How to Filter Your Mail (page 231)

1. Click `Tools` → `Inbox Assistant`.

2. Click the Add button.

3. Define the criteria for your filter, and then click OK.

How to Apply a Filter to Mail Already in Your Inbox (page 232)

1. In the Properties dialog box, select the filter to be applied.

2. Click Apply To and then click the Inbox icon to apply this rule to all mail in the Inbox.

3. Click OK.

CHAPTER 13

How to Get to Newsgroups (page 240)

1. Click the Outlook Express icon on the Quick Launch toolbar.
2. Click `Go` → `News`.

How to Subscribe to a Newsgroup (page 242)

When You Know the Address   In the Newsgroups dialog box, enter the newsgroup address on the All tab and click Subscribe.

When You Know the Subject   In the Newsgroups dialog box, click the All tab. Type a subject in the "Display newsgroups which contain" box. Click a matching newsgroup and click Subscribe.

How to Delete a Newsgroup (page 244)

＊ In the newsgroup folder, right-click the newsgroup listing and then click `Unsubscribe from this newsgroup`.

Or

＊ In the newsgroup itself, right-click the newsgroup icon on the right of the Title bar. Click `Unsubscribe from this newsgroup`.

CHAPTER 14

How to Read Newsgroup Messages (page 253)

1. Go to the newsgroup folder in Outlook Express.
2. Double-click the newsgroup you want to read to open it.
3. Click a subject that interests you. The message appears in the preview pane at the bottom of the window.
4. Click the + to the left of a message to expand the thread.

How to Post a Newsgroup Message (page 257)

To start a new thread, click .

To send a reply to the entire newsgroup, click .

To send a message to the author but not to the group, click the Reply to Author icon.

To forward a newsgroup message to someone not in the newsgroup, click
.

How to Sort Messages (page 260)

* Click View in the menu bar and then click Sort By. Select the appropriate method.

Or

* Click the column heading for the method you want. For example, click the Sent heading. The ▼ sorts with most recent dates at the top of the column and the oldest dates at the bottom. The ▲ sorts with the oldest dates at the top of the list and the most recent at the bottom.

How to Mark a Message (page 262)

Right-click the message, then click the appropriate choice.

How to Switch Between Newsgroups (page 262)

1. Click the down arrow to the right of the newsgroup name. A list of folders within Outlook Express appears with the current newsgroup highlighted.

2. Switch to another newsgroup by clicking its name at the bottom of the list.

How to Download Messages for Offline Reading (page 267)

1. Mark selected messages that you want to download.

2. While you're in the newsgroup, click Tools → Download this Newsgroup . The Download Newsgroup dialog box appears. If you've marked

messages, there will be a check beside "Get marked messages" at the bottom of the dialog box.

3. Click "Get the following items" to enable the choices below it, and then click the appropriate choice.

4. Click OK. An Outlook Express dialog box appears showing the progress of the download. Click the Stop button if you want to stop the download.

5. Click the ⊠ to close the dialog box.

6. The next time you boot up Outlook Express, don't connect. You can read downloaded messages offline.

CHAPTER 15

How to Set Options in Microsoft NetMeeting (page 280)

1. Open NetMeeting and click Tools → Options to open the Options dialog box.

2. Click the General tab to set automatic startup options.

3. Click the My Information tab to change your directory information.

4. Click the Calling tab to set directory and SpeedDial options.

How to Make a NetMeeting Call (page 282)

NetMeeting calls can be made in several different ways, including any of the following:

* Double-click a listing on the SpeedDial tab.
* Double-click a listing on the Directory tab.
* Double-click a listing on the History tab.
* Click the Call toolbar button or select Call → New Call to open the New Call dialog box, type the e-mail or IP address that you want to call, and click Call.

How to Set Up the Windows Address Book for NetMeeting (page 284)

1. Open your Windows Address Book.

2. Click the entry for the person you will be making a call to.

3. Click the Properties toolbar button to open the person's Properties dialog box.

4. Click the NetMeeting tab.

5. Select the person's e-mail address under Conferencing E-Mail, and add his or her server under Conferencing Directory Servers.

6. Click OK to save your settings and close the Properties dialog box.

CHAPTER 16

How to Use Chat (page 290)

1. While in the Current Call window, click the Chat button.

2. Type your message in the Message box at the bottom of the window.

3. Click the Enter key. It appears on the Chat screen where everyone in the meeting can see it.

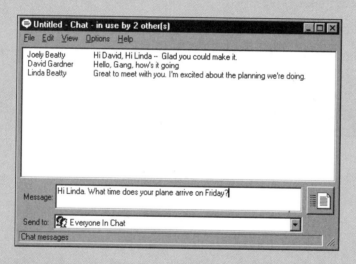

How to Whisper to One Person in a Meeting (page 292)

1. Click the down arrow to the right of the Send to box at the bottom of the Chat window. A list of people in the chat session appears.

2. Click the name of the person you want to whisper to.

3. Type your comment and send it as usual. Your comment appears on your screen and the screen of the person to whom you whispered. It's preceded by the word *private* (in italics and parentheses).

How to Use the Whiteboard (page 294)

1. Click the Current Call tab.

2. Click the Whiteboard icon in the toolbar. (If you don't see a Whiteboard icon, you're not in Current Call.) You'll see a message that says its searching for other Whiteboards. When NetMeeting locates them all, the Whiteboard appears.

3. Click the Maximize button to enlarge the Whiteboard.

4. Click a tool in order to use it.

5. If the tool uses line width or color, click the appropriate choices.

How to End a NetMeeting (page 299)

Click the Hang Up button and close the NetMeeting window.

CHAPTER 17

How to Initiate Sharing a File (page 304)

As the leader, or host, of the meeting:

1. While you are in the current call, open the file you want to share and then minimize it.

2. Click the Share button and then the filename.

3. Maximize the file. What you see on your screen is what the other people in the meeting will see.

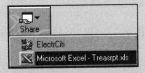

How to See a Shared File (page 305)

As a participant in a meeting: Click the file icon in the taskbar. The file appears on your screen. You can see what the leader does but you cannot interact with the file in any way.

How to Stop Sharing a File (page 306)

The leader clicks the Share button and then clicks the shared file to remove the ✓.

How to Collaborate on a File (page 307)

1. Complete the steps to share a file.

2. Click the Collaborate button on the NetMeeting toolbar or on the Quick Access toolbar.

3. Each person in the meeting clicks the Collaborate button. The file appears on everyone's screen.

4. Click your mouse to take control.

How to Send a File to People in a Meeting (page 309)

1. Select `Tools` → `File Transfer` → `Send File`.

2. Select the file and click `Send`.

3. The recipients see the transfer take place on their screens and can do one of the following:

   ✳ Open the file in the transfer dialog box.

   ✳ Close the dialog box and open the file with `Tools` → `File Transfer` → `Open Received Files Folder`.

   ✳ Delete the file.

How to Browse Collaboratively (page 311)

1. In the current call, click the icon to launch the Internet Explorer browser.

2. While the browser is on your screen, click the NetMeeting icon on the right of the taskbar and then click Share and the site name.

3. After you've shared the file, click the NetMeeting icon again and click Start Collaborate.

4. Each person in the meeting must click the Start Collaborate button on his or her screen.

CHAPTER 18

How to Find Web Models (page 318)

1. Type **http://www.netscape.com/home/gold3.0_templates.html**

2. Scroll about half-way down the Netscape Web Page Templates page until you see the following categories of templates:

   * Personal/Family
   * Company/Small Business
   * Department
   * Product/Service
   * Special Interest Group
   * Interesting and Fun

3. Click any link that interests you to open the associated template. If you like the looks of a particular layout, or some facet of the layout interests you, print the page.

How to Make a Web Site Folder (page 325)

1. Go to Windows Explorer and click the name of the drive on which you want to create the folder.

2. Click File → New → Folder .

3. Type the name of the folder in the Contents window.

How to Search for Free Artwork (page 322)

1. Click the Search button on the Internet Explorer toolbar.

2. Choose any of the search engines listed and use the search box to locate "free clipart."

How to Save a Graphic (page 325)

1. Right-click the graphic.
2. Click `Save Image As` on the shortcut menu.
3. Save to the appropriate folder.

How to View HTML Coding (page 328)

1. Right-click a Web page.
2. Click `View Source` on the shortcut menu.

How to Save the Source Document (page 328)

Click File→Save As and save in the appropriate folder as a text file.

CHAPTER 19

How to Start Your HTML Document (page 332)

1. Click `Start`. A menu appears.
2. Click `Programs` → `Internet Explorer` → `FrontPage Express`. FrontPage Express opens with an untitled HTML document ready for editing.

How to Add Background and Text Color (page 333)

1. Click `Format` → `Background`. A Page Properties dialog box appears with the Background tab in front.
2. Click the ▼ to the right of the Background text box to open the background color selection menu.
3. Click the color of your choice. The color menu closes.
4. Click the OK button to complete the process.
5. You can follow Steps 1 through 4 to change the text color.

How to Insert and Format a Heading (page 335)

1. Type some text on the blank page.

2. Drag the cursor over the text to highlight it.

3. Click the arrow in the first list box on the left (with the word Normal in it) to open it.

4. Click Heading 1. The list will close and the text becomes larger.

How to Change Fonts, Font Styles, Size, and Color (page 335)

1. Highlight the text whose font you want to change.

2. Click `Format` → `Font` to open the Font tab.

3. Click the Font, Font Style, and Size you want to select them.

4. Click the ▼ next to Color in the lower left corner of the tab. A drop-down list appears.

5. Click the font color you want in the drop-down list to select it.

6. Click the OK button.

How to Change Text Alignment (page 335)

1. Highlight the text whose alignment you want to change.

2. Click `Format` → `Paragraph` to open the Paragraph Properties tab.

3. Click the ▼ to the right of the Paragraph Alignment text box. A drop-down list appears.

4. Click your alignment choice (left, right, center).

5. Click the OK button.

How to Insert and Format a Horizontal Line (page 336)

1. Click `Insert` → `Paragraph` → `Horizontal Line`. A horizontal line appears instantly on the page.

2. Right-click the line. A menu appears.

3. Click `Horizontal Line Properties`. The Horizontal Line Properties dialog box appears.

4. Select the width, height, alignment, and color of the line.

5. When you have finished, click the OK button.

How to Insert a Graphic Image (page 336)

1. Click the page to set the cursor where you want to place the image.

2. Click Insert → Image or click the Insert Image toolbar button. In either case, the Image dialog box appears with the Other Location tab at the front.

3. Click From File to put a dot in the circle if it is not already there.

4. Click the Browse button and browse to the folder where the image is located.

5. Open the image into FrontPage Express. The image appears on the page where you placed the cursor.

How to Link a Page You Made to Another Page (page 339)

1. Save both pages in the same folder.

2. Open both pages in FrontPage Express.

3. Type a name or phrase for the page-to-page link in your master page. Any name or phrase will do. It doesn't have to be the name of the file to be linked.

4. Highlight the name or phrase that you have given the link.

5. Click Insert → Hyperlink. The Create Hyperlink dialog box appears.

6. Click the Open Pages tab to bring it to the front.

7. Click the name of the page you want to link to highlight it.

8. Click OK. The page is linked.

How to Link Your Page to a Graphic Image (page 340)

1. Create a new page and save it.

2. Follow the steps in the section entitled, "How to Insert a Graphic Image," to insert a graphic image into the new page.

3. Size the graphic so that it will be displayed the way you want it to look when the page is opened.

4. Repeat the steps in the previous section entitled, "How to Link a Page You Made to Another Page," to link the page containing the graphic file to your master page.

How to Get Ready to Publish Your Page on the WWW (page 345)

Complete the following steps *before* opening the Web Publishing Wizard:

1. Call your ISP to find out if they are compatible with Explorer's Web Publishing Wizard Program. If so, go on to Step 2.

2. Get the following information from your ISP and write it down:

   * How much space is available for your pages and graphics
   * The URL for their server
   * What the procedures are for signing onto their server
   * Your user name and password for access to their server, if it is different from your user name and password for other Internet access
   * The path to the folder (or directory) on the server where you can store your files
   * The URL you should use to view your page(s) using Internet Explorer

How to Use the Web Publishing Wizard (page 346)

1. Click `Start` on the taskbar. The Start menu pops up.

2. Click `Programs` → `Internet Explorer` → `Web Publishing Wizard`. The first of a number of Wizard dialog boxes appears.

3. Type the information requested in each dialog box as it appears.

4. Once you are satisfied that you have filled in the correct information in a dialog box, click Next to move to the next one.

5. Fill in your password and user name when asked.

6. When you get to the Publish Your Files dialog box, click the Finish button.

VISUAL INDEX

Using the Active Desktop

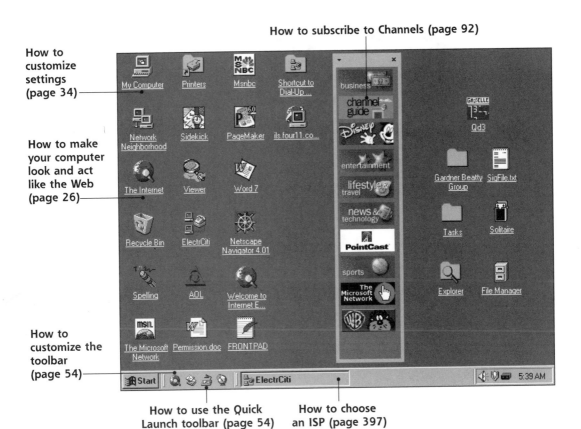

How to subscribe to Channels (page 92)

How to customize settings (page 34)

How to make your computer look and act like the Web (page 26)

How to customize the toolbar (page 54)

How to use the Quick Launch toolbar (page 54)

How to choose an ISP (page 397)

Surfing the Web with Internet Explorer

How to create and manage Favorites (page 128)

How to move around quickly (page 109)

How to print a frame or page (page 117)

How to use a URL (page 107)

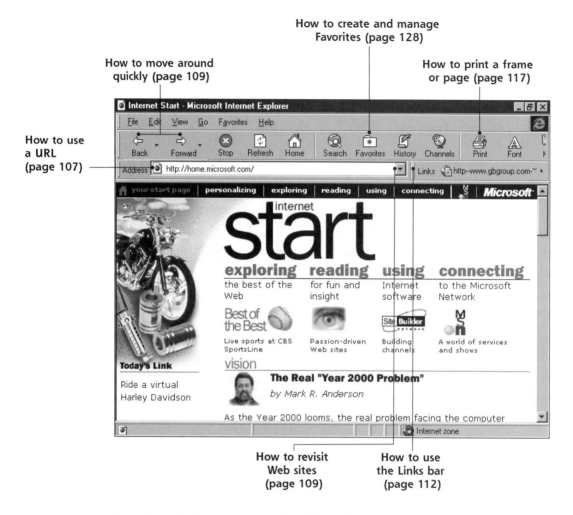

How to revisit Web sites (page 109)

How to use the Links bar (page 112)

Screen shot reprinted by permission from Microsoft Corporation.

Searching the Web

How to search
the Web
(page 146)

How to
show a list
of Favorites
(page 129)

How to
show
Channels
(page 90)

How to
show
or hide
toolbars
(page 21)

How to use
AutoSearch
(page 157)

How to
choose a
search engine
(page 146)

How to work
with frames
(page 116)

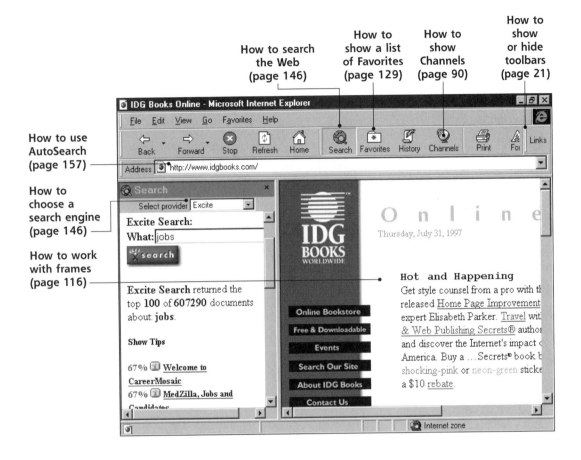

Viewing New Mail in the Inbox

How to forward a message (page 226)

How to send outgoing mail and get new mail (page 214)

How to delete a message (page 230)

How to use special stationery (page 185)

How to set up the Outlook Express window (page 183)

How to reply to the author (page 223)

How to file a message in a folder (page 231)

How to use Internet acronyms (page 212)

How to include a signature (page 186)

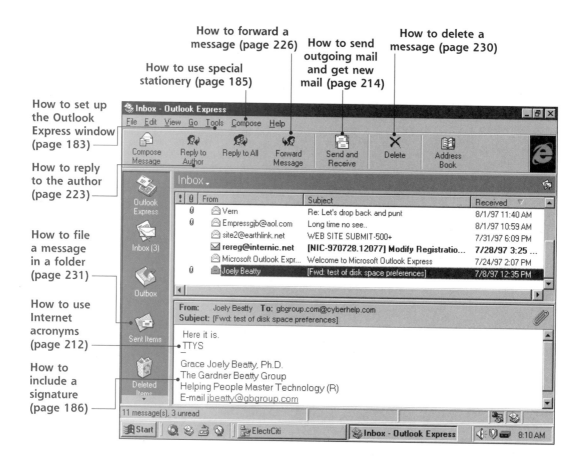

Composing Messages

How to send
a message
(page 215)

How to set up
mail options
(page 183)

How to spell
check a message
(page 213)

How to attach
a business card
(page 199)

How to create
a personal
address book
(page 195)

How to
address e-mail
(page 208)

How to send a
copy of e-mail
(page 209)

How to quote
part of a
message
(page 225)

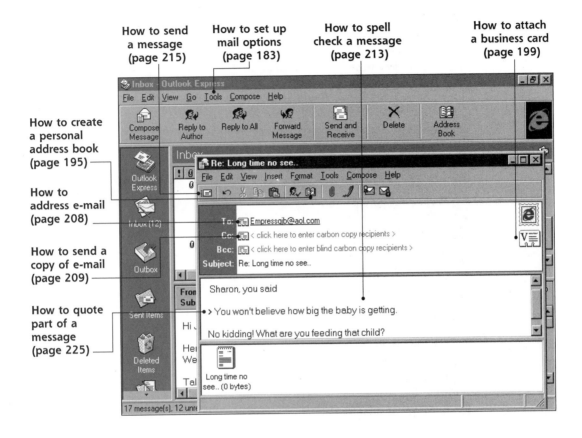

Setting Up Newsgroups in Outlook Express

How to set
newsgroup
options
(page 236)

How to go to
a different folder
in Outlook Express
(page 262)

How to subscribe
to a newsgroup
(page 242)

How to read
newsgroups
offline
(page 266)

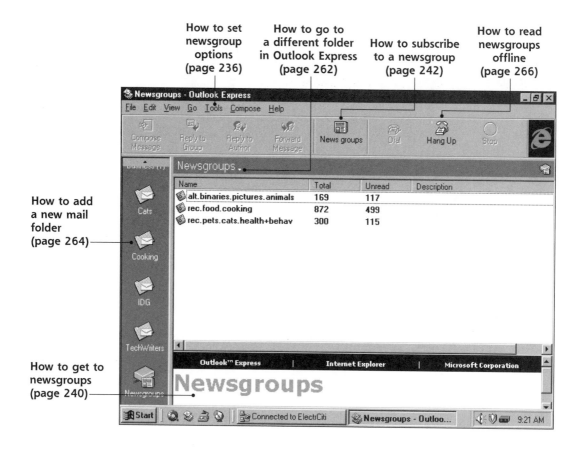

How to add
a new mail
folder
(page 264)

How to get to
newsgroups
(page 240)

Reading Newsgroup Messages

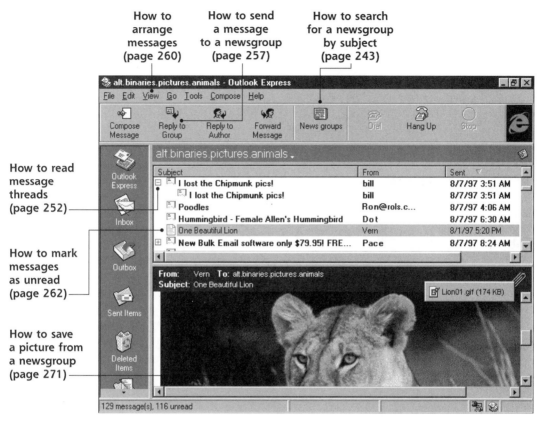

How to arrange messages (page 260)

How to send a message to a newsgroup (page 257)

How to search for a newsgroup by subject (page 243)

How to read message threads (page 252)

How to mark messages as unread (page 262)

How to save a picture from a newsgroup (page 271)

Photo taken by Jo A. Moore while in the Masai Mara, Kenya during July 1997. Photo scanned and published on "A World Travels, Safaris and Wildlife" Web site at http://www.inficad.com/~vmoore by Vern Moore.

Using NetMeeting

How to call people
for a NetMeeting
(page 282)

How to type
text in the
Whiteboard
(page 296)

How to
use Chat
(page 290)

How to open
the Whiteboard
(page 294)

How to
choose a
directory
service
(page 279)

How to use
SpeedDial to
call people
(page 282)

How to
draw shapes
(page 294)

How to use
the remote
pointer
(page 298)

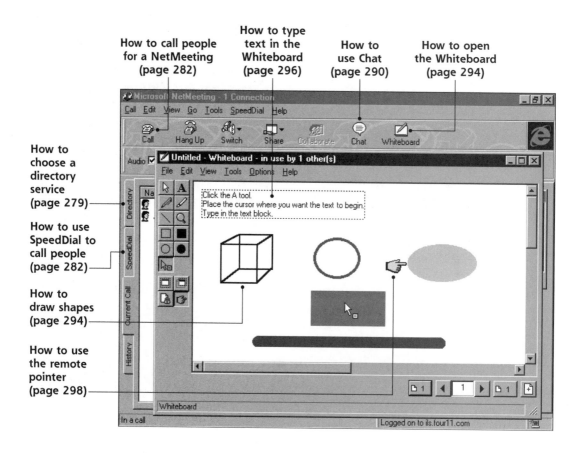

Sharing and Collaborating
in NetMeeting

**How to
end a call
(page 299)**

**How to
share a file
(page 304)**

**How to
work together
on a file
(page 307)**

**How to use
audio and video
(page 289)**

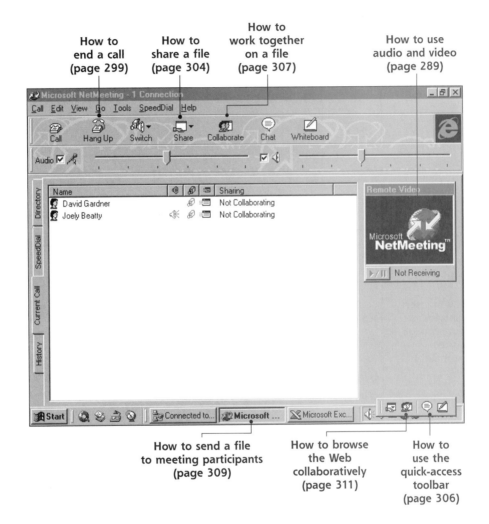

**How to send a file
to meeting participants
(page 309)**

**How to browse
the Web
collaboratively
(page 311)**

**How to
use the
quick-access
toolbar
(page 306)**

Creating a Home Page in FrontPage Express

How to
insert a reply
e-mail link
(page 342)

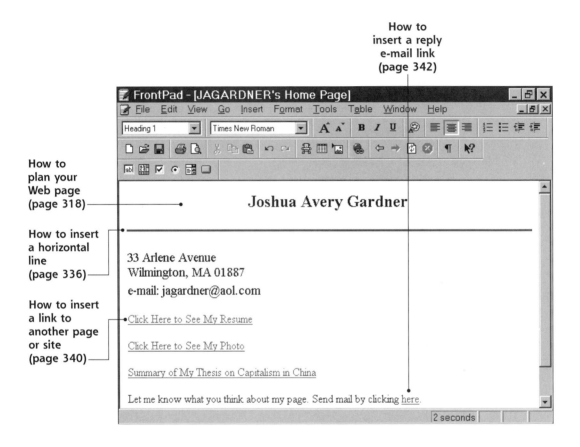

How to
plan your
Web page
(page 318)

How to insert
a horizontal
line
(page 336)

How to insert
a link to
another page
or site
(page 340)

Creating a Web Page in FrontPage Express

How to open
FrontPage Express
(page 332)

How to
customize
the text
(page 335)

How to make
a colored
background
(page 333)

How to insert
graphics
(page 336)

How to create
a table
(page 343)

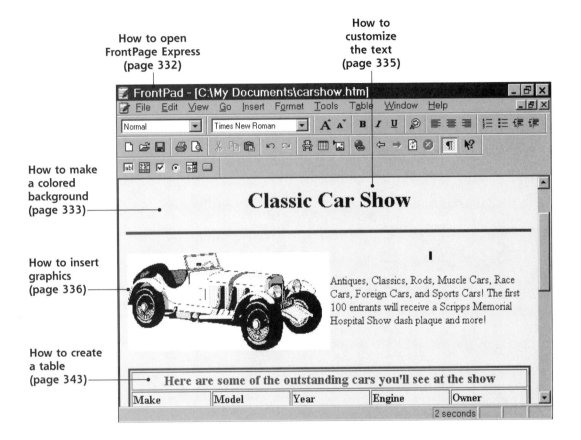

INSTALLING AND SETTING UP EXPLORER

Most of the Internet Explorer 4 installation process is automatic and you should have no problems with it. Updating or adding components to IE 4 should also be a trouble-free experience. There are a few points, however, that we think you'd like to know about in advance, and some fine-tuning you can do to the program after it's installed.

Before You Start

To run IE 4 your computer needs to have a 486 processor runnning at 66MHz or better.

The version of IE 4 discussed in this book is the one produced for Windows 95, Windows NT 4.0, and Windows 98.

Although Microsoft says that IE 4 will run on computers that have only 8MB of RAM (16MB for Windows NT), our advice is that, in order to support IE 4 and other memory-hungry programs running at the same time, your computer needs at least 16MB (32 for NT) and, ideally, should have 32MB of RAM.

Your computer must have lots of free hard disk space for IE 4. You will need from about 70MB to nearly 90MB free for installation, depending on what components you choose to install. Most of this space is used by temporary files that are deleted when you're done. The installed program will permanently take up between 10MB and 25MB of space depending on what components are installed.

Getting Explorer

There are several different ways you can obtain IE 4. We'll discuss these from the least complicated to the most:

* You may receive IE 4 already installed and set up when you buy your computer. If this is the case, skip the installation part of this appendix and go right to the section titled "Fine-Tuning Explorer."

* You may purchase or receive IE 4 on a CD-ROM. Installation is very easy in this case, and you may have little to do except watch the light on your CD drive flicker while the program is installed on your computer. If you received IE 4 on a CD, proceed with the installation instructions that accompany the CD. Read through the more detailed procedures involved in downloading IE 4 below. Some of the steps you will see there are duplicated, at a much more rapid pace, in the CD installation. Then proceed to the "Fine-Tuning" section to customize Explorer's operation.

* You may download the IE 4 installation program, run it to select the components you want to install, then download and install the components. This method can take quite a while, even if your modem works at 28,800 bps. The files required for a complete installation are very large and the download (at 28,800) could take over two hours. If you're the impatient sort, you may start to think that it will never end.

Downloading and Installing Explorer

Microsoft offers IE 4 for free at their Web site. The IE 4 download and installation procedures changed recently with the introduction of the "Active Setup Wizard." This program is fairly small, relatively speaking (about 425 kilobytes), and downloads in a fairly short time. When you run the Active Setup Wizard program, it presents you with several setup options.

Follow these steps to download and install IE 4:

1. Go to Microsoft's IE 4 home page at `http://www.microsoft.com/ie/ie40` and select the download link. You will have the option of downloading and automatically running the Active Setup Wizard, or just downloading it and running it later. We recommend downloading only. This allows you to keep a copy of the Wizard program so that you can run it quickly and easily later should you need to reinstall IE 4 or install it on another computer.

2. Follow the instructions on the download Web pages to copy the Active Setup Wizard to your computer's hard disk.

3. Close your browser, disconnect from your ISP, and run the IE 4 Active Setup Wizard program. The Internet Explorer 4 Active Setup dialog box opens.

4. Click Next. The Wizard's Installation Option screen appears (see Figure A-1).

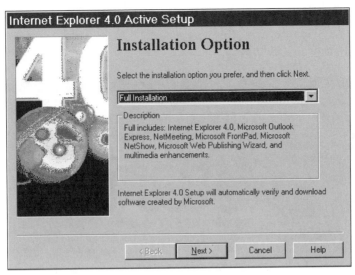

Figure A-1 The Active Setup Wizard automates the download and installation process.

5. Click the down arrow in the option box to see your installation options. Click each one in turn to see the description for each option. Click the one you want, and then click Next. The Wizard's Web Integrated Desktop screen appears. This screen gives you the option of installing the "Web" interface for your desktop. You can install it and turn it off or modify it later if you don't like it (see Chapter 1).

6. Click Yes or No in the Web Integrated Desktop screen, and then click Next. The next screen that appears shows the default path and folder for storing IE 4 files on your computer's hard disk.

7. You can type in the path and folder of your choice or click Browse and browse to the folder you want to use, or make no changes, accepting the default path and folder. Click Next. The program connects to the Internet and eventually presents you with a list of download sites.

8. Select a download site and click the link that begins the download. The files are downloaded, extracted, and installed. Some of the previous steps (for installation options and the Web Integrated Desktop) may be repeated after the files are downloaded and before they are installed.

After installation, IE 4 asks you to restart your computer. After the computer restarts, IE 4 finishes setup by updating shortcuts, opens IE 4, and connects to the Welcome to Internet Start page.

The Welcome page introduces you to the Internet and IE 4. Read through the information on the page and then scroll to the bottom of the page and click the link for the regular Start page (see Figure A-2). The Start page's design and content change regularly, so it may not look exactly like our example when you see it. The regular start page can be customized and designated as your "home page." (The "Fine-Tuning the Browser" section tells you how to set your home page and other IE 4 options.)

Figure A-2   The IE 4 Internet Start page.
Screen shot reprinted by permission from Microsoft Corporation.

X-REF   To update IE 4 or to add components to it that you did not initially install, see the Bonus section at the end of Chapter 3, "Updating Explorer."

Fine-Tuning the Browser

After you install Explorer, you'll want to investigate the many ways in which you can personalize its operation with settings in its Properties dialog box. Some of these settings may not make any sense to you if you're new to browsing the Web. Just remember that you can come back to the Properties dialog box and alter the settings after you've used IE 4 for a while and better understand how making changes here will affect it.

We'll tell you a little about the IE 4 properties that you can change. For more information on the options in the Properties dialog box, click the question mark in the upper-right of whatever dialog box is open, and then click the option you want to know more about.

Follow these steps to access the Properties dialog box:

1. Right-click the icon on your desktop named The Internet and select
   [**Properties**] from the shortcut menu that appears.

   You can also open this dialog box when the browser is open by selecting
   [**View**] → [**Options**].

2. The Internet Properties dialog box appears with the General tab at the
   front (see Figure A-3).

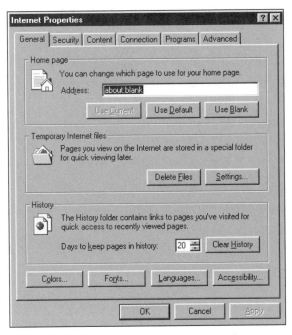

Figure A-3   The Internet Properties dialog box.

General Properties

The General tab in the Properties dialog box includes seven different groups of
options:

✳ *Home page.* This is the Web page that IE 4 displays when you start it up.
  If you do not want IE 4 to automatically connect to the Internet when it
  starts up, click Use Blank (IE 4 opens with a blank page), or use a page
  that's stored on your computer.

  To use a page on your computer, make the page with FrontPage Express
  and save it on your computer's hard disk. Then open it in IE 4 (select
  File→Open, browse to the file, and double-click it) and click the Use
  Current button. To use a favorite page on the Web as your home page,

go to it, and then click the Use Current button. If you click Use Default, IE 4 uses the Start page shown in Figure A-2.

* *Temporary Internet files.* These files are used to store copies of the Web pages you visit and the graphics that appear on them. This reduces the time it takes to redisplay the pages the next time you visit them. Click Delete whenever you want to delete these files to free up hard disk space. Click Settings to adjust how much hard disk space is used for the files, to change the folder (or hard disk) where the files are stored, or to change how often IE 4 checks for newer versions of the files.

* *History.* This is a list of Web pages that you have visited. You can limit the number of days that pages remain on the list, and you can clear the list by clicking Clear History.

* *Colors.* To change the colors used for text, background, or links in the browser, click this button, and then click the color buttons on the dialog box that appears.

* *Fonts.* To change the fonts and font size used in the browser, click this button, and then use the drop-down lists on the dialog box that appears.

* *Languages* and *Accessibility*. These settings generally don't need to be changed.

Security Properties

IE 4 uses "zones" to assign different levels of security to different pages you may encounter with the browser. The Security tab is where you set these up. Generally, the default settings under "Set the security level for this zone" should be adequate.

Click the arrow at the right end of the Zone box and select a zone. For the Trusted sites and Restricted sites zones, click the Add Sites button and enter the URLs for specific Web pages that you either trust a lot ("Trusted Sites") or don't trust at all ("Restricted Sites") in the dialog box that appears. The dialog box that appears when you click Add Sites for the Local intranet zone gives you options specific to your local company network (ask your network administrator about these if you're on one). All other Web sites that you may encounter fall under "Internet Zone."

Content Properties

The Content tab in the Properties dialog box has settings for four things:

* *Ratings.* See "Controlling What Your Kids See," in Chapter 5 for information about Ratings.

* *Certificates.* Certificates are encrypted files that are used to "show some ID." A personal certificate would be used to identify you to a Web site where you may be conducting business, and a site certificate identifies

the site to you so that, for instance, you can be certain you're not downloading a file from a hacker posing as a site.

There are several varieties of certificates, and the difficulty in obtaining one and its cost varies depending on the degree of security that you or a business may need. The most basic ones cost under $10 per year and require no more verification from you than an e-mail address. Often, you can get a "free trial" period for basic certificates. More advanced certificates can require substantial annual fees and such precautions as notarized applications, personal interviews, or even background checks.

The certificate is linked to your browser. When you visit a Web site that requires a digital ID, your browser sends it to the site automatically. Similarly, some commercial Web sites will automatically send a digital certificate to your browser before you start to download software from them. This is their proof that they are who they claim to be and that the software they are offering to send you over the Internet is the genuine product.

 WEB PATH **For more on computer security in general, check the listings in Yahoo! at:**

```
http://www.yahoo.com/Computers_and_Internet/
Security_and_Encryption/
```

* *Personal information — Microsoft Profile Assistant.* This lets you store personal information in a file on your hard disk and control how and when that information is transmitted over the Internet. The Profile Assistant lets you determine what, if any, of this information goes out when a request for data is received from a Web site. Click Edit Profile to set up or edit your profile.

* *Personal information — Microsoft Wallet.* For more information about Wallet, see "Get Out Your Wallet," in Chapter 8.

Connection Properties

The Connection tab controls how you connect to the Internet. If you connect through a company network, your network administrator will tell you if you should use most of these settings, and how to use them. There are two settings you would deal with if you dial into the Internet through an ISP (Internet Service Provider):

* *Use the Connection Wizard...* Click Connect to start the Wizard if your ISP connection has not been set up yet. The Wizard will ask you for information such as phone numbers to use, domain names, and Internet addresses for domain name servers, which should be provided to you by your ISP.

* *Connect to the Internet using a modem.* Click Settings to make adjustments to an ISP connection that has already been set up. You can change phone numbers, passwords, etc., in the Dial-Up Settings dialog box that appears.

X-REF See Appendix B, "Choosing an Internet Service Provider," for more on ISPs and dial-up connections.

Programs Properties

The Programs tab lets you designate which, if any, program you want to use for Internet mail, newsgroups, and "calls" (online conferencing) over the Internet. In addition, you can designate a personal calendar program, such as SideKick, or an Address Book to use with Internet mail, on this tab.

At the bottom of the Programs tab is a curious little checkbox for "Internet Explorer should check to see whether it is the default browser." The default browser is the one that opens automatically when you click a shortcut to a Web page on your desktop or in Windows Explorer. If you have other browsers installed, or install one after you install IE 4, IE 4 may not be the default browser. If this is the case and you want IE 4 to be the default, check this box and open IE 4. You'll see a dialog box that lets you designate IE 4 as the default browser.

Advanced Properties

The Advanced tab includes dozens of options, but we'll only cover a few of them here. In general, the default settings (the ones made for you by IE 4 during installation) should be OK. You may, however, want to check the following:

* *Browsing.* Several of these options affect the way IE 4 looks and acts. They include Use AutoComplete, Show friendly URLs, Use smooth scrolling, Highlight links when clicked, and Browse in a new process. Try them out to see what difference they may make.

* *Cookies.* See the Bonus at the end of Chapter 5 for more information about cookies.

* *Toolbar — Small Icons.* Click this to try out smaller icons on your IE 4 toolbar.

CHOOSING AN INTERNET SERVICE PROVIDER

Competition among Internet service providers (ISPs) is fierce, which is to your advantage. Though it was predicted that the large ISPs offering nationwide service would drive local ISPs out of business, local ISPs are still coming online and thriving. It is not uncommon to have more than 50 ISPs to choose from in metropolitan areas of the U.S. Most of the points raised here apply even if you are considering using an online service such as America Online, CompuServe, or The Microsoft Network for access to the Internet.

Finding an Internet Service Provider

Because there are so many ISPs, the process of choosing one can be daunting. Some offer services nationwide, some are local concerns. Often the lower rate of a national ISP is offset by the personal service of a local one. Following are some sources for ISP names:

* Local newspapers or magazines
* The Yellow Pages under Internet, Computers, or Telecommunications
* Local computer clubs and publications
* Friends who have computers
* Staff at local computer stores
* "Internet Cafes," if available, where you can log onto the Internet while you gather with friends or have something to eat

In addition to the sources listed above, if you have access to the World Wide Web, check `http://thelist.com`. You can search this site for ISPs by city or area code.

Evaluating Internet Service Providers

Once you've found the names of several ISPs, you're ready to compare them. ISPs fall into two categories: those that only provide access to the Internet and those that give you additional services.

You should consider four components of service when evaluating an ISP: costs and payment policies, connections, added services, and customer service and technical support. Because each ISP's offerings and rates will probably be different, you may want to make up a table before calling the ISPs for information. List each ISP along one side of the table, with services and rates along the top. Then, as you are making your calls, you can make notes for comparing them later.

Comparing Costs and Payment Policies

The old adage that time is money has never been more true than with time spent online. Virtually all ISPs give you a set number of hours online with your monthly fee. Once you go beyond the specified number of hours, you are charged extra. Also, you may have to keep track of local phone company toll charges, which can add up quickly. It's easy to get so immersed in your online activities that you lose sight of the time, and that can become very expensive. It's a good idea to learn how to compose your e-mail and participate in newsgroups offline (see Chapters 9 through 14) and save your online time for exploring the Web.

Most ISPs offer a variety of service plans at different rates. Before deciding on one, you should think about how much you plan to use the Internet and what you'll be using it for. For example, browsing the Web at home requires less online time and fewer services than using the Web for a business. Also ask about what Internet services are supported. While nearly all ISPs support Web browsing, for example, some do not support Telnet, a program used for direct connections to other computers.

Many ISPs offer special rates if you commit to an annual service package up front. While this may seem like the most economical way to go, it's not a good idea unless you've heard that the ISP is reliable from people you trust, or you've had time to use the service for a while and evaluate it. Ask if you can try their service for a while at the monthly rate before committing to a long-term package.

Questions to ask about costs and payment policies:

✓ Is there an installation or startup charge?
✓ How much free online time do you get for your monthly fee?
✓ How much does additional time cost?
✓ Is there any limit on file transfers?
✓ Do they support Internet Relay Chat and Telnet?
✓ Are there fees for special services?
✓ Do they offer a variety of plans?
✓ Are there payment options such as check, credit card, and bank account debit?
✓ What is the refund policy if you cancel your account?
✓ Is there a discount for quarterly or annual payment?

Comparing Connections

Connection speed, or bandwidth, is a hot topic in the online world because it affects the speed with which you can interact while online. There are two points to your Internet connection: The first is your connection to the ISP. It is determined by the speed of your modem and the ISP's modems that you dial into. As of the time of this writing, to get the most out of your Web browsing experiences, both should support at least a 28.8 Kbps connection. Anything slower and you'll be incredibly frustrated when you try to connect to an elaborate Web site and have to wait for ages while graphics, audio, and other "bells and whistles" are downloaded.

The second connection point is the ISP's connection to the Internet. According to Kim Clark, a sales support engineer at our ISP, ElectriCiti, you should expect your ISP to have a T1 line. This, combined with a fast modem on your computer, will give you all the power you need at the most cost-effective price.

Be sure to ask if there is a local toll-free number for your area. If you have to pay tolls each time you call the ISP, your telephone bill can get out of hand quickly. If you travel extensively and use a laptop to do business, ask the ISP if they have an 800 number or point of presence (POP) sites. POPs are local numbers across the country that get routed into your ISP, thus avoiding toll calls.

Finally, don't be afraid to ask about "down time;" that is, how often their system can't be used because of technical problems. Most systems have to shut down for routine maintenance from time to time, but a schedule for such shutdowns should be available.

Questions to ask about connections:

✓ Do they have a T1 line?
✓ Do their modems support the fastest speeds currently available?
✓ Is there a local toll-free phone number for connecting to the ISP?
✓ If you travel, do they have POPs? If so, where?
✓ How often has their system been down in the last week? In the last month?

Comparing Added Services

Added services offered by ISPs may include such things as storage space on their computer for your own Web page and other files, Web page design services, and domain name registration.

If you want your own Web page, ask if they offer a template that you can simply fill in. If you're setting up service for a business, ask if they offer professional design services. You should not have to pay extra just to store a Web page on your ISP's computer, but the amount of space included in your monthly fee will vary. Most ISPs can also track your Web site's *hits,* the number of times your Web site is visited.

Do you want a domain name—that is, your own special address—on the Internet? For example, we use an Internet service provider called ElectriCiti. A standard Web address with them takes the form: `www.electriciti.com/yourname`. With your own domain name, your Web address would be `www.yourcompany.com` and you could have your e-mail addressed to `yourname@yourcompany.com`. Your mail still goes through the ISP, but people see your domain name instead of the ISP's.

Questions to ask about added services:

✓ Do they offer Web page services?
✓ How much storage space on their computer do you get for your Web page?
✓ Do they have a template or software to help you create a Web page?
✓ Do they have a design service to create a Web page for you?
✓ What other Web page support services do they provide?
✓ Do they offer domain name registration?

Comparing Customer Service and Technical Support

Consider the amount of help the ISP will give you to set up and use your connection. At a minimum, they should provide you with a printed guide of step-by-step connection instructions and live assistance for getting connected. Some ISPs offer free training for new users. You should also expect to receive free of charge any software you may need to make your connection.

Your ISP should provide you with everything you need to set up your Internet connection. Depending on your computer skills, it may be necessary to talk with a competent person who will walk you through the entire connection process.

If you're using an online service such as AOL or CompuServe as your ISP, check whether their software is compatible with all of Explorer's functions.

Questions to ask about customer service and technical support:

✓ What kind of help will you get in setting up your connection?
✓ Do they provide written instructions?
✓ Will someone walk you through the setup?
✓ Will they work with you until your connection works?
✓ If you need additional software, do they supply it? Do you have to download it?
✓ Do they have live technical assistance on weekends? Twenty-four hours a day?
✓ Is their software compatible with Internet Explorer?

Many ISPs have different packages with different levels of service and features. Compare the ISPs in your area carefully. Don't sign up for more features than you realistically will use. And don't commit yourself to a long-term deal until you've had time to use and evaluate the ISP's services.

APPENDIX C

TROUBLESHOOTING GUIDE

Internet Explorer represents an evolving technology, integrating several Internet-related programs with each other, and integrating your computer with the Internet. With any program this complex and inclusive, you're bound to run into the occasional problem. Here are some of the more common problems we've encountered and some things to try if they happen to you.

General Connection Problems

Why can't I dial into the Internet any more? Or, What happened to my Connect To (or Connection Manager) dialog box? It doesn't come up anymore when I try to get on the Internet.

Check your Internet Properties and Dial-Up Networking settings. We have found that these can sometimes get changed by setup and installation programs or other software quirks, so that dial-up networking is no longer automatic. If you run into this problem, check your Internet settings by completing the following steps:

1. Right-click the icon on your desktop named The Internet and select `Properties` from the shortcut menu, or click `Start` → `Settings` → `Control Panel` to open the Control Panel window, and double-click the Internet icon. The Internet Properties dialog box appears.

2. Click the Connection tab to bring it to the front.

3. If "Connect to the Internet using a modem" is not selected (i.e., doesn't have a dot in the circle next to it), click it to select it.

4. Click the Settings button. The Dial-Up Settings dialog box appears.

5. Make sure that your ISP is in the "Use the following Dial-Up Networking connection" box; select it from the drop-down list if it isn't.

6. Click the Properties button. The Properties dialog box for your ISP appears.

7. Check the phone number and all of the settings for your ISP for accuracy, including those on the Server Types tab and the TCP/IP

settings. Check that the correct script is linked to your ISP connection on the Scripting (or Script) tab if you need to use a script for the connection.

8. If you have to make any changes, remember to click OK to save your changes when you close the dialog boxes.

If you still have the connection problem, contact your ISP's help desk. Ask for their latest connection settings, and request that someone walk you through these settings.

How can I stop my computer from dialing into the Internet all by itself?

IE 4 automatically sets up subscriptions to a Web site for IE 4 updates and to the Microsoft Channel Guide when it is installed. These subscriptions are set by default to automatically dial into the Internet and update themselves. To change the update schedule for these subscriptions, open IE 4, My Computer, or Windows Explorer. Select Favorites→Subscriptions→Manage Subscriptions to open the Subscriptions folder. Right-click each subscription in turn and select Properties from its shortcut menu. Click the Schedule tab, and then click the "Update Now (LAN and modem)" option to place a dot in the circle next to it. This option changes the subscriptions so that they have to be updated "manually." (See Chapters 4 and 6 for details about subscriptions and how to update them.)

Browser Problems

W*hat are the strange error messages with numbers in them that I sometimes get instead of the Web page I'm expecting?*

* **Unauthorized 401** — The site you're trying to reach is restricted, or the password you entered was not recognized by the server. Try entering the password again or contact the site's administrator.

* **Forbidden 403** — The Web page you are trying to get is restricted.

* **Not Found 404** — The Web page you are trying to get may not be there anymore. Check the address you entered for accuracy and try again. Also, if IE 4 can't find a URL that you typed into the Address box, try its new automatic search feature: click View→Options, and then click the Advanced tab; under "Search" click "Autoscan common root domains," and under "Search when URL fails," click "Always ask" or "Always search." IE 4 will try to find similar URLs for you when it can't find the one you typed.

* **Unable to Locate the Server** — IE 4 can't find the computer you are trying to reach. Check the URL for accuracy and try again.

* **Too Many Connections — Try Again Later** — What can we say? The Internet simply has become too popular.

Where can I find a complete list of these error messages?

Try the list available from W3 (the ultimate source):

```
http://www.w3.org/pub/WWW/Library/src/HTError.html
```

Another outstanding source that we found through Yahoo! is Comm Corner, by John Woody (Alamo PC Organization Telecommunications Special Interest Group):

```
http://www.alamopc.org/comm.htm
```

How can I stop Explorer from connecting to the Internet every time I open it?

When you install it, IE 4 is set by default to automatically connect to the IE 4 Start page on the Web. To change this, right-click the icon on your desktop named The Internet, or select View→Options when IE 4 is open to open the Internet Properties (or Options) dialog box. On the General tab, in the section named Home page, click the Use Blank button. This sets IE 4 to open and display a blank page when it starts up. It won't connect to the Internet until you select one of your Favorites or enter a URL into the Address box.

My browser stopped working, but all the other IE 4 components (Mail, News, etc.) are still OK. What's wrong?

This problem usually occurs when the Work Offline setting in IE 4 has been changed. (We have discovered that this setting can get changed by some mysterious process.) Open IE 4 and click File on the menu bar to open the File menu. If there is a ✓ next to Work Offline, click Work Offline to remove the ✓.

Channel Problems

How can I stop my channels from connecting to the Internet and updating when I don't want them to?

Apparently, some of your subscriptions are set to automatically dial into the Internet and update themselves. To change the update schedule for subscriptions, open IE 4, My Computer, or Windows Explorer. Select Favorites→ Subscriptions→Manage Subscriptions to open the Subscriptions folder. Right-click each subscription in turn and select Properties from its shortcut menu. Click the Schedule tab, and then click the "Update Now (LAN and modem)" option to place a dot in the circle next to it. This option changes the subscriptions so that they have to be updated "manually." (See Chapters 4 and 6 for details about subscriptions and how to update them.)

Why doesn't a Channel that I thought I subscribed to show up in my Subscriptions folder?

The Channels feature is new and may have a bug or two that still needs to be worked out, or it may not be cooperating with your computer model. Try subscribing again, and then reboot your computer. If the Channel still doesn't show up but others that you subscribed to do, try sending e-mail to the Channel's provider and asking them about the problem. If no Channels that you subscribe to show up, call Microsoft. They may have a fix that applies to your particular computer.

Mail and Newsgroup Problems

W*hy doesn't Outlook Express dial into my ISP when I start it up?*

There are two places to check on settings for this problem: Internet Properties and Outlook Express options. Open Outlook Express, select Tools→Options, and click the Dialup tab. Make sure that "Dial this connection" is selected, and that the correct dialup connection is listed. For Internet Properties, right-click the icon on your desktop named The Internet, select Properties from the shortcut menu, and click the Connection tab. Make sure that "Connect to the Internet using a modem" is selected, and then click the Settings button, making sure that the correct dialup connection is listed in the Dialup Settings dialog box.

Why can't I send or receive e-mail when I'm connected to my ISP? or Why can't I see any newsgroups when I'm connected to my ISP?

First, make sure that you have the latest connection information from your ISP. An ISP we once used was bought by another ISP and transferred its customers' accounts to new servers without notice. Only after a frantic call did we discover that we were customers of the new ISP, and that the connection settings for our e-mail and newsgroups were different! ISPs may also add new servers or change IP addresses, though they usually give you lots of advance warning when this happens. Go to your ISP's Web site, look for a link to customer service or troubleshooting information, and copy down their phone numbers, IP numbers, port numbers, server names, etc.

Open Outlook Express, click Tools→Accounts, click the Mail tab (or News tab), and then click Properties. Check all of the settings on the General, Server, Connection and Advanced tabs for each account to be sure that they match the latest information from your ISP.

FrontPage Express and Web Publisher Problems

W*hy does the wrong HTML editor open when I click "Customize This Folder?"*

One of the many vile aspects of the software wars that torment computer users is that software installation programs almost always set the program being installed as the default program for opening particular types of files. This is called *file association,* and it means that any time you click a file that the program can open—in Windows Explorer, for example—the program starts up and displays the file.

In the case of browsers, HTML editors, and other programs where competition is fierce, it's easy to believe that these programs are equipped with subroutines that regularly "steal" file associations from one another when your back is turned. There may even be several different programs associated with particular file types on your computer.

To check the file associations for files with the ".htm" or ".html" extension on their names, complete the following steps:

1. Open Windows Explorer or My Computer, click [View] → [Options], and click the File Types tab to bring it to the front.

2. Scroll through the list of Registered file types until you see HTM, HTML, Web Pages, or some similar designation and click it. The file extension and the name of the program associated with the file type appears below the scrollable list, under "File type details." The file type name and the file extension are usually different, so check any file types that seem related to HTML files to be sure you find them all.

3. If there are two or more associations for the file type, click each one in turn and click the Remove button to remove the wrong ones (click Yes in the confirmation dialog box) so that only the association for the program you want to use is left. Alternately, you can follow Steps 4 and 5 for all of the associations so that they all refer to the same program.

4. If there is only one association for the file type, and the program you want associated is not the one listed, click the Edit button, and then click the Edit button in the Edit File Type dialog box.

5. Click the Browse button next to the box named "Application used to perform action," browse to the program you want to use, and select it.

6. Click OK in all of the dialog boxes to close them and save your settings.

Removing all file associations for a file type will not disable the programs that can open the file. This only takes away the ability to open the file by clicking (or double-clicking) it in My Computer, Windows Explorer, or File Manager.

Why doesn't my page show up at my Web site after I run the Web Publishing Wizard?

Contact your ISP's help desk and ask if their server or setup does not support using the Web Publishing Wizard. Ask the technical service person to walk you through the process of setting the server name, URL, and other necessary information in the Wizard.

NetMeeting Problems

How do I keep NetMeeting from connecting to the Internet as soon as I open it?

In NetMeeting, click Tools→Options to open the Options dialog box, and then click the Calling tab to bring it to the front. There are three settings on this tab that should not have a ✓ next to them if you don't want to automatically log on to the Internet when you open NetMeeting: "Log on to the directory when NetMeeting starts," "Refresh directory listing when NetMeeting starts," and "Refresh SpeedDial list when NetMeeting starts." Click each of these to remove the ✓. (See Chapter 15 for more details about setting up NetMeeting.)

Why can't I see part of a shared application's window clearly?

The person running the application may have other programs open, overlapping its window. Tell the other person to close or minimize all other programs.

Why can't I save or print from a shared application?

Saving and printing only work on the computer that's sharing the application. Ask the person running it to send you a copy of the file by using the file exchanger.

Why can't I talk with one of the people in the meeting?

You can talk to only one person at a time. Select Tools→Audio and Video to switch to the person you want to talk to.

Why can't anybody hear me (or hear me clearly)?

Make sure your microphone is plugged in and not muted (double-click the little speaker in the taskbar tray to check your Volume Control). Make sure that the microphone icon is checked, and try adjusting its volume. Don't get too close to the microphone. If the problem is severe, quit the meeting and run the Audio Tuning Wizard.

Miscellaneous Problems

My computer slowed down to a crawl after installing Explorer; how can I get it back up to speed?

Turn off the Active Desktop when running memory-hogging programs such as games and programs that edit or make use of lots of graphics. If this doesn't help, you may have to buy more memory (RAM) for your computer.

How do I turn off the Active Desktop?

Right-click the desktop and select Active Desktop→View as Web Page to remove the ✓ next to View as Web Page.

How do I turn off Hover Select and the Web View features?

Read through the "Going Retro" sections in Chapter 1.

How can I get the Task Scheduler icon to go away from the taskbar tray?

1. Click [Start]→[Programs]→[Accessories]→[Schedule Tasks] to open the Scheduled Tasks folder.

2. Click [Advanced]→[Stop Using Task Scheduler].

GLOSSARY

ADN Advanced Digital Network. A network of high-speed lines linking computers and networks.

anonymous FTP See FTP.

Archie An Internet search program for locating files at *FTP* sites.

ARPANET Advanced Research Projects Agency NETwork. A computer network developed in the 1960s by the U.S. Department of Defense that led to the Internet.

bandwidth A measure of how much data you can send through a line.

baud The speed at which information can move over an analog line or through a *modem*.

BBS Bulletin Board System. A computerized system that lets people read and post messages to one another and upload and download files.

bit Binary digIT. The smallest piece of electronic data; either a zero or a one.

BITNET Because It's There NETwork. A research network separate from but connected to the Internet. E-mail discussion groups, often called *mailing lists* or *listservs,* originated on BITNET.

Bps Bits Per Second. The speed at which information can move over a digital line or through a modem.

byte A group of *bits* (usually 8) that stands for one character of data. For example, a three-letter word would be represented by three bytes.

Channel An Internet source for continuously updated information, analogous to a television channel.

Chat Computerized, text communication between two or more users at the same time.

client A computer or program that receives data or services from another computer or program, called a *server.*

DLS   Dynamic Lookup Service. A computer, or a database and search program on a computer, for looking up e-mail addresses.

DNS   Domain Name Server or Service. A computer, or a program on a computer, that translates *domain names*, or Internet addresses, from words to *IP numbers* and vice versa.

domain name   The unique name of each Internet site, sometimes referred to as an Internet address.

e-mail   Electronic mail. Messages sent from one person to another by computer.

Ethernet   A method of linking computers in a network.

FAQ   Frequently Asked Questions. Lists of questions and answers on a particular subject.

FDDI   Fiber Distributed Data Interface. A standard for moving data over optical fiber lines, at about 100,000,000 *bits* per second.

finger   An Internet program used to locate or find out about people at other Internet sites.

firewall   Internet hardware and software that protects a computer or network by restricting access or the kind of data that can move into and out of it.

flame   To engage in immature, uncivil behavior; in particular, making derogatory comments in online discussion groups, or the comments themselves.

floating frame   A frame that can be moved to different parts of the screen.

frame   A rectangular portion of a browser display area that contains a Web page and can be used independently of the other parts of the display area.

FTP   File Transfer Protocol. A protocol (set of rules), or an Internet program, for moving files back and forth between two Internet sites.

gateway   Hardware or software that provides access between different computer systems or networks. For example, most online services, such as CompuServe, provide a gateway to the Internet.

GIF   Graphics Interchange Format. A type of graphics image file, often used to display graphics on Web pages.

gopher An Internet program that organizes information into text menus. By selecting a choice on a gopher menu, you go to either another menu of choices or to a text file. Computers that store this information are called gopher *servers*.

host A computer that stores programs and/or data files on a network.

HTML HyperText Markup Language. The code that is used to create Internet Web pages or to link files to other files.

HTTP HyperText Transport Protocol. The rules for transferring *hypertext* (*HTML*) files over the Internet.

hyperlink An element, such as a word, icon, or graphic, on a Web page or in an electronic document that leads to another Web page or document when clicked.

hypertext Files or documents that are linked to other files or documents. When a link, usually a word or an icon in the file, is selected, another file with more information about the word or icon is displayed.

Hytelnet An Internet program that organizes numerous *Telnet* links into a menu.

Internet The global, decentralized network of other interconnected networks that connects millions of computers. The Internet allows users to share electronic mail, transfer files, access Web pages, and cooperatively use other computerized resources.

IP Number (or IP Address) Internet Protocol Number. The unique, numerical address for each machine on the Internet.

IRC Internet Relay Chat. A system that lets many people communicate with one another simultaneously, using text messages, over the Internet.

ISDN Integrated Services Digital Network. A way to move more data over regular phone lines at speeds up to about 128,000 *bits* per second.

ISP Internet Service Provider. A corporation or institution that provides access to the Internet.

Java A general-purpose programming language developed to be used on any computer or with any operating system. Java is often used for animation or interactive effects on Web pages.

JPEG Joint Photographic Experts Group. A type of graphics image file, often used to display graphics on Web pages.

Jughead Jonzy's Universal Gopher Hierarchy Excavation And Display. A program, developed by a man named Jonzy, that searches through the titles of gopher menus on a specific set of gopher servers.

Kbps Kilobytes Per Second. A measure of line capacity, or *bandwidth*.

LAN Local Area Network. A network in your immediate vicinity, e.g., within the building you are in.

link See Hyperlink.

listserv The most common kind of *maillist*.

maillist (or mailing list) An automated system that lets people send e-mail on a particular topic to one address, where it is copied and sent to all of the other subscribers to the maillist.

Mbps Megabits Per Second. A measure of line capacity, or *bandwidth*.

MIME Multipurpose Internet Mail Extensions. A standard that was developed for attaching nontext files to Internet e-mail. MIME is also used by World Wide Web *servers* and browsers to identify files that are being sent or received over the *WWW*.

modem Modulator, DEModulator. A device, connected to a computer and to a phone line, that converts computer data into an audio signal and vice versa, so that computers can communicate with other computers over phone lines.

MOO MUD, Object Oriented. A type of *MUD*, a computerized, text-based, multiuser role-playing environment.

Mosaic The first WWW *browser*.

MUD MultiUser Dungeon or Dimension. A text-based, multiuser simulated environment that people can connect to through telephone lines or the Internet.

MUSE A type of *MUD*.

netiquette Etiquette on the Internet.

newsgroup Discussion groups on *Usenet*.

NFS Network File System. A protocol, or set of rules, that allows computers to share files over a network.

NIC Networked Information Center. Any central office that handles information for a network, such as InterNIC, where new *domain names* are registered.

NNTP Network News Transport Protocol. A standard for transferring news messages over *Usenet*.

node A single computer connected to a network.

packets; packet switching The method for breaking electronic data down into pieces, or packets, that can be transferred over the Internet. Each packet includes the addresses of where it came from and where it is going. Because of this, data from many different sources can share the same lines, directed by devices called *routers*.

PING Packet INternet Groper. An Internet program used for testing network connections by sending out a signal to a specific host and expecting a reply in a certain amount of time.

POP Point of Presence, or Post Office Protocol. A Point of Presence is a local connection to a network, such as America Online, Sprint, or the Internet. Post Office Protocol is an Internet standard for retrieving e-mail from a computer, called a mail *server*.

PPP Point-to-Point Protocol. A protocol, or set of rules, that allows a computer access to the Internet using a *TCP/IP* connection over phone or network lines.

protocol A set of very detailed, specific rules or standards for sending and receiving electronic data.

push A system for delivery of information over the Internet without the information being repeatedly requested. With push, you select information sources in advance and schedule times when the information will be "pushed" to your computer. The term was coined to contrast with the traditional method in which you have to request information; that is, search for it and "pull" it back to your computer.

RFC Request For Comment. Documents on the Internet that discuss issues associated with Internet protocols.

router A computer that manages the connection between two or more networks. Routers examine addresses in the *packets* of data that pass through them and send them where they are supposed to go.

server A computer or program that provides data or services to other computers or programs, called *clients*.

SLIP Serial Line Internet Protocol. A protocol, or set of rules, that allows a computer access to the Internet using a *TCP/IP* connection over phone or network lines.

SMDS Switched Multimegabit Data Service. A standard for high-speed data transfer.

SMTP Simple Mail Transport Protocol. A protocol, or standard, for delivering mail over a computer network.

spam (or spamming)   Use of a newsgroup or mailing list to send the same message to a large number of people who didn't ask for it. The term probably comes from the famous Monty Python skit in which the word "Spam" was repeatedly used.

Sysop   SYStems OPerator. The person responsible for tasks related to the operation of a computer system or network.

T1   A line equivalent to 24 regular telephone lines, with a *bandwidth* of 1.5 *Mbps*.

T2   A line equivalent to four T1 lines, with a *bandwidth* of 6.3 *Mbps*.

T3   A line equivalent to 28 T1 channels, with a *bandwidth* of 45 *Mbps*.

T4   A line equivalent to 168 T1 lines, with a *bandwidth* of 274 *Mbps*.

TCP/IP   Transmission Control Protocol/Internet Protocol. The protocol, or standard, for transmitting data over the Internet.

Telnet   An Internet program used to connect to another computer that allows you to use programs running on the other computer.

UNIX   A multiuser, multitasking computer operating system that includes *TCP/IP*. Though it's available for PCs, UNIX is used most widely on larger computers, including most Web servers.

URL   Uniform Resource Locator. The address of any resource on the Internet, consisting of the transport protocol (usually "http" on the Web), the type of resource (www, gopher, etc.), followed by the rest of the resource's address. A typical URL for a Web page would look like this: `http://www.typicalwebpage.com/webpage`.

Usenet   A worldwide system of electronic discussion groups organized by subject into *newsgroups*. Though sometimes called "Internet newsgroups," not all Usenet machines are on the Internet.

Veronica   Very Easy Rodent Oriented Net-wide Index to Computerized Archives. An Internet program used to search a continuously updated database that contains the names of almost every menu item on the thousands of *gopher* servers.

Virtual Reality (VR)   Electronic simulation of reality with three-dimensional graphics.

WAIS   Wide Area Information Server. A program that indexes large quantities of information and lets people search the indices over networks such as the Internet.

WAN   Wide Area Network. A network that covers an area larger than a single building or group of buildings.

Whiteboard   A window, or an area in a window, where more than one person can write or draw at the same time.

WWW   World Wide Web. The Internet system for hypertext linking between computers. WWW browsers like IE 4 make it possible to combine text, graphics, sound, and animation on documents that are linked to other documents on computers anywhere in the world.

Online Glossaries on the Web

Here are a couple of glossaries on the Web that you may wish to consult:

NetGlos: The Multilingual Glossary of Internet Terminology, copyright ©1995 by WorldWide Language Institute

`http://wwli.com/translation/netglos/netglos.html`

ILC Glossary of Internet Terms, copyright ©1994-96 by Internet Literacy Consultants™

`http://www.matisse.net/files/glossary.html`

INDEX

IDG BOOKS WORLDWIDE REGISTRATION CARD

Visit our Web site at http://www.idgbooks.com

ISBN Number: 0-7645-3067-4

Title of this book: Discover Internet Explorer 4

My overall rating of this book: ❑ Very good [1] ❑ Good [2] ❑ Satisfactory [3] ❑ Fair [4] ❑ Poor [5]

How I first heard about this book:

❑ Found in bookstore; name: [6] ❑ Book review: [7]

❑ Advertisement: [8] ❑ Catalog: [9]

❑ Word of mouth; heard about book from friend, co-worker, etc.: [10] ❑ Other: [11]

What I liked most about this book:

What I would change, add, delete, etc., in future editions of this book:

Other comments:

Number of computer books I purchase in a year: ❑ 1 [12] ❑ 2-5 [13] ❑ 6-10 [14] ❑ More than 10 [15]

I would characterize my computer skills as: ❑ Beginner [16] ❑ Intermediate [17] ❑ Advanced [18] ❑ Professional [19]

I use ❑ DOS [20] ❑ Windows [21] ❑ OS/2 [22] ❑ Unix [23] ❑ Macintosh [24] ❑ Other: [25]_____

(please specify)

I would be interested in new books on the following subjects:

(please check all that apply, and use the spaces provided to identify specific software)

❑ Word processing: [26] ❑ Spreadsheets: [27]

❑ Data bases: [28] ❑ Desktop publishing: [29]

❑ File Utilities: [30] ❑ Money management: [31]

❑ Networking: [32] ❑ Programming languages: [33]

❑ Other: [34]

I use a PC at (please check all that apply): ❑ home [35] ❑ work [36] ❑ school [37] ❑ other: [38] _____

The disks I prefer to use are ❑ 5.25 [39] ❑ 3.5 [40] ❑ other: [41]_____

I have a CD ROM: ❑ yes [42] ❑ no [43]

I plan to buy or upgrade computer hardware this year: ❑ yes [44] ❑ no [45]

I plan to buy or upgrade computer software this year: ❑ yes [46] ❑ no [47]

Name: _____ Business title: [48] _____ Type of Business: [49]

Address (❑ home [50] ❑ work [51]/Company name: _____)

Street/Suite#

City [52]/State [53]/Zip code [54]: _____ Country [55]

❑ **I liked this book!** You may quote me by name in future IDG Books Worldwide promotional materials.

My daytime phone number is _____

IDG BOOKS WORLDWIDE

THE WORLD OF COMPUTER KNOWLEDGE®

☐ YES!

Please keep me informed about IDG Books Worldwide's World of Computer Knowledge. Send me your latest catalog.

BESTSELLING
BOOK SERIES
FROM IDG